GREGG

Speed Building Simplified

John R. Gregg

Louis A. Leslie

Charles E. Zoubek

Shorthand written by Charles Rader

Gregg Publishing Division

McGraw-Hill Book Company, Inc.
NEW YORK CHICAGO CORTE MADERA, CALIF.
DALLAS TORONTO LONDON

GREGG

SPEED BUILDING SIMPLIFIED

SECOND EDITION

GREGG SPEED BUILDING SIMPLIFIED, SECOND EDITION

Library of Congress Catalog No. 56-12267

July, 1961-RRD-5
24517

PUBLISHED BY GREGG PUBLISHING DIVISION
McGraw-Hill Book Company, Inc.
Printed in the United States of America

PREFACE

Gregg Speed Building Simplified,
Second Edition, has two major objectives:

1. Further development of the student's shorthand skill.

2. Further development of the student's ability to spell and punctuate, to the end that he will be a more rapid and accurate transcriber.

Gregg Speed Building Simplified, Second Edition, like its predecessor, is a lesson-planned text. It contains four parts divided into 16 chapters, which in turn are divided into 80 lessons. The features that made the first edition so popular with teachers have been retained in this Second Edition, and many new ones have been added.

Practice Material. 1. *Gregg Speed Building Simplified,* Second Edition, contains 67,806 words of practice material — 36,026 in shorthand and 31,780 in type.

2. The material in each chapter is devoted to a specific line of business or industry. Chapter 1, for example, is built around advertising and selling; Chapter 2, around insurance, etc.

3. The practice material consists of representative business letters and articles, which have been chosen not only for their shorthand values but for their informative and inspirational content as well.

4. The practice material that appears in type is preceded by a shorthand preview of the more difficult words and phrases that it contains. The letters are counted in such a way that the teacher may dictate them either separately, to develop speed by using short spurts; or consecutively, to develop endurance. The letters are printed in a large, readable type from which it is easy to dictate.

Progressive Speed Builders. A feature of this revision that will especially appeal to teachers is the Progressive Speed Builder that appears in the fifth lesson of each chapter. It consists of five one-minute letters (preceded by a shorthand preview) counted at progressively increasing speeds. In Progressive Speed Builder, Lesson 5, for example, the first letter is counted at 50 words a minute; the second, at 60; the third, at 70; the fourth, at 80; and the fifth, at 90.

The speeds of the Progressive Speed Builders increase after each four chapters, until in Chapters 13 through 16 the student is writing at the rates of 120, 125, 130, 135, and 140 words a minute.

The letters in each Progressive Speed Builder are related to the same transaction and contain substantially the same vocabulary. Consequently, after the student has taken from dictation the first letter in the Progressive Speed Builder, his problem in taking the succeeding, faster letters is simplified.

Review Drill Cycle. Each of the 16 chapters of *Gregg Speed Building Simplified*, Second Edition, contains a five-drill cycle designed to help the student develop further his ability to construct new outlines under stress of dictation:

FIRST LESSON: Principles of Outline Construction
SECOND LESSON: Recall Drill
THIRD LESSON: Word Families; Proper Names
FOURTH LESSON: Frequent Phrases; Geographical Expressions
FIFTH LESSON: Penmanship Practice

Suggested procedures on how to practice each of these drills are provided for the student.

Marginal Reminders. A complete review of the spelling, punctuation, and typing style is included in the marginal reminders. The reminders that have been presented to the student in his previous shorthand textbooks are reviewed in Chapters 1, 2, and 3. Three new, more advanced uses of the comma are introduced in Chapter 4.

All marginal reminders appear in red to impress them on the mind of the student.

Part Openings. Each of the four part openings of the book contains information that will be helpful to the student in the development and application of his shorthand speed. The subjects covered in these part openings are:

PART I: Self-dictation
PART II: Dictation Problems
PART III: Devising Shortcuts
PART IV: Shorthand Reporting

Each part opening is attractively illustrated.

Appendix. The appendix contains:

1. A chart of brief forms
2. A complete review of word beginnings and endings
3. A complete review of phrasing principles
4. A list of 534 names and addresses that may be used in the transcription room

The authors of *Gregg Speed Building Simplified*, Second Edition, wish to express their appreciation for the many helpful suggestions that they have received from teachers who have used the first edition. The authors are confident that *Gregg Speed Building Simplified*, Second Edition, will enable teachers to do an even more effective job of shorthand speed development.

LOUIS A. LESLIE
CHARLES E. ZOUBEK

CONTENTS

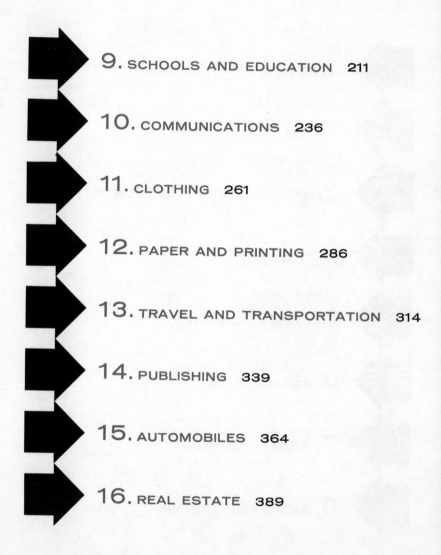

Self-dictation

As you have no doubt discovered, a major factor in your shorthand speed development is large quantities of the right kind of dictation. The more dictation practice you get, the more rapidly will your shorthand speed increase.

Of course, you will receive a great deal of dictation practice in class, and it is there that your greatest growth will take place.

However, if you can supplement that class dictation with additional practice at home, your progress will be even more rapid.

There are a number of ways in which you can obtain this additional dictation practice:

1. Draft a member of the family as a dictator. This, however, has some disadvantages. First, a member of the family may not be available when you want to practice; and, second, his inexperience as a dictator may retard rather than increase your shorthand speed.

2. Use the television or the radio. In general, people on television and radio speak too rapidly, with the result that your efforts in trying to "take" them may be discouraging. However, you may occasionally be able to tune in on someone who speaks approximately at your dictation speed.

3. Use records and tapes. This is by far the most satisfactory way to obtain home dictation practice. There is available today a large selection of records and tapes. Their use has two definite advantages: first, you can choose records and tapes that contain dictation within

the range of speed that you are writing; second, they are dictated by experienced dictators. Ask your teacher about the dictation records and tapes that are on the market.

4. Use the "self-dictation" method that will enable you to practice by yourself. Here are the steps you should follow.

(a) Select a magazine or other reading matter that is printed in a fairly large-size type. (Full-page advertisements in some of the leading national magazines are ideal for this purpose.) Select material that deals with many different types of subject matter — automobiles, radios, books, airplanes, etc. — so that you will encounter the widest possible vocabulary.

(b) Read through the material quickly to be sure that you can write the outlines for each word. If you find you do not know the outlines for some of the vocabulary, look up those words in the *Gregg Shorthand Dictionary Simplified* or construct an outline of your own. By thus eliminating all the stumbling blocks, you will be able to write continuously as you dictate to yourself.

(c) Read the material aloud at the fastest rate that you can write fairly good notes, writing slightly below the words that you read. The exact point at which you write each outline is not important.

This type of self-dictation may seem a little strange to you during the first few attempts, but you will soon be able to adjust your self-dictation to the speed that you can write.

(d) After you have self-dictated the material once, redictate it a second time, faster. Write over the outlines that you originally wrote.

(e) Occasionally, dictate a piece of material slowly, striving for perfection of outline rather than for increased speed.

On page 12 you will find an illustration of how your "self-dictation" will look.

Whenever you have the urge to practice at home, try this method of self-dictation; you will be pleased with the effect it will have on your shorthand writing speed.

Illustration of Self-Dictation

The typical beginning worker does not like to ask questions. I suppose his is a normal fear. He does not want to appear to be a beginner; he does not want anyone to think that he is a novice; he is afraid of revealing his inexperience. So, he goes ahead blindly with the tasks that are assigned him, holding his breath and hoping for the best. He probably does not realize that, if he does make a mistake because he did not understand what he was to do, his supervisor will wonder why on earth the newcomer did not ask questions.

To protect yourself and at the same time to get in your mind the exact details of a set of instructions, grab a pencil and jot down enough notes to make sure you will be able to complete the assignment. If several steps are involved, do your best to get them down in a very clear one, two, three order. As you work, then, check off the steps as you complete them so that, if you are interrupted, you will know where to pick up. This careful procedure will be of help in other ways. Some jobs assigned you are done once a week or once a month or at some other typical interval; because you may have to work the steps several times before you master the routine, particularly if the procedure is rather involved, your written guide will save you the need of running around and asking what to do if you get lost when you are halfway through.

Add your own notes as you do the job or when you review it. There may be some information that will be helpful the next time you do this work. Keep your description sheet for future reference. You can never tell; you might want to use it to help the next newcomer, in case you are promoted and have to orient him to the work you have been doing.

12

In *Gregg Speed Building Simplified*, Second Edition, you will continue to improve your ability to spell and punctuate as you strive to increase your dictation speed. In the first three chapters you will review those points of punctuation and typing style with which you are already familiar; in the fourth chapter you will take up a number of new points.

In *Gregg Speed Building Simplified*, Second Edition, you will once again find the familiar red circle around each punctuation mark, and in the margin the reason for the use of the mark. In the margin also will appear those words to which you should give special spelling attention.

Suggestions for Practice: To be sure that you derive the most benefit from the marginal reminders, let us review briefly the procedure you should follow.

1. Read the explanations and the illustrative examples of the marginal reminders that follow these explanations.

2. When you meet an encircled punctuation mark and are not sure why the punctuation mark was used, glance in the left margin of the page, where you will find the reason. By this time many of the punctuation marks will be so familiar to you that you will have to glance into the margin only occasionally.

3. As you copy the Reading and Writing Practice, insert each punctuation mark in your shorthand notes and encircle it.

4. Spell all words in the marginal reminders once, preferably aloud.

In Chapter 1, you will review the following uses of the comma:

, parenthetical

A writer will sometimes insert in a sentence a word or an expression that could be omitted without changing the meaning of the sentence. These added words or expressions are parenthetical and are set off from the rest of the sentence by commas.

I cannot, of course, accept the fee.

, apposition

Sometimes a writer mentions a person or thing and then, in order to make his meaning clear, says the same thing in different words. This added explanation is known as an expression "in apposition." An expression in apposition is set off by two commas, except when it occurs at the end of the sentence, in which case only one comma is necessary.

Our sales manager, Mr. Green, resigned.
I gave the papers to Mr. Smith, the treasurer.

, series

When three or more similar expressions (words, phrases, or clauses) occur in a series with a conjunction before the last expression, a comma should be placed before the conjunction as well as between the items.

I have arranged for a blackboard, chalk, and an eraser.
He made payments on June 1, on June 15, and on June 30.

, conjunction

A comma is used to separate two independent clauses that are joined by a conjunction.

The television set will be delivered on April 15, and our serviceman will install it on April 16.

, *when clause*
, *as clause*
, *if clause*
, introductory

A comma is used to separate a dependent, or subordinate, clause from a following main clause. Each subordinate clause beginning with *when, as,* or *if* has been marked as such in the marginal reminders. All other dependent clauses have been grouped under the general marginal reminder ", introductory."

When he comes, please inform me.
As you know, the meeting has been canceled.
If you will be late, please call me.
Before I can take any action, I shall need more information.

A comma is also required after such introductory words and phrases as *frankly, consequently, on the contrary, for instance.*

> Frankly, I am unhappy about the situation.
> On the contrary, he is the one who is wrong.

These introductory words and phrases are also indicated in the marginal reminders as ", introductory."

, *and* **omitted**

Two adjectives preceding a noun are separated by a comma.

> He gave an interesting, informative talk.

The comma is not used if the first adjective modifies the combined idea of the second adjective plus the noun.

> He wore an attractive red tie.

, **nonrestrictive**

Nonrestrictive clauses or phrases are set off by commas. A nonrestrictive clause or phrase is one that may be omitted without changing the meaning of the sentence. The nonrestrictive clause or phrase might be classified as parenthetical.

> Mr. Green, who is a successful businessman, lives in
> Chicago.

LESSON 1

▶ **Principles of Outline Construction.** The first lesson in each chapter contains principles of outline construction. You will quickly see how the application of these principles will help to develop your power to construct outlines for new words. In practicing this list of words, as well as all lists in the following lessons, cover the type key and read the words. When you come to an outline you cannot read, spell it. If the spelling does not immediately give you the meaning of the outline, refer to the key.

At this stage of your shorthand course, you should be able to read all the lists rapidly.

1. Omission of unaccented vowel from word endings -ER, -AR, -OR. When the vowel in the endings -ER, -AR, -OR is not stressed or accented, it is omitted.

-er

1

-ar

2

-or

3

1. Customer, printer, clever, former, manner.
2. Sugar, similar, popular, circular, grammar.
3. Author, humor, honor, error, supervisor, operator, factor.

2. Inclusion of accented vowel in ending -ER. When the E in the end-

CHAPTER 1 — **ADVERTISING AND SELLING**

ing -ER is stressed or accented, it is written. It is also written in derivatives, even though the E may no longer be accented.

-er

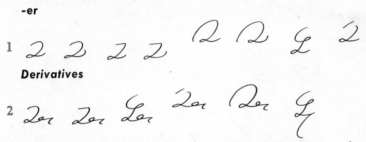

Derivatives

1. Confer, conferred, infer, inferred, defer, deferred, prefer, transfer.
2. Conference, inference, preference, transference, deference, preferable.

Reading and Writing Practice

The more good shorthand you read and copy, the more rapidly will your skill grow. Through your reading and copying of good shorthand, you will be constantly reviewing the system as well as learning new words.

Be sure that you read each Reading and Writing Practice before you make a copy of it.

3. Courtesy — The Oil of Business

(shorthand) — Harold Whitehead (337)

Letters

4.

, apposition
territory

receive
, conjunction

, and omitted
enjoyable

displays
, if clause

, nonrestrictive
assistance

(128)

5.

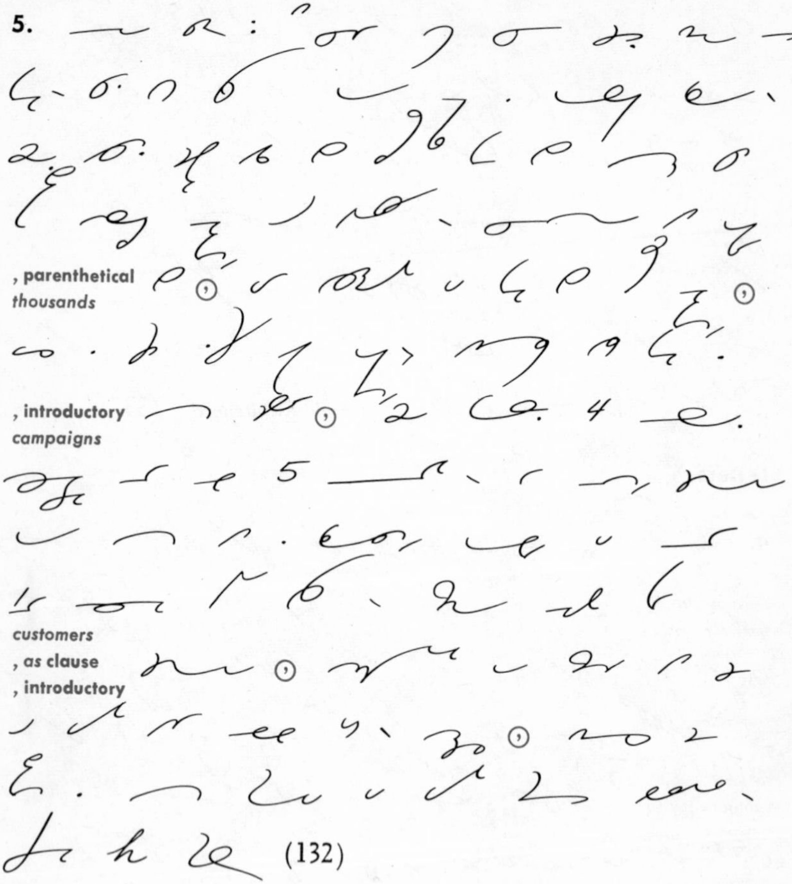

[shorthand outlines]

, parenthetical
thousands

[shorthand outlines]

, introductory
campaigns

[shorthand outlines]

customers
, as clause
, introductory

[shorthand outlines] (132)

6. Recall Drill (Sh). This drill illustrates the different word beginnings and endings that are represented by the alphabetic stroke SH. Read the list, referring to the key whenever you cannot immediately read an outline.

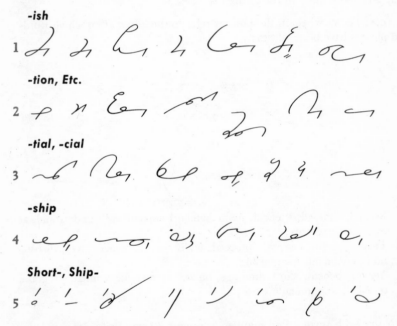

-ish

1

-tion, Etc.

2

-tial, -cial

3

-ship

4

Short-, Ship-

5

1. Vanish, finish, abolish, furnish, blemish, Spanish, accomplish.
2. Nation, station, experimentation, dictation, investigation, definition, omission.
3. Credential, differential, palatial, initialed, official, social, commercial.
4. Relationship, workmanship, hardships, partnership, friendship, airship.
5. Shortly, shorten, shortsighted, shortage, shortened; shipwreck, shipshape, shipyard.

7. Previews and Writing Practice. The following preview contains the more difficult words and phrases that appear in the Writing Practice, which consists of letters in type. If you practice this preview before you take the letters from dictation, the letters should give you no difficulty.

Here is the practice procedure you should use:

1. Cover up the type key to the preview and read the entire list.

2. Spell any outline that you cannot immediately read. If the spelling does not give you the outline, refer to the key. Don't stop more than a few seconds to puzzle out an outline.

3. Make one copy of the entire list.

Note: The numbers in the preview refer to the letters from which words and phrases have been selected.

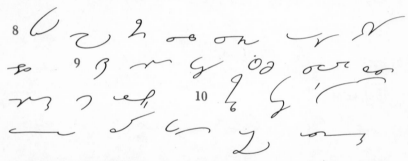

8. Beyond, compelled, effect, immediately, I am sure, will understand, at this time, necessity.
9. Thank you for, contract, proceed, highway, accordance, erect, instructions, confident, relationship.
10. Agency, benefit, short time ago, on the market, he wanted, program, revealed, recommendations.

Note: Each small raised number represents 20 standard words.

8. Mr. Palmer: Conditions beyond our control have compelled us to raise our advertising rates. Please give the enclosed[1] rate card your careful attention. The new rates are going into effect immediately on all new business.[2]

I am sure that our customers will understand the necessity for raising rates at this time. J. P. Green.[3]

---

9. Gentlemen: Thank you for sending us your contract so promptly. We will proceed with the building of the highway signs[4] advertising your cars.

In accordance with the contract, we will do the following:

1. We will erect the signs[5] in the best available spots.

2. We will keep them in good condition for five years.

3. In preparing the copy[6] for the advertising on the signs, we will follow closely the instructions in the contract.

We are confident[7] that this will be the beginning of a long, profitable relationship for both of us. Sincerely yours,[8]

---

10. Dear Mr. Price: Our advertising agency does more than write copy to sell your products. It gives you the benefit[9] of the experience of its large staff.

For example, a short time ago a businessman came to us[10] with a new product that he planned to put on the market. He wanted to start an immediate national[11] advertising program. Our Research Department revealed that his product was overpriced and poorly designed, and it[12] pointed out ways in which it could be improved. We recommended a complete overhauling of the product itself[13] before releasing a program of advertising. Our client accepted our recommendations and saved[14] himself a good deal of hardship and money.

This is just one illustration of the type of service you will receive[15] if you entrust our organization with the advertising of your products. Very cordially yours,[16] (320)

Reading and Writing Practice

11.

pictures

, introductory

, nonrestrictive
received

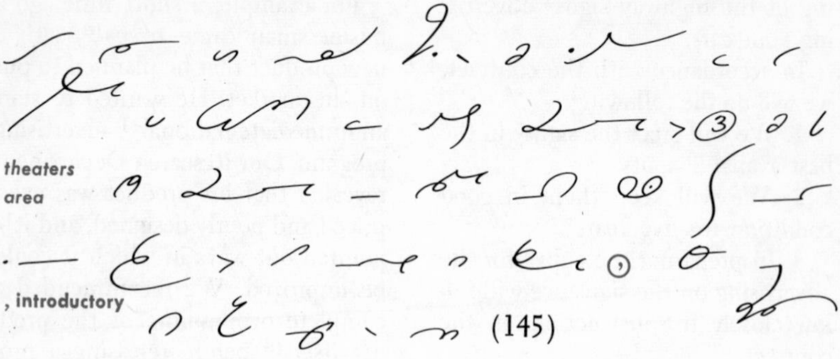

theaters
area

, introductory

(145)

12.

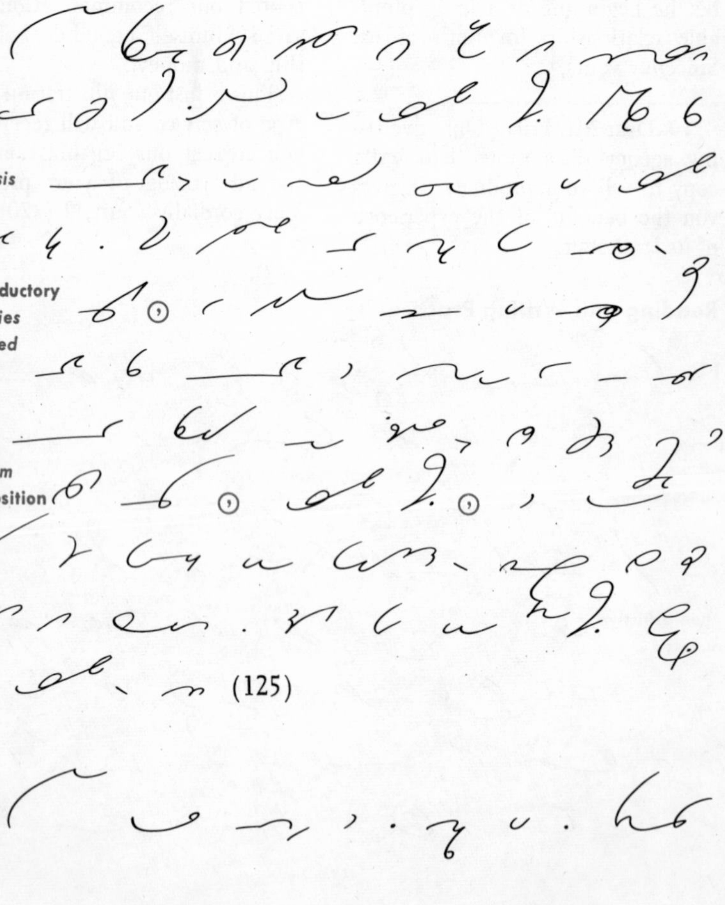

analysis

, introductory
inquiries
received

6 =

medium
, apposition

(125)

13.

cereal
sufficient

, if clause
, introductory

territory
personally

, if clause
notify

outlined
, as clause

(184)

▶ **Word Families.** Word families enable you to take advantage of analogy in the construction of new outlines. The third lesson in each chapter contains two word families, and a number of illustrations of these word families appear in your practice material.

Read the illustrations given in each word family. Refer to the key whenever you are in doubt about an outline.

14. -tified

Gratified, notified, fortified, justified, unidentified, testified.

15. -sive

Impressive, inexpensive, impulsive, extensive, intensive, defensive.

16. Frequent Names. The third lesson in each chapter contains (1) a number of frequently used last names and (2) a number of frequently used women's first names, or a number of frequently used men's first names. Many of these names are used in the practice material of the lesson.

Just read through the list, referring to the key whenever you cannot immediately read a name.

Last Names

1

Women's First Names

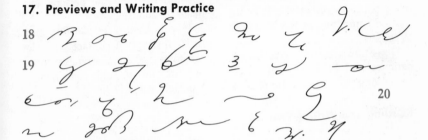

2

1. Adams, Anderson, Baker, Barry, Becker, Bennett, Brennan, Brown.
2. Adeline, Agnes, Amelia, Annabell, Augusta, Barbara.

17. Previews and Writing Practice

18

19

20

18. To thank you for the, accuracy, especially, prospect, as you know, represents, advertising, pleasant.
19. Persuade, assembled, binder, 300, recent, minor, selected, repay, if you will, gladly, approval.
20. One of our, executives, industrial, experience, consulting, established.

18. Dear Mr. Dodge: I wish to take this opportunity to thank you for the completeness and accuracy with[1] which you have taken care of our requirements. We are especially grateful for the fine manner in which you have[2] kept our prospect file. As you know, this file represents our most important source of new business.

The success of our[3] advertising and promotion program depends in a large measure on your efficient service.

It is our hope[4] that we may continue our pleasant and profitable business relationship for many years. Cordially yours,[5]

19. Dear Mr. Anderson: Are you looking for effective sales letters that you can use to get direct orders, obtain[6] leads for your salesmen, or persuade dealers to purchase your line?

We have carefully assembled a binder of[7] more than 300 of the most successful sales letters submitted to us in recent years. Every one of[8] these letters is a winner. With minor changes, you can use many of these sales letters in your own business.

The[9] binder costs $10.50. A single letter selected and used by you will more than repay the cost.[10] If you will return the attached postal card, we will gladly send you the binder on approval. Cordially yours,[11]

---

20. Dear Mr. Brown: One of our advertising executives is retiring after 30 years of service. During[12] that time he has had contact with the top executives of the large industrial companies of the Middle[13] West.

He is now eager to make his experience and knowledge of advertising and sales promotion avail-able[14] on a consulting basis to some organization that can use them.

Through the years he has established[15] a personal friendship with the officials of many companies throughout the Middle West. These contacts place[16] him in an excellent position to reach the persons who make decisions.

If you need a responsible man for[17] this type of contact work, let me know and I will arrange a meeting for you at your convenience. Sincerely yours,[18] (360)

Reading and Writing Practice

21.
impressive
, and omitted

, conjunction
colored

, when clause

, series
truest

(140)

22.

development
response
amazing

29

, parenthetical
approximately

250/ 250/

(157)

29

23.

verify
arrangement

confident
profitable
, parenthetical

15

reputation
dependability

, introductory
extensive

connection
, if clause

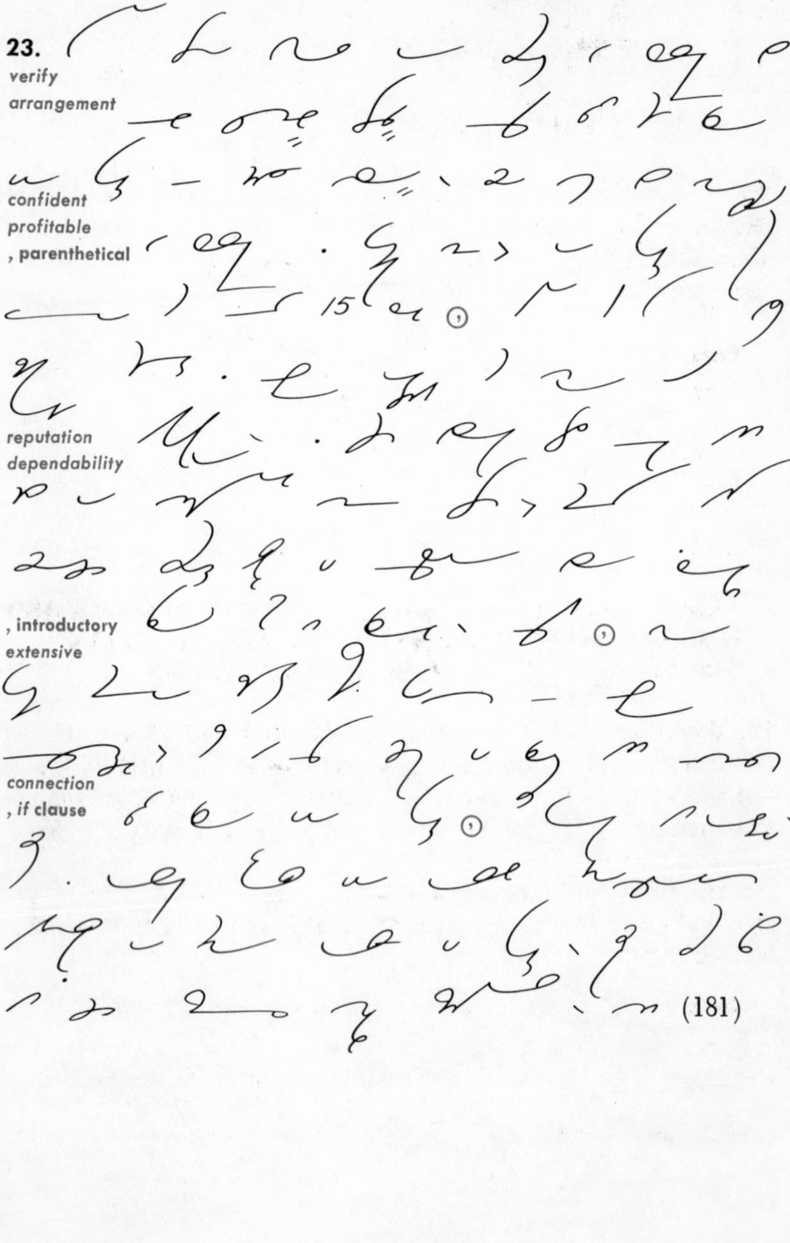

(181)

30

24. Frequent Phrases. The fourth lesson in each chapter contains illustrations of two phrasing principles. As you are already familiar with these phrases, they are given here for a quick review. It should not take you more than a few seconds to read through the list.

Been

1. I have been, you have been, who have been, have not been, would have been, could have been, he might have been, has been, it has been.
2. Some time ago, months ago, weeks ago, years ago, days ago.

25. Geographical Expressions. The fourth lesson of each chapter also contains a list of geographical expressions, divided into three parts — names of: (1) cities containing a common beginning or ending; (2) states and territories of the United States; and (3) foreign countries or foreign cities.

Read through the list quickly. You will find several of these geographical expressions in the practice material of this lesson and of the following lessons.

-field

States and Territories

3 *[shorthand]*

1. Springfield, Plainfield, Greenfield, Fairfield, Winfield, Westfield, Deerfield.
2. South Dakota, North Carolina, Missouri, Kentucky, Delaware, Guam.
3. Argentina, Australia, Belgium, Bolivia, Brazil, Canada.

26. Previews and Writing Practice

27 *[shorthand]*

28 *[shorthand]*

29 *[shorthand]*

27. Bulletin, sketch, I understand, will you please, let me, I should like to have, territory, essential.
28. Considerable, toward; $1,000,000; strengthening, we should be able, duplication, described, affected, personnel.
29. Conference, Springfield, session, previous, prepared, editorial, Westfield, forward.

27. Mr. Dark: As you know, we try to include in the monthly company bulletin a brief sketch of the salesmen[1] who have been added to the staff recently. I understand that you have added two men to your department.

Would[2] you please let me have a few lines about each man. I should like to have some information about the experience[3] of each, and the territory he will cover for you. Even though it is not essential, please include a[4] recent picture if you have one available.

Can you let me have this material by April 1? John Trees[5]

---

28. To the Staff: As you know, considerable progress has been made toward the achievement of the $1,000,000[6] sales goal we have set for ourselves for next year. Much planning and building and hard work will be required to reach this goal;[7] but, with the continued strengthening of our sales efforts, we should be able to realize it.

At the last meeting[8] of the Planning Committee several decisions were made that should strengthen our staff further and help us avoid[9] duplication. These changes, which will be effective on September 1, are indicated in the enclosed[10] organization charts.

If any of the changes described on the chart are not clear to any of the personnel[11] affected by them, I shall be glad to hear from these persons and answer any questions they may have. John A. Smith[12]

---

29. To the Sales Staff. Our annual sales conference will be held this year in Springfield, Missouri, from August 4 to[13] 15. Please arrange your travel plans so that you will be in Springfield in time to take part in the first session at[14] 10 a.m. on Monday, August 4. It is our hope that this sales meeting will be even more helpful than our[15] previous meetings.

Before you come to Springfield, be prepared to discuss three things:

1. Your most important sales problems.[16]

2. Your most important editorial needs.

3. Your most important general problems.

Our meetings will be[17] held at the Hotel Westfield.

I am looking forward to seeing you all at the sales conference. James R. Ramsey[18] (360)

Reading and Writing Practice

30.

previous
, as clause

its
circulation

, if clause

, when clause
attractive

(127)

31.

, parenthetical
machine

21

, as clause

(117)

32.

, as clause

, and omitted
dependable

, as clause
experience

, introductory
, parenthetical

recommended
medium

advice
, parenthetical

someone
, if clause

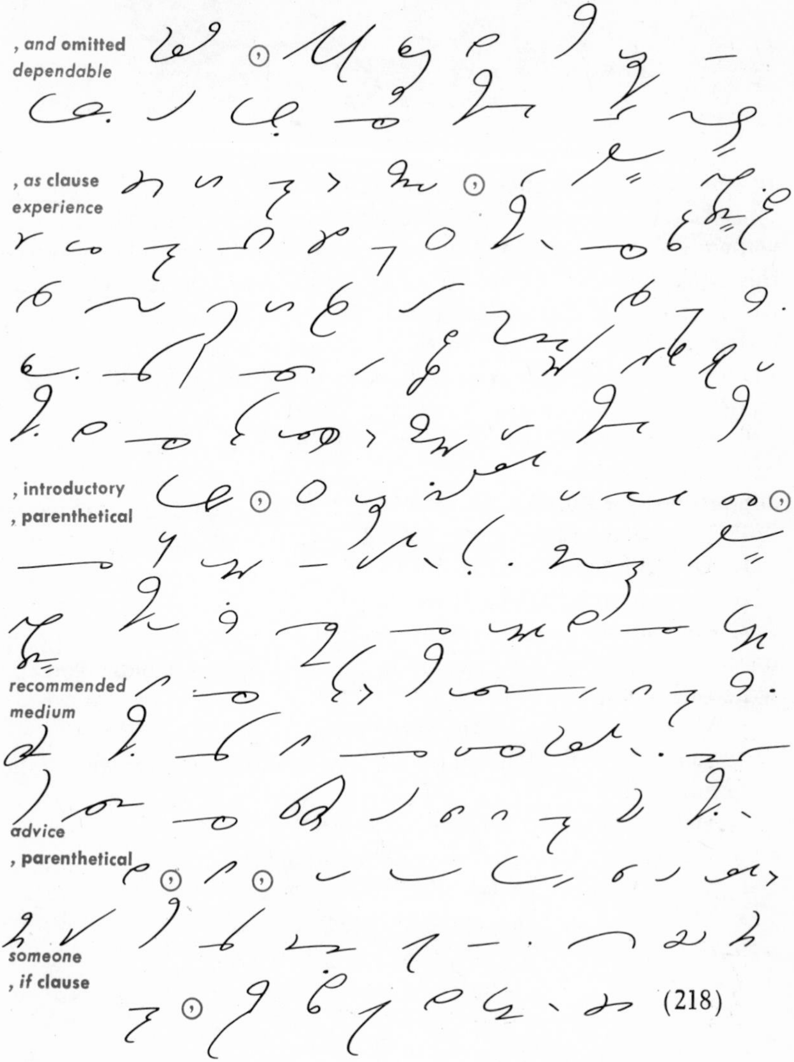

(218)

LESSON 5

33. Penmanship Practice. The speed and accuracy with which you can read your shorthand notes depend to a large extent on how well you write them. Your notes do not have to be as beautiful as those in this book, but they should be readable. They will be readable if you will be careful about one important thing — proportion.

The penmanship lessons in this book are designed to help you develop accurate proportion as well as to point out to you the correct joinings of the various strokes in Gregg Shorthand.

In this penmanship practice, you will work with proper proportions of individual strokes.

Suggestions for Practice: In practicing this and the other penmanship drills in this book, here is the procedure you should follow:

1. Read through the entire drill to be sure that you know the word or phrase that each stroke represents.

2. The outlines in each drill are written in groups. Write each group once, striving to see how accurately, rather than how rapidly, you can write each outline.

3. Make another copy of the entire list.

As you practice the following drill, here are a few pointers you should keep in mind:

1. Make strokes like TED and MEN very long; strokes like T, SH very short. Try hard to keep each straight line *straight*.

2. Make all curves *deep*.

3. Make the A circle *huge*; the E circle *tiny*.

1)))   ((⌒ ⌒ ⌒   ○ ○

2 ∪ ∪ ∪ ∪   ∩ ∩   ∪ ∪   ))

3 — — —   ⁄ ⁄ ⁄   ⁄⁄

1. Is-his, for, have; put, be-by; you-your, can, go-good; I, he.

2. Of, are-our-hour, will-well; you-your, this; of, gentlemen; their-there, and-end.
3. In-not, am-more, men; it-at, would, did-date; shall-ship, which.

▶ **Progressive Speed Builder (50-90).** In each fifth lesson you will find a Progressive Speed Builder, the purpose of which is to force you to write faster. Each Progressive Speed Builder consists of five letters or memoranda, all related to the same transaction. Each letter is counted at a slightly higher speed. In this lesson, the letters are counted progressively at 50, 60, 70, 80, and 90 words a minute.

Your first step always should be to practice the preview for the Progressive Speed Builder by reading it, with the help of the key when necessary, and making a copy of it. This will refresh your recollection of the shorthand outlines for the more difficult words and phrases that it contains. The numbers within the preview refer to the letters to which each group applies.

You should find the first two or three letters quite easy; you may have to work a little harder on the fourth and fifth letters, especially in the later lessons.

The important thing to remember is *to get something down* for every word, even though the legibility of your outlines may suffer at the higher speeds.

34. Preview

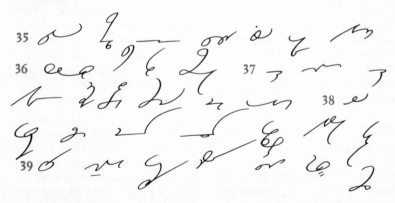

35. I told, agency, more and more, acute, hired, report, discuss.
36. I realize, however, best, available.

37. News, contract, enough, department, sufficient, expansion, vacant, as soon as, location.
38. Third, private, exact, sometime, meantime, preparations, disturb, possible.
39. I had, quarters, provided, started, week or two, Friday, conveniently.

Note: One diagonal indicates the end of a quarter minute's dictation; two diagonals, the end of a half minute's dictation; three diagonals, the end of a three-quarter minute's dictation; the number after each letter, the end of a minute's dictation.

(1 Minute at 50)

35. Mr. Davis: As I told you, the problem of space in our advertising/agency is becoming more and more acute. Two weeks ago//we hired two new girls. When they report, we shall have no place to put them.///

May I suggest that we have a meeting to discuss this matter. Harry Lee (1)

(1 Minute at 60)

36. Mr. Lee: I realize that the space problem in our advertising agency/is becoming more and more acute. For the present, however, I am afraid you//will have to get along as best you can with the space you have available. It will///be a few weeks before we can take any action on the matter of space. James Davis (2)

(1 Minute at 70)

37. Mr. Lee: I have good news for you. We have just signed a contract for the purchase of a new building./The building is large enough so that each department will have sufficient space. We shall have a great//deal of room for ex-pansion. The building is now vacant and we can move in at once. I will write///you as soon as we have made definite plans for the location of each department. James Davis (3)

(1 Minute at 80)

38. Mr. Lee: Our plans for moving to our new building are now complete. Your department will be located on the/third floor. You will have a private office.

I do not know the exact date on which you will move, but it will be sometime//during the week of July 12. In the meantime, please make whatever preparations you feel are necessary///so that the moving will disturb the operation of your department as little as possible. James Davis (4)

(1 Minute at 90)

39. Mr. Davis: I had an opportunity today to look over our quarters in the new building. For the first time in/more than 10 years, our advertising agency will have all the space it needs. I was pleased with the office that you have provided// for me.

I think, too, that the staff will be happy because there is plenty of light.

We have started packing those things that we shall///not have to use during the next week or two. By Friday, we shall finish all the packing we can conveniently do. Harry Lee (5) (350)

Reading and Writing Practice

40.

, as clause
, introductory
excise

, introductory
original

already
, conjunction

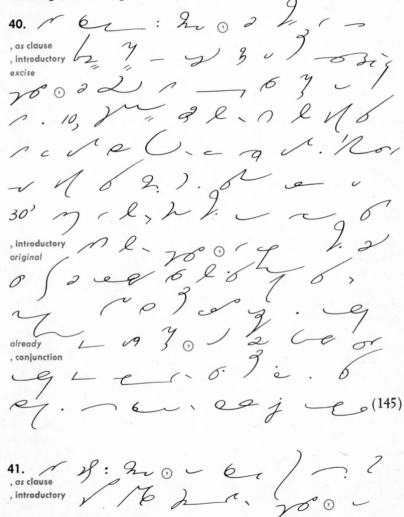

(145)

41.
, as clause
, introductory

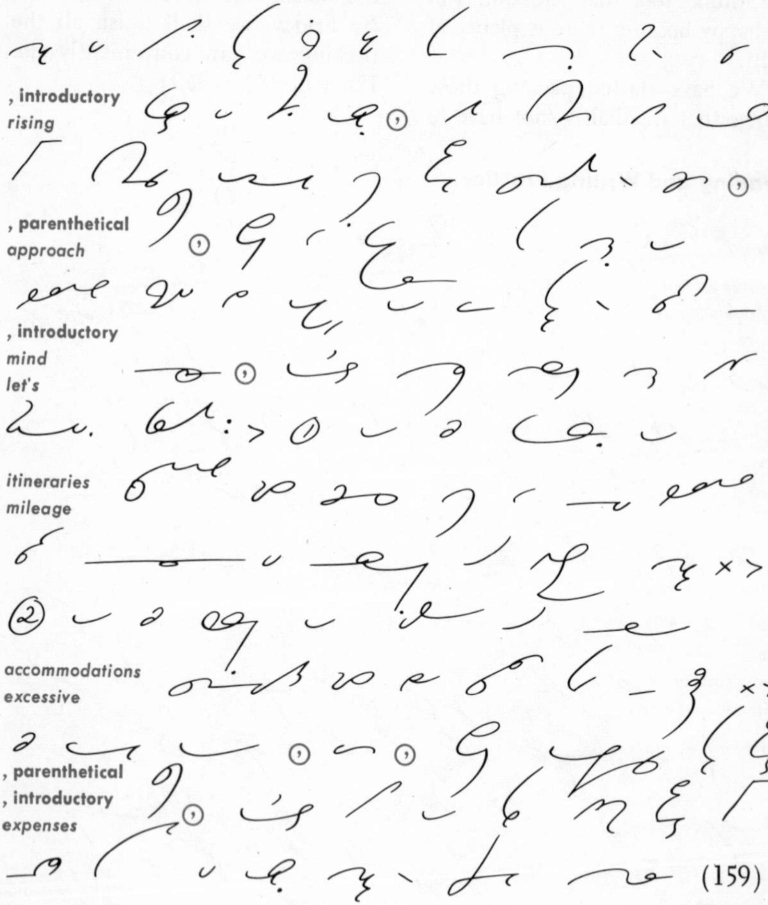

, introductory
rising

, parenthetical
approach

, introductory
mind
let's

itineraries
mileage

②

accommodations
excessive

, parenthetical
, introductory
expenses

(159)

In the following chapter you will review three uses of the semicolon and one use of the colon. You will also review hyphenated words.

; because of comma

As you already have learned, a comma is used to separate two independent clauses that are joined by a conjunction. When a comma occurs within one of or both the independent clauses, a semicolon is used to separate the two clauses.

> According to my records, we placed six orders with you last year; and every one of them was delivered within five days.

; no conjunction

A semicolon is used to separate two independent, but closely related, clauses when no conjunction is used to connect the clauses.

> Harry has brown eyes; Mary has blue eyes.

The above sentence could be written as two sentences, with a period after the first *eyes*. However, because the two thoughts are closely related, the semicolon seems more appropriate.

; illustrative ,

When an illustration is introduced by some such expression as *namely, that is,* or *for example,* the expression should be preceded by a semicolon and followed by a comma.

> John has one objective; namely, to complete the work on time.

: enumeration

A colon is used after an expression that introduces some following material, such as an explanation of a general statement, a list, or an enumeration.

> He was absent on three days this year: March 1, April 15, and June 20.

The new book has this improvement over the old one:
it has fewer blank pages.

hyphenated before noun
no noun, no hyphen
no hyphen after *ly*

You can quickly decide whether to use a hyphen in expressions such as *worth while* and *well trained* by observing these rules:

1. If a noun follows the expression, use a hyphen.

    I attended a worth-while meeting.

2. If *no* noun follows the expression, no hyphen is used.

    The meeting was worth while.

No hyphen is used, however, in a compound modifier where the first expression ends in *ly*. For example, no hyphen would be used in the expression *widely read magazine*.

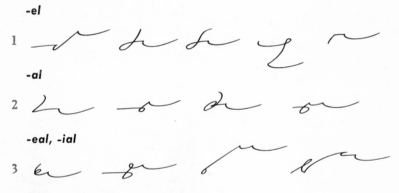

LESSON **6**

▶ **Principles of Outline Construction**

42. Omission of unaccented vowel in word endings -EL, -AL, -EAL, -IAL. *When the vowel is not accented or stressed in the endings* -EL, -AL, -EAL, -IAL, *it is omitted.* This omission results in outlines that are easy to write and at the same time readable.

-el

1

-al

2

-eal, -ial

3

1. Model, channel, panel, level, tunnel.
2. Formal, metal, final, natural.
3. Cereal, material, editorial, testimonial.

43. Vowel written in word endings -ER, -AR, -OR. *When* -ER, -AR, *or* -OR *follow* ī; *left* s; *or* SH, CH, J, *more legible outlines result by writing the vowel.*

ī

1

CHAPTER **2** INSURANCE

Sh, Ch, J

1. Prior, drier, crier, flyer, liar, buyer.
2. Eraser, condenser, appraiser, closer, nicer, announcer.
3. Washer, polisher, teacher, richer, manager, danger, larger.

Reading and Writing Practice

44. It's the Little Things That Count

(230)

Letters

45.

benefits
model

, if clause
envelope

assistant

(78)

46.

pictures
, apposition

; no conjunction

; no conjunction
neglected

, when clause

, if clause
; illustrative ,
, introductory

worth-while
  hyphenated
  before noun
, introductory

; because of comma

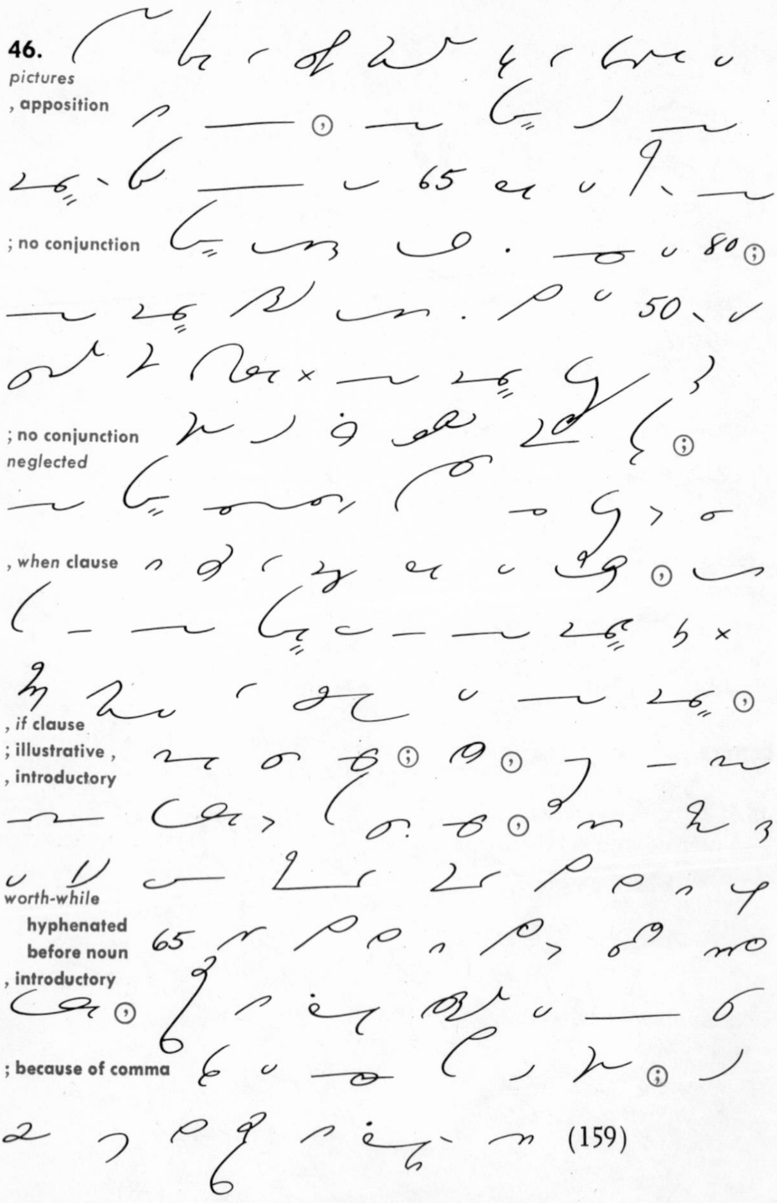

(159)

46

47. Recall Drill (K). This drill is a review of the word beginnings and endings that are represented by the alphabetic stroke к.

Con-

1 [shorthand outlines]

Com-

2 [shorthand outlines]

-ical, -cle

3 [shorthand outlines]

-ic

4 [shorthand outlines]

1. Congratulate, control, contract, confront, contemplate.
2. Companion, combine, combination, comfort, complete, complex, complicated.
3. Chemical, technical, critical, skeptical, article, particle.
4. Basic, scientific, tragic, civic, logic, specific, magic.

48. Previews and Writing Practice

49 [shorthand outlines]

50 [shorthand outlines]

49. Liability, policy, medical, period, injury, servants, we hope that, enclosed, entirely, sincerely, privilege.
50. Thank you for your letter, representative, he will be glad, advantages, organization, in the market, figures, compare, decisions, occur.
51. Discontinue, investigate, dividends, studied, reconsider, elsewhere.

49. Dear Mr. Stern: Enclosed is personal liability policy No. 17415. This[1] policy is made out for $10,-000. It includes medical payments up to $350[2] for a period of three years.

This policy covers your liability for any injury to the[3] public or to any servants in your house.

We hope that you find the enclosed policy entirely satisfactory,[4] and we wish to thank you sincerely for the privilege of handling your insurance. Cordially yours,[5]

50. Dear Mr. Brown: Thank you for your letter of June 19 in which you ask us to send a representative to[6] discuss our policies with you.

We shall be very glad to have our represenative, Mr. Martin, call to[7] talk with you next Friday evening as you suggest. He will be glad to tell you about the advantages of dealing[8] with an organization like ours when you are in the market for insurance.

You will be interested[9] in the figures that Mr. Martin will show you. We hope that you will compare them with those of other companies[10] before you make a decision.

Feel free to ask Mr. Martin any questions that may occur to you. Sincerely yours,[11]

51. Dear Mr. Crowder: We were sorry to receive your letter of January 8, informing us that you[12] plan to discontinue your insurance with us when your present policy expires on February 3. We assume[13] that you are planning to place your insurance with some other company.

Before you do so, be sure to investigate[14] the dividends paid by that company. Because of the careful way in which we select the persons whom[15] we insure, we have been able to pay a high dividend each year. The actual rates that we have paid during[16] the last 20 years are given on the enclosed folder.

We hope that, after you have studied the whole important[17] matter of insurance, you will reconsider your decision to transfer your insurance elsewhere. Sincerely yours,[18] (360)

Reading and Writing Practice

52.

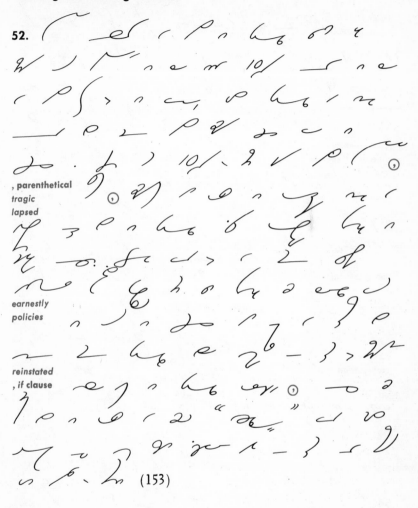

, parenthetical
tragic
lapsed

earnestly
policies

reinstated
, if clause

(153)

53.

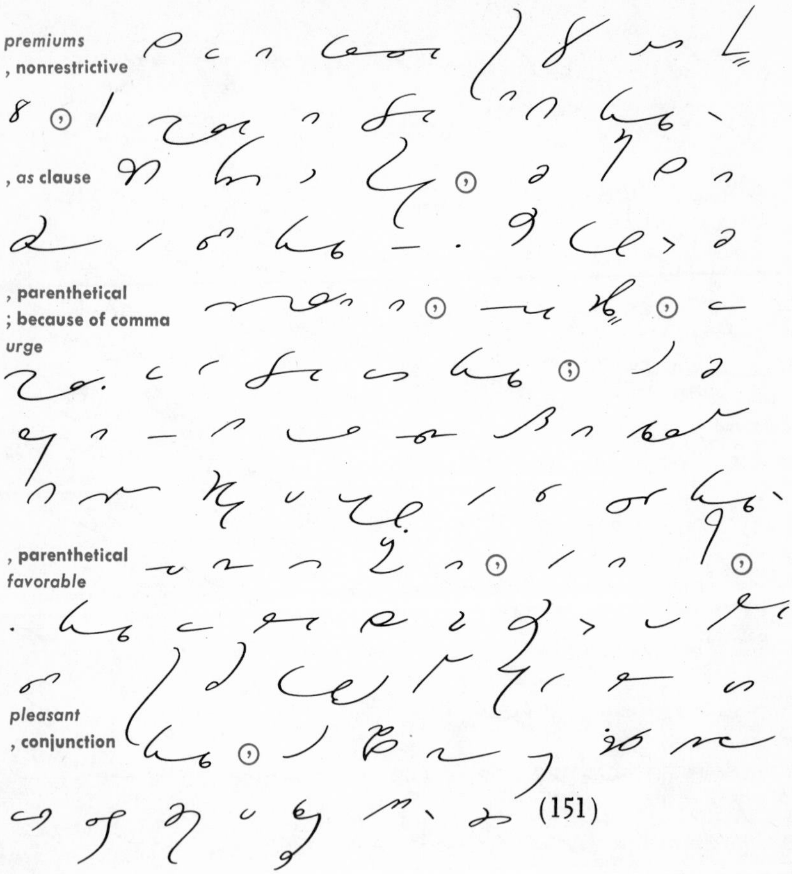

premiums
, nonrestrictive

(shorthand outlines)

, as clause

(shorthand outlines)

, parenthetical
; because of comma
urge

(shorthand outlines)

, parenthetical
favorable

(shorthand outlines)

pleasant
, conjunction

(shorthand outlines) (151)

54. 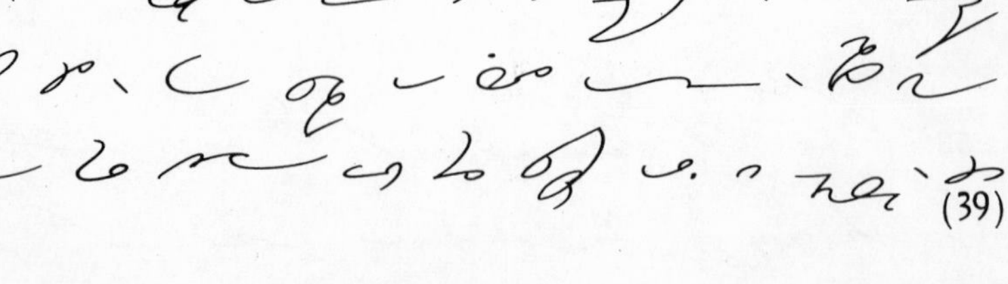 *(shorthand outlines)* (39)

LESSON **8**

► **Word Families**

55. -serve

Observe, deserve, conserve, serve, preserve, reserve, undeserved.

56. -dent

Student, accident, resident, president, incident, coincident.

57. Frequent Names

Last Names

1

Men's First Names

2

1. Burke, Callahan, Cameron, Campbell, Carroll.
2. Abraham, Adam, Adolph, Albert, Alfred, Andrew.

58. Previews and Writing Practice

59

60

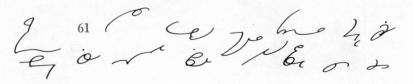

59. Conversation, dwelling, garage, provision, damage, explosions, riots, confidence.
60. Superstitious, walking, accidents, precaution, wouldn't, mishap, I shall be glad.
61. To make, pleasant, inventory, booklet, furnishings, white, inasmuch, higher, contents, hazards, don't, expires, act, Sincerely yours.

59. Dear Mrs. Adams: In accordance with our telephone conversation this afternoon, I am enclosing a fire[1] insurance policy, written by the Mutual Insurance Company, covering your dwelling and garage[2] in the amount of $18,000 for a period of three years beginning April 27.[3]

This policy also contains a provision that protects you up to $18,000 for any loss[4] or damage by explosions, riots, and airplanes.

Thank you for your confidence in us. Very cordially yours,[5]

---

60. Dear Mr. Cameron: Today is Friday, the 13th. Perhaps you are one of those people who are not superstitious.[6] Perhaps you pay no attention to black cats walking across your path or to walking under a ladder or to breaking[7] a mirror. Perhaps Friday, the 13th, is just like any other day for you.

Accidents happen on Friday,[8] the 13th, however, and on every other day. Wise people take the precaution to insure themselves against[9] expenses resulting from accidents.

Wouldn't you like to see a plan that, for only a few cents a day,[10] would pay all your bills if you had a mishap?

If you would, I shall be glad to give you all the facts. Cordially yours,[11]

---

61. Dear Mr. Albert: Would you like to make a pleasant discovery? Then write for our inventory booklet; it is[12] free. In this booklet list all your home furnishings at their value today. You will probably be amazed as most[13] people are, when you see in black and white exactly how much they are worth. Your home furnishings are now worth many[14] times the amount you paid for them.

This means that it will take more insurance to protect these goods, inasmuch as their[15] replacement value is so much higher now than it was on the day you bought them.

Our agent can take care of this[16] for you. Let him tell you about the policies that we offer, policies that cover your home and its[17] contents against fire and many other hazards.

Don't wait until your present policy expires; act now. Sincerely yours,[18] (360)

Reading and Writing Practice

62.

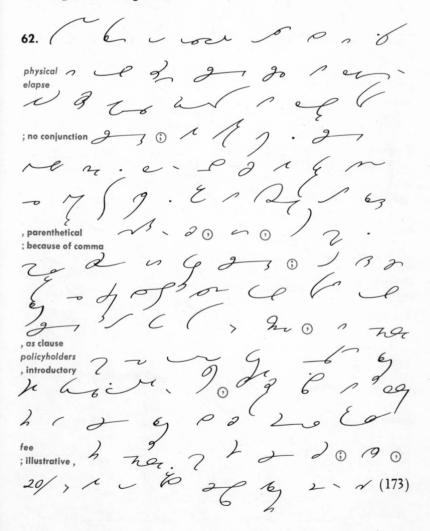

physical
elapse

; no conjunction

, parenthetical
; because of comma

, as clause
policyholders
, introductory

fee
; illustrative ,

20/

(173)

63.

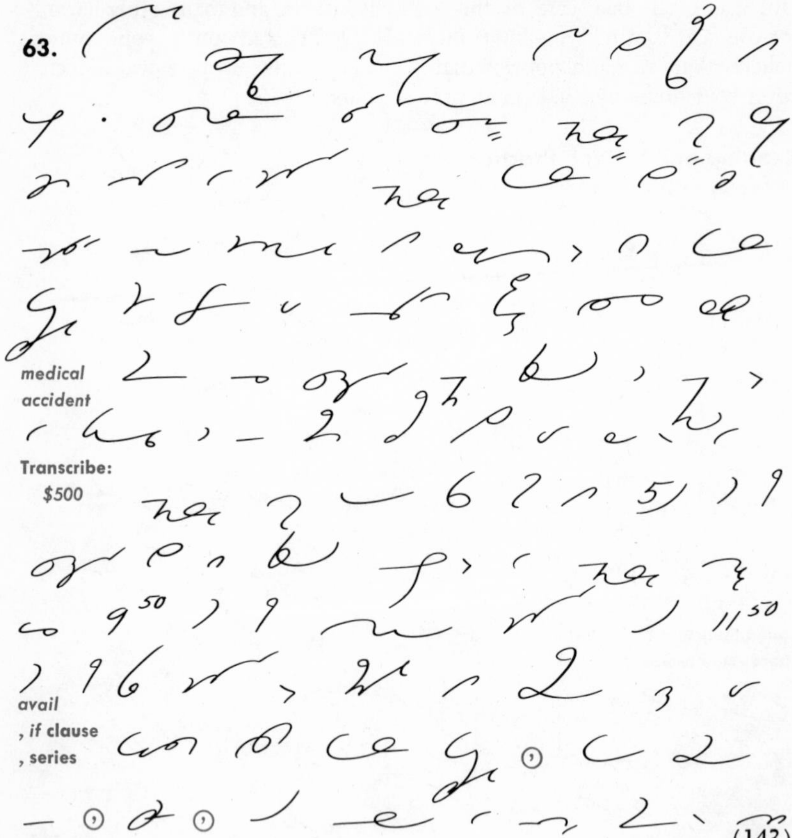

medical
accident

Transcribe:
$500

avail
, if clause
, series

(143)

64.

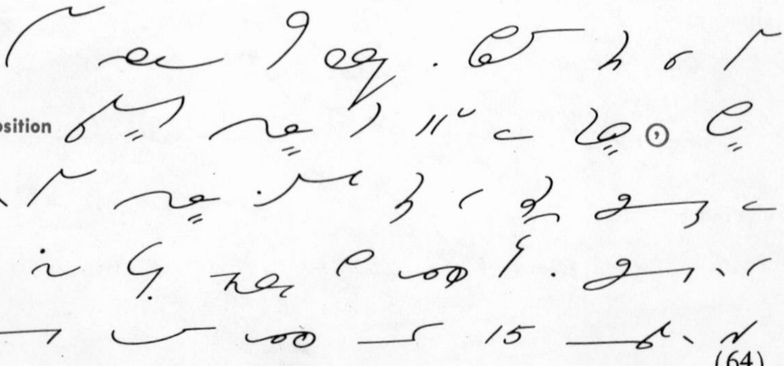

, apposition

10.

(64)

54

65. Frequent Phrases

In-law

1 *(shorthand outline)*

Few

2 *(shorthand outline)*

1. Son-in-law, brother-in-law, mother-in-law, father-in-law, sister-in-law.
2. Few minutes, few days, few months, few moments, few times.

66. Geographical Expressions

-ford

1 *(shorthand outline)*

States

2 *(shorthand outline)*

Foreign Countries

3 *(shorthand outline)*

1. Bedford, Bradford, Oxford, Hartford, Stamford, Cranford.
2. West Virginia, Rhode Island, New Mexico, Minnesota, Iowa, Colorado.
3. Ecuador, Egypt, France, Greece, India, Iran, Iraq.

68 [shorthand outlines]

69 [shorthand outlines]

70 [shorthand outlines]

68. Recently, heard, $300,000, son-in-law's, burden, dependent, daughter, thousands, young, anyone, retirement, insurance, assure, attached, coupon, description.

69. Everyone, partnership, successful, in the past, heirs, preservation, worth while.

70. Interested, arithmetic, New Mexico, advantage, longer, protection.

68. Dear Mr. Trees: We recently heard of the sad case of a man who earned $300,000 in his[1] day but who is now just his son-in-law's burden. He is a man without a home of his own.

Perhaps you have seen men[2] like him, dependent on a son or a daughter.

Thousands of young men today are making sure that they will never[3] become burdens to anyone; they are investing in retirement insurance.

Under our plan, you, too, can assure[4] yourself of an old-age income.

Send the attached coupon for a description of this plan. Cordially yours,[5]

been very successful in the past few years. It[6] is our hope that it will continue to be successful for many years to come.

It is good business, however,[7] for you to give some thought to the time when your partner's share will pass to his heirs, who may not know anything about[8] business. When your partner passes away, you will, no doubt, wish to purchase his share of the business. Will you be able[9] to do this? You will if you hold our business-preservation policy.

No matter what your present situation[10] may be, we believe that you will find it well worth while to learn just what this new policy will do for you. Yours truly,[11]

69. Dear Mr. Norris: As everyone knows, your partnership has

70. Dear Mr. Perry: Would you be interested in a plan that, for only $5 a week, will give you[12] $1,300 at the end of five years, as well as $1,000 worth of insurance starting[13] immediately. Of course, simple arithmetic will tell you that when you save $5 a week for five years, you will[14] have $1,300. But when you place that amount with the New Mexico Bank each week, you will not only have the[15] $1,300 at the end of that time, but you will have a $1,000 life insurance policy[16] as well.

These figures are based on your present age—thirty. If you act within the next two months, you can take[17] advantage of the present low rate. If you delay longer than two months, you will have to pay more to get this same[18] protection.

You can handle the entire transaction by mail if you wish. Send for our free booklet. Cordially yours,[19] (380)

Reading and Writing Practice

71.

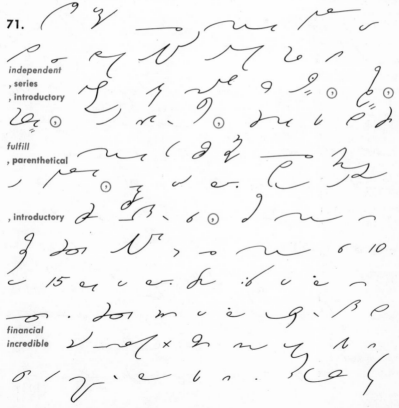

independent
, series
, introductory

fulfill
, parenthetical

, introductory

financial
incredible

accumulate
, series

5/ ⊙ 10/ ⊙

strain
. courteous
request

— ⊙ (140)

72.

lose
family

: enumeration
low-cost
hyphenated
before noun

⊙

②

③

difficulty
threatens

; no conjunction

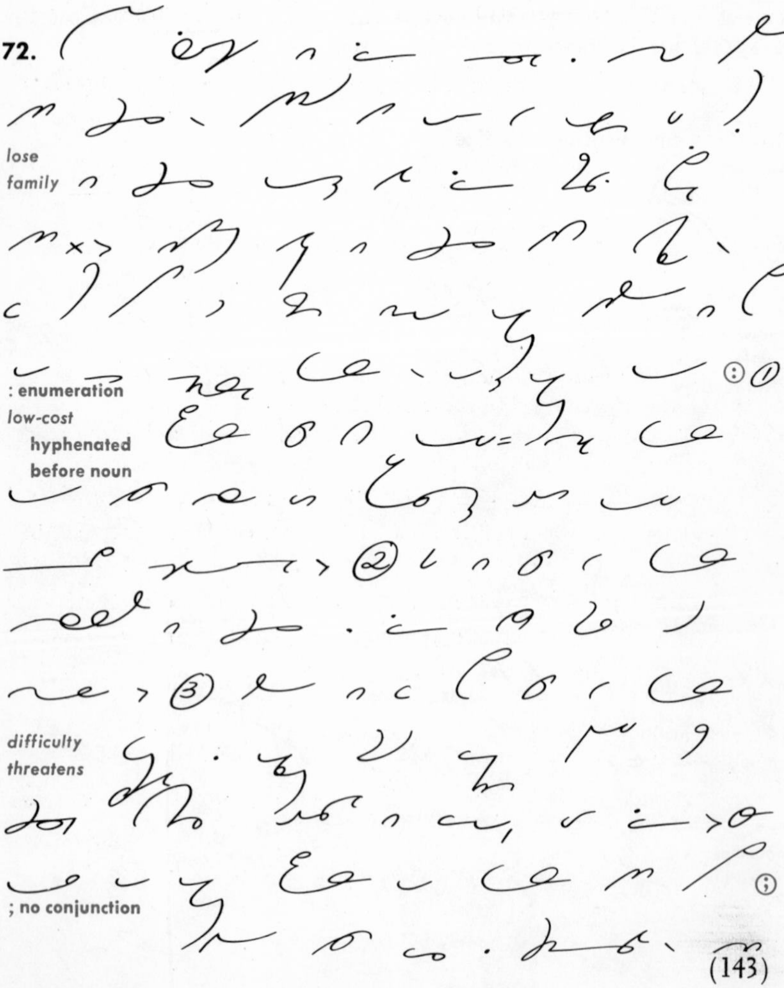

(143)

58

73. Penmanship Practice. The drills in this lesson deal with groups of outlines that tend to look alike when they are written under the pressure of rapid dictation. Practice each group following the suggestions given on page 36.

The secret to writing these outlines legibly is to keep the straight lines *straight* and the curves *deep*.

1. All, of; or, on, home; whole, old.
2. With, when, yet; hear, heard; write-right, lie.
3. They, that; the, than-then, them; thin, theme; though, although.

▶ **Progressive Speed Builder (50-90).** The letters in this Speed Builder again range in speed from 50 to 90 words a minute. Remember to:

1. Practice the preview before taking the letters from dictation.

2. Get something down for every word, even though some of your outlines may be "shaky." Do not stop writing!

74. Preview

75. Insurance, honor, retiring, I hope that, you will be able, card.
76. Glad to hear, it has been, for some years, of course, to buy, contribute.
77. Thank you for, promptly, you will find, without, offer, toward, watch.
78. There has been, slight, manager, informed, available, meant, surprise, party, anything.
79. How much, enjoyed, to me, forget, wonderful, needless to say, include.

(1 Minute at 50)

75. Dear Mr. Green: You will be happy to learn that on May 5 our/ insurance company will hold a dinner in honor of Mr. Smith. He// is retiring on June 1.

I hope that you will be able to be///present. If you can come, please return the enclosed card. Cordially yours, (1)

(1 Minute at 60)

76. Dear Mr. Jones: I was glad to hear that your insurance company is planning a/dinner for Mr. Smith. It has been my pleasure to work with him for some years, and I//shall be sorry to see him go.

I shall, of course, be present. My card is enclosed. If///you are planning to buy him a gift, I shall be glad to contribute. Sincerely yours, (2)

(1 Minute at 70)

77. Dear Mr. Green: Thank you for returning your card so promptly. I am glad that you will find it/possible to be with us. The dinner would not be complete without you.

Thank you also for your offer// to contribute toward a gift. We are planning to give him a watch, but it will be paid for by///the insurance company.

We shall look for you at the head table on May 5. Sincerely yours, (3)

(1 Minute at 80)

78. Dear Mr. Green: There has been a slight change in our plans for the dinner we are going to give Mr. Smith. The/manager of the hotel informed us that they will not have a dining room available on May 5. We are, therefore,//changing the date to May 8.

I hope that this change in plans will not prevent you from being with us.

As this dinner///is meant to be a surprise party, please do not say anything about it to Mr. Smith. Cordially yours, (4)

(1 Minute at 90)

79. Dear Mr. Jones: This is just a note to tell you how much I enjoyed the dinner you and my other friends gave me on May 8./The party was a complete surprise to me. I can assure you that I shall never forget it. Nor shall I forget the many//wonderful people with whom I have worked during my 30 years with the company. Needless to say, I shall miss them very/// much.

I have not yet made definite plans for the future, but you may be sure that they will include many hours of fishing. Sincerely, (5) (350)

Reading and Writing Practice

80.
recall
, parenthetical
; because of comma

ceases
worry
, parenthetical

, when clause
long-lasting
  hyphenated
  before noun

, if clause

judgment
up to date
  no noun,
  no hyphen

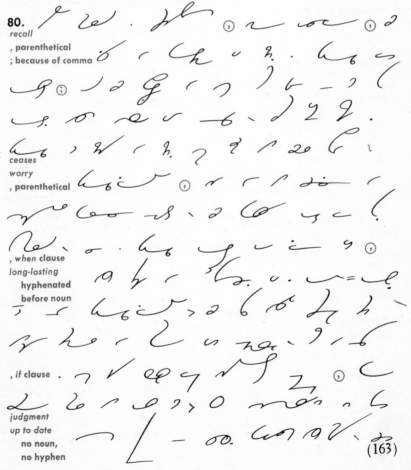

(163)

81.

cellar

, if clause
overnight

, parenthetical
, introductory
worth-while
hyphenated
before noun

. courteous
request
jot

; no conjunction
mailbox

(133)

In the following chapter you will review punctuation with quotation marks; the typing of dates, amounts, and street addresses; and the use of a period instead of a question mark in a courteous request.

, introducing short quote

Short quotations are introduced by a comma.

> John said, "I am hungry."

: introducing long quote

Long quotations are introduced by a colon.

> John said: "I shall not be able to attend the meeting on Wednesday. I have an examination scheduled for Thursday, and I want to spend Wednesday night preparing for it."

, inside quote
. inside quote

The comma and the period are *always* typed inside the final quotation mark.

> He said, "I cannot accept the present."
> The pamphlet, "Tabulation Made Easy," is now available.

The question mark is placed inside the closing quotation mark if only the quoted material is a question. The question mark is placed outside the closing quotation mark if the entire sentence is a question.

> She asked, "Will you take my check?"
> Did she say, "The job is too difficult for me"?

Semicolons and colons are *always* placed outside the final quotation mark.

dates

The correct form for transcribing dates is *January 15,* with no *th* after the figures when the month precedes the day.

amounts

The correct form for transcribing amounts of dollars is $120, with no decimal point and no zeros for cents.

street address

In transcribing a street address, the form recommended is 115 East 72 Street—without a d after the street number. More and more authorities are recommending the omission of th, st, and d from numbered streets because the omission adds to the readability of the address.

courteous request

Very often one businessman may wish to persuade another to take some definite action. He could make his request for action with a direct statement like this:

Send me your check today.

A direct statement of this type, however, might antagonize the reader. Many businessmen, therefore, prefer to make such a request in the form of a question.

Won't you please send me a check today.

Where a request for definite action is put in the form of a question, a period is used at the end of the sentence.

LESSON **11**

▶ **Principles of Outline Construction**

82. Vowel written in word endings -ANCE and -ENCE. *The vowel is written in the endings* -ANCE, -ENCE *when those endings follow* ī, N, R, *or* L.

Ī

N

R

L

1. Compliance, alliance, appliance, defiance, reliance, self-reliance.
2. Maintenance, dominance, eminence, prominence.
3. Recurrence, conference, difference, endurance, appearance, assurance.
4. Balance, brilliance, resemblance, violence, silence.

83. Vowel omitted in word endings -ANCE and -ENCE. *The vowel in* -ANCE, -ENCE *is omitted in the following words because its omission gives much more fluent, and at the same time legible, outlines.*

CHAPTER **3** BANKING AND INVESTMENTS

2 [shorthand outlines]

1. Assistance, accordance, issuance, resistance, annoyance, acquaintance.
2. Negligence, insistence, essence, independence, indulgence, influence.

Reading and Writing Practice

84. Money

[shorthand outlines]

25

Croesus

550

13

1368 (330)

—The Story of Uncle Sam's Money

Letters

85.
Transcribe:
  $50
. inside quote

, parenthetical
Transcribe:
  April 5

its
recurrence

(65)

86.
Transcribe:
  June 5

compliance
, introductory

: enumeration

(97)

87. Recall Drill (S). In this drill you will review the word beginnings and endings that are represented by the two forms for s.

Self-, Circum-

1 [shorthand outlines]

Super-, Etc.

2 [shorthand outlines]

Sub-

3 [shorthand outlines]

-ings

4 [shorthand outlines]

Amounts

5 [shorthand outlines]

1. Selfish, self-supporting, self-reliance, self-confident, self-satisfied, self-educated, circumstances.
2. Superior, supervise, supervision, supervisory, supreme, supremacy, support, supporter.
3. Substantial, sublease, suburb, suburban, subway, submit, subnormal.
4. Savings, feelings, shavings, findings, sayings, shortcomings, helpings.
5. 8 cents, 3 per cent.

88. Previews and Writing Practice

89. You have been, courage, finance, one of the, useful, welcome, sensible, prefer, nearest.
90. Millions, however, difference, between, commercial, constantly, substantial, avoid, profits, discounts, exceeds, interest, invited.
91. Convenience, account, certain, sincerely, hope that, personal.

89. Dear Mr. March: If you have been longing for a car but have not had the courage to buy one, let the County Trust[1] Company finance it for you. It is one of the many useful banking services that we perform every[2] day. You will welcome the lack of red tape as well as our sensible monthly repayment plan.

In your monthly[3] payments we include a small charge to cover insurance. If you prefer, you can place this insurance through your own[4] broker. For further details phone Main 4-6000, or visit our nearest office. Very sincerely yours,[5]

---

90. Dear Mr. Smith: There are times when people talk very lightly about millions of dollars. The wise businessman and[6] his banker, however, know that attention to small amounts makes the difference between profit and loss.

The[7] commercial bank is constantly helping its customers to make small savings as well as substantial ones, to avoid[8] small losses as well as great losses, to reap small profits as well as large profits.

It is good business practice to borrow[9] in order to take advantage of cash discounts when the saving exceeds the interest on a bank loan.

You are[10] invited to come in and discuss with us ways in which you can make use of our services and save. Sincerely yours,[11]

---

91. Dear Mr. Fisher: Would it be a convenience to you if you did not have to come to the bank to make payments[12] on your real estate loan? If so, you can do just that by opening a checking account with us.

As a service[13] to our real-estate customers, we are happy to arrange to charge your monthly payments against your checking account[14] and mail you a copy of the charge.

We have two types of checking accounts, one of which is certain to fit your[15] needs.

We wish you to feel that this is your bank, and we sincerely hope that you will make full use of all our departments.[16] A checking account can be opened for you by mail or by a personal visit to this bank. Cordially yours,[17] (340)

Reading and Writing Practice

92.
, parenthetical
, and omitted
, parenthetical

, introductory
, apposition
. inside quote

, and omitted
stories

, nonrestrictive
self-supporting

, introducing
short quote
. inside quote

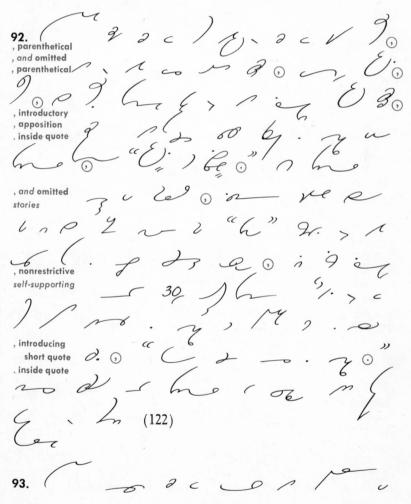

(122)

93.

carefree
permanent

, parenthetical
substantial

, parenthetical

(126)

94.

emergencies
, introductory

(70)

LESSON **13**

▶ **Word Families**

95. -ually

(shorthand outlines)

Equally, perpetually, annually, actually, virtually.

96. Unm-

(shorthand outlines)

Unmolested, unmarried, unmatched, unmindful, unmake.

97. Frequent Names

Last Names

1 *(shorthand outlines)*

Women's First Names

2 *(shorthand outlines)*

1. Clarke, Cohen, Cohn, Collins, Connell, Cooper.
2. Beatrice, Belle, Bertha, Bridget, Caroline, Catherine, Celia.

98. Previews and Writing Practice

99 *(shorthand outlines)*

100 *(shorthand outlines)*

101 *(shorthand outlines)*

[shorthand outlines]

99. Pleased, latest, financial, convince, letting us, completed, operation, interesting, approximately, I hope that.
100. Combine, entirely, Washington, whatever, prepared.
101. Receiving, up-to-the-minute, Social Security Act, available, retire, to know, benefits, wife, we shall be glad, troubling, obligation.

99. Dear Mr. Henry: We are pleased to enclose our latest financial statement showing the fine condition of our[1] bank. This statement should convince you that you will be taking the right step by letting us handle your banking business.[2]

We might add that our organization has just completed 50 years of operation in this state. It is[3] interesting to note that approximately 30 per cent of our business comes from out of the state.

I hope that[4] you will give us an opportunity to look after your banking business in the near future. Cordially yours,[5]

---

100. Dear Mr. White: Many of us have doctors' bills and other obligations to pay, but some months we just cannot[6] seem to make our pay check cover them all. With a personal loan from the County Trust Company at low[7] interest rates, you can combine several debts into one that you can repay in convenient monthly installments.[8]

Most business organizations combine their debts in this way. You will find it good business, too.

Visit our nearest[9] office. If it is more convenient, arrange a loan entirely by telephone and mail. Simply call Washington[10] 3-3456.

Whatever your banking needs may be, our bank is prepared to take care of them. Cordially yours,[11]

---

101. Dear Mr. Nelson: Would you be interested in receiving the latest, up-to-the-minute information[12] about your benefits under the Social Security Act? Would you like to know what amount of money will[13] be available to you when you retire in March, 1965? Would you like to know what benefits[14] your wife would receive before reaching the age of sixty-five if anything should happen to you in the[15] meantime?

We shall be glad to answer these as well as any other questions that may be troubling you about the[16] Social Security Act. This service is rendered by our bank without cost or obligation to you.

For full[17] details on the Social Security Act and how it affects you, fill in and mail the enclosed slip. Sincerely yours,[18] (360)

102. *[shorthand outlines]*

, when clause
securities

[shorthand outlines]

, conjunction
promptly

[shorthand outlines]

, when clause
mind

[shorthand outlines]

(124)

103. *[shorthand outlines]*

, introductory
safe-deposit
  hyphenated
  before noun

[shorthand outlines]

, parenthetical
, series

[shorthand outlines]

[shorthand outline]

[shorthand outline]

[shorthand outline]

[shorthand outline]

[shorthand outline]

[shorthand outline] (176)

104. *[shorthand outline]* (35)

105. Frequent Phrases

Want

1   ✧ ✧ ✧ ✧ ✧ ✧ ✧ ✧

Year

2   ✧ ✧ ✧ ✧ ✧ ✧ ✧

1. I want, he wants, he wanted, you wanted, who wanted, if you want, do you want.

2. Last year, during the last year, past year, during the past year, next year, some years.

106. Geographical Expressions

-ington

1   ✧ ✧ ✧ ✧ ✧ ✧

States and Territories

2   ✧ ✧ ✧ ✧ ✧ ✧ ✧ ✧

Foreign Countries

3   ✧ ✧ ✧ ✧ ✧ ✧ ✧

1. Arlington, Bennington, Bloomington, Irvington, Burlington.

2. Virginia, Oregon, New Hampshire, Massachusetts, Illinois, Arkansas, Kentucky, Hawaii.

3. Peru, Poland, Siam, Sweden, Turkey, Ukraine.

108

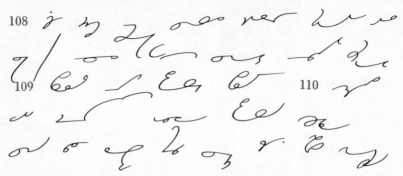

109

110

108. Whether, successfully, infallible, accurately, strengthen, folder, three, enable, judge, namely, program, analysis, methods, facilities.
109. Apparently, undue, explanation, appointment.
110. Constantly, although, some time ago, recall, explained, cancel, account, within, elapsed, you have not yet, anxious, extending, we hope that, you will find.

108. Gentlemen: How can you tell whether a business is operating successfully or not?

There is no infallible[1] way, but there are means of testing accurately the strength of an organization. The enclosed folder[2] deals with three services that we render that enable you to judge the success of a business; namely,[3] a carefully planned financial program, an analysis of methods of operation, and suggestions for[4] improvement.

May we discuss with you how the facilities of our bank can be put to work for you. Just return[5] the post card that is enclosed, and a representative will call at your convenience. Very truly yours,[6]

you have not had an opportunity to give much thought to our letter of May 6.[7] I am writing you again just in case the contents of that letter have slipped your mind.

I am firmly convinced that our[8] financing plan is the best one for your particular needs. It is the best one because you can arrange[9] payment over a long period of time. It does not require any fixed payment dates; therefore, it does[10] not place an undue strain on the funds of your organization.

There is no obligation in asking for an[11] explanation of our plan. Why not call Main 7-4500 and arrange an appointment. Cordially yours,[12]

---

109. Dear Mr. Fox: Apparently

110. Dear Mr. Adams: Up to

the present time your name has not been listed among our constantly increasing number[13] of new friends, although we sent you one of our steel banks some time ago.

As you will recall, we explained that we would[14] charge your account with the purchase price of the bank; but we promised to cancel the charge of $2 if you opened[15]

an account within ninety days. This time has elapsed, but you have not yet opened an account. We are anxious[16] to keep our part of the agreement; therefore, we are extending the time for opening your account for[17] another ten days. We hope that you will find it possible to call soon and open an account. Cordially yours,[18] (360)

Reading and Writing Practice

111.

bearing
foreign

: introducing
    long quote
, conjunction

10 /

Transcribe:
  15 per cent
. inside quote

incur
, conjunction

, if clause

(137)

112.

(156)

113. Penmanship Practice. The Penmanship drills in this lesson also deal with groups of outlines that tend to look alike when they are written under the stress of rapid dictation. Practice the drills following the suggestions given on page 36.

Writing these outlines legibly will give you no problem if you will:
1. Keep the straight lines *straight*, the curves *deep*.
2. Make the A circle very *large*, the E circle *tiny*.
3. Watch your proportions carefully.

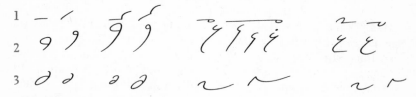

1. In-not, at-it; in the, at the; any, many; one, no-know.
2. As, if, I have, ever; object, subject, such, hope; opinion, opportunity.
3. Say, see; we, way; you will, it will; you are, to our.

▶ **Progressive Speed Builder (60-100).** The speed range of the letters in this Progressive Speed Builder is slightly higher than the previous two Speed Builders with which you have worked. The first letter is counted at 60 words a minute and the last at 100 words a minute.

Because the vocabulary of the 100-word letter is similar to that of the other four letters, that letter should give you no trouble.

114. Preview

115 *[shorthand outlines]*

116 *[shorthand outlines]*

117 *[shorthand outlines]*

118
119

115. This morning, application, position, secretary, reference, shorthand, opinion.
116. One of the best, in fact, one time, reporter, in addition, typist, hesitation, recommending.
117. Thank you for your letter, to whom, highly, I might say, efficient.
118. You will be glad, encouraging, letters, convenient, I am sure, enjoy, anxious.
119. Accepted, physical, examination, necessary, details, disposed, judging.

(1 Minute at 60)

115. Dear Miss Lee: This morning I received a letter of application from Miss Helen/Green. She is applying for a position as my secretary and gave your name//as a reference. She tells me that you were her shorthand teacher.

I wonder whether///you would write us your opinion of Miss Green. A stamped envelope is enclosed. Yours sincerely, (1)

(1 Minute at 70)

116. Dear Mr. Gates: It is a pleasure to give you my opinion of Miss Helen Green, who is/applying for a position as your secretary. Miss Green is one of the best students I have ever//had. In fact, at one time she was thinking of becoming a shorthand reporter. In addition,///she is a fast typist.

I have no hesitation in recommending her to you. Cordially yours, (2)

(1 Minute at 80)

117. Dear Miss Lee: Thank you for your letter telling us that you have no hesitation in recommending Miss Green for/a position with our bank. All the people to whom we have written about her speak highly of her, and I plan//to offer the position to her.

I might say that we have in our department of the bank several of the///girls you have trained; and if Miss Green is as efficient as these girls, I know that we shall be pleased with her. Sincerely yours, (3)

(1 Minute at 90)

118. Dear Miss Green: You will be glad to know that all the people you listed as references on your application form have written/us very encouraging letters about you. It is a pleasure, therefore, to offer you the position as my//secretary.

If it is convenient for you, please

come to my office on Monday, April 10, so that we may make final/// arrangements.

I am sure you will enjoy being with us. You will find all your fellow workers anxious to help you succeed. Cordially yours, (4)

(1 Minute at 100)

119. Mr. Smith: Miss Helen Green has just accepted the position as my secretary. She will come to the bank on April 10 to make final/arrangements. She will report on April 15.

Would you be good enough to arrange to have her take the usual physical examination//while she is here on April 10. Also, have her fill out all the necessary forms so that all these details will have been disposed of///when she reports.

Judging by the excellent reports I have received about Miss Green, she should be able to handle the job nicely. A. C. Gates (5) (400)

Reading and Writing Practice

120.

, conjunction
mighty

, if clause
. courteous
  request

, conjunction
, introductory

(134)

121.
response
, introductory

, parenthetical
systematically

, conjunction
balance

, if clause
, series
self-addressed

(154)

Marginal Reminders, 4

In the following chapter you will study three new uses of the comma. The following explanations will help you understand these uses. Their frequent occurrence in the Reading and Writing Practice exercises will help you master them.

, words omitted

A comma is used to indicate the omission of a word, or several words, that are completely understood from the meaning.

> One model sells for $35; the other, for $45.
> The first job is easy; the second, difficult.
> In June our volume was up 20 per cent; in July, 15 per cent.

Whenever one of these uses occurs in the Reading and Writing exercises, it will be indicated in the margin by ", words omitted."

, contrast

Contrasting expressions are set off by commas.

> He wanted help, not advice.
> I am going to the meeting, not because I want to, but because it is my duty.
> The harder you work, the more you will earn.

Whenever one of these uses occurs in the Reading and Writing exercises, it will be indicated in the margin by ", contrast."

, intervening phrase

When two phrases modify the same expression, the second, or intervening, phrase is set off by commas.

> The last book is as interesting as, if not more interesting than, his other books.
> No one can equal, or even approach, his skill in typing.

Caution: Be sure to enclose the *complete* intervening expression, not just part of it.

> *Wrong:* Our business is as large as, if not larger, than
> it was a year ago.
> *Right:* Our business is as large as, if not larger than,
> it was a year ago.

Each time one of these uses of the comma occurs in the Reading and Writing exercises, it will be indicated in the margin by ", intervening phrase."

LESSON **16**

▶ **Principles of Outline Construction**

122. Vowel written in word endings -ANT, -ENT. *The vowel is written in the endings* -ANT, -ENT *when those endings follow* ī, N, R, *or* L.

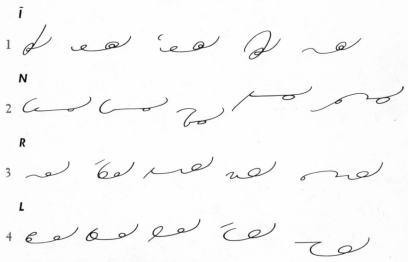

1. Giant, reliant, self-reliant, defiant, client.
2. Prominent, permanent, component, dominant, indignant.
3. Current, transparent, tolerant, warrant, ignorant.
4. Excellent, silent, talent, transplant, implant.

Reading and Writing Practice

123. Yesterday—Today—Tomorrow

(158)

Letters

124.
, introductory
: enumeration

, series
selection

[shorthand outline]

, if clause
, contrast
compliments

(96)

125. [shorthand outline]

; no conjunction
, words omitted

shelves
, if clause

especially
frequently

(127)

126.

maximum
, introductory
currently

, introductory
guarantee
, contrast

, introductory

, if clause

(107)

127.

grocery
: enumeration

guaranteed
, introductory

(53)

128. Recall Drill (F). In this drill you will review the word beginnings and endings that are represented by the alphabetic stroke F.

-ful

1 *[shorthand outlines]*

-ify

2 *[shorthand outlines]*

Fur-, For-, Fore-

3 *[shorthand outlines]*

-ification

4 *[shorthand outlines]*

-field

5 *[shorthand outlines]*

1. Wonderful, grateful, thoughtful, dreadful, beautiful, tactful, shameful.
2. Simplify, amplify, classify, clarify, verify.
3. Furniture, furnace, furnished; forgot, forgotten, forfeit; foresee.
4. Notification, modification, fortification, classification, ratification, specifications.
5. Deerfield, Greenfield, Westfield, Plainfield, Garfield, Littlefield.

129. Previews and Writing Practice

130 *[shorthand outlines]*

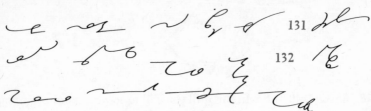

130. One of the most, manager, trained, kind, you should have, you want, listen, criticism, count, happiest, next time.

131. Few days ago, rendered, needless to say, employ, responsible.

132. During the past year, complimentary, comments, men and women, employees.

130. Dear Mrs. Parks: One of the most important men in our stores is the manager. He is trained to give you the kind[1] of service that we think you should have. He is our representative and is charged with the duty of satisfying[2] you.

He is in the store to see that you get what you want—and he is there to listen when you have something[3] on your mind.

If you have a question or a suggestion or a criticism, he is there to hear it. You can count[4] on him to do all he can to please you. That is part of his job. When he can be of help to you, he is happiest.[5]

The next time you are in one of our stores, make it a point to meet the manager; he is your friend. Cordially yours,[6]

---

131. Mr. Smith: A few days ago we received a very nice letter from Mrs. E. H. Brown, of 10 Main Street in[7] Cambridge, in which she tells us that for more than 25 years you have supplied her with our milk

and dairy products.[8] She says that during that time the service you rendered to her was so satisfactory that she almost regrets[9] moving.

This surely speaks well for you as one of our salesmen. Needless to say, we are proud to have you in our employ.[10] I am attaching a carbon of the letter that we wrote Mrs. Brown.

It is the co-operation of[11] men like you that has been responsible for the growth of our company during the past 30 years. J. H. Abbey[12]

---

132. Dear Mrs. Burns: During the past year, we received more than 5,000 complimentary comments about the men[13] and women who serve you daily in our stores— almost three times as many favorable comments about our[14] employees as there were the year before.

That makes all of us very happy indeed, for it indicates that we are[15] giving you the kind of service you want.

If you have any ideas as to how we can make your shopping even[16] more satisfying, please write to our Customer Relations Department at 14 West Broadway. Sincerely yours,[17] (340)

Reading and Writing Practice

133.

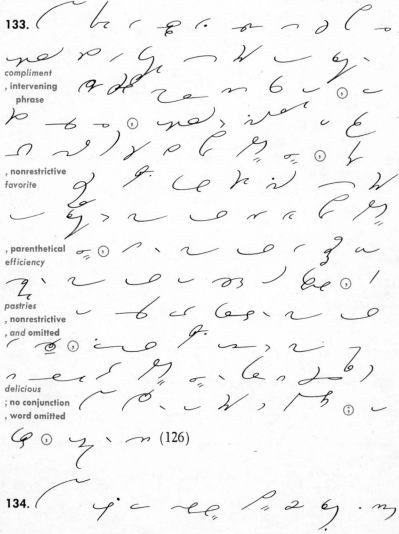

compliment
, intervening
    phrase

, nonrestrictive
favorite

, parenthetical
efficiency

pastries
, nonrestrictive
, and omitted

delicious
; no conjunction
, word omitted

(126)

134.

(shorthand outline)

(shorthand outline)

(113)

135.
Inn
luncheon

(shorthand outline)

(shorthand outline)

(63)

94

► **Word Families**

136. *-sure*

Sure, insure, assure, pressure, pleasure, reassure, reinsure.

137. *-stic*

Plastic, elastic, drastic, artistic, mystic.

138. Frequent Names

Last Names

1

Men's First Names

2

1. Crowley, Daly, Davidson, Davis, Donovan, Doyle.
2. Arthur, Benjamin, Charles, Clarence, Daniel, David.

139. Previews and Writing Practice

140

141

95

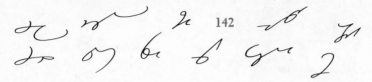
140. I am sure, you want, one of the, Connecticut, quality, won't.
141. Description, manager, co-operation, attempt, neighborhood, profitable, sampled, scheduled, efforts.
142. No doubt, reputation, families, attractive, buyers, in addition, procedures, convenience.

140. Dear Mrs. Arthur: I am sure you want the best when it comes to dairy products for your family. If you should like[1] these products delivered fresh from one of the finest farms of Connecticut, return the enclosed card telling us what[2] we can deliver to you as a trial order. I am sure you and your family will be so delighted with the[3] freshness and quality of the products you receive that you will want us to take care of all your dairy needs.

You[4] will be interested to know that we serve many of your neighbors.

Won't you give our products a trial? Sincerely yours,[5]

---

141. Dear Mr. Davidson: Enclosed with this letter is a complete description of Daniel's Soup Sale that will start on Monday,[6] May 6.

As sales manager of the Charles Soup Company, I want to take this opportunity to thank you for[7] your offer of co-operation in our attempt to get a sample of Daniel's Soup into the home of as many[8] families in your neighborhood as possible.

We have tried to make our plan profitable to you as the dealer.[9] We realize, of course, that the quantity of soup sold and the number of families sampled depend on you. The[10] advertising scheduled for May will help; but the displays in your store and the efforts of your clerks will help determine[11] the amount of soup you sell and the profit you make.

Many thanks for your co-operation. Cordially yours,[12]

---

142. Dear Mrs. Drake: As you no doubt know, our store has made a fine reputation for itself as a meat market. For[13] years we have been supplying local families with the finest cuts of meat.

We wonder, however, whether you[14] have had an opportunity to visit our fruit corner recently. You will find it more attractive than ever[15] before.

Our fruit buyers make every effort to buy only the finest of fruits. Our clerks keep the fruit displays[16] neat and fresh. In addition, we have improved our packing procedures to insure freshness and shopping convenience.[17]

On your next visit to our store, stop at the fruit corner. You will be pleased with what you find there. Cordially yours,[18] (360)

Reading and Writing Practice

143.
economics
, conjunction

up to date
no noun,
no hyphen
, inside quote

, words omitted
, parenthetical
adopt

suitable
, if clause

February
, as clause

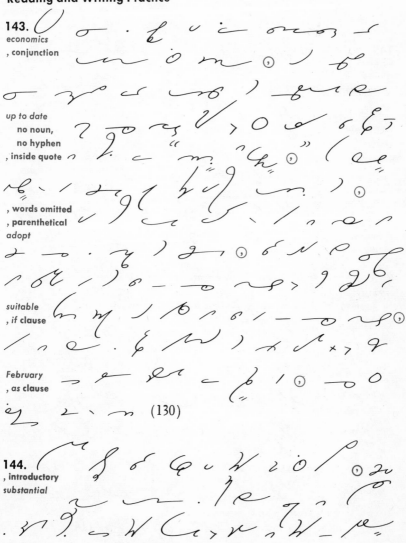

(130)

144.
, introductory
substantial

(54)

145.

workers'
midday
, introductory

, introductory
, contrast

employees
morale

successful
, intervening
  phrase

— 16 — 45 —

, introductory

, apposition
. inside quote

(149)

LESSON **19**

146. Frequent Phrases

Time

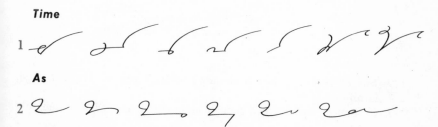

1

As

2

1. Next time, same time, any time, one time, at a time, few times, several times.
2. As well, as good, as many, as much, as low, as little.

147. Geographical Expressions

-ingham

1

States and Territories

2

Foreign Countries

3

1. Birmingham, Framingham, Nottingham, Effingham, Cunningham.
2. Utah, Oklahoma, Nevada, Maryland, Idaho, Arizona, Alaska.
3. U.S.S.R., Uruguay, Venezuela, Albania.

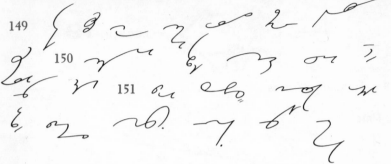

149. Budget, wisely, quality, coupons, already, if you are not, delighted, favorites.

150. Customers, busiest, good enough, announce, interested, any time, substantial.

151. Users, Alaska, you might be, results, experienced, uniformly, gratifying, encouraging, in addition to the, invaluable.

149. Dear Mrs. Knight: Your food budget is a mighty important item to both of us. It is important to you[1] because it is your job to use it wisely; it is important to us because we strive to bring you the very[2] finest quality for your money.

We are enclosing several coupons in this letter to help you stretch your[3] food dollar. The coupons may be used for the purchase of a number of new Smith products that we know you will want[4] to try.

If you already are a user of these products, you will be happy to save in the purchase of them.[5] If you are not, we know you will be delighted to add these products to your list of favorites. Sincerely yours,[6]

150. Dear Mr. Gray: Because of the increased business that we expect during the summer months, we shall need four boys to[7] handle stock and work with customers. Two of the boys would work from nine to one and the other two from one to five.[8] All four would work a full eight hours on Saturday, which is our busiest day.

I wonder whether you would be good[9] enough to announce these jobs to your class of senior boys and invite any who are interested to come in[10] to see me at any time that is convenient to them.

By doing this, you will be helping some boys to earn a[11] substantial sum during the summer and at the same time learn a good deal about the food business. Cordially yours,[12]

151. Dear Mr. Murphy: In view of the fact that we were one of the first users of the Alaska Ice-Maker,[13] I thought you might be interested in the results we experienced.

During the past year we have installed one[14] of your units in every Smith Hotel. Our results with them have been uniformly good. The satisfaction[15] of our guests with the ice now supplied in our restaurants and in the hotel rooms is most gratifying.

Since [16] these machines were installed, our savings have been encouraging.

In addition to the savings we are making, the [17] advantage of having all the ice we want when we want it is invaluable in our business. Yours truly,[18] (360)

Reading and Writing Practice

152.

, introductory
Restaurant

, nonrestrictive
whether

, parenthetical
; because of comma
pleasant

; no conjunction
, words omitted

privilege ‿ ᧐ ⌒ ᒐ ᒐᵒᵒ ⌐ ⎯⎯ ⎴
  ᶆ ⟍ ᶆ (147)

153. ⎛⎝ ⎛ ℓ ⟋ ⟍ ‿ ᶄ ⎝ ⮝ ⎯ ⟋

, introductory
, contrast
75 ᥱᧄ ᥱ ⊙ ⟋ ‿ ⌐₆ ⊙ — ⎠

⎬ ⟋ ⊙ ᒐ ⎝ ᧄ ⟋ ⎨ — ⟍

‿ ⟋ ℬ ᠈ ᥱ ⌐ᥱᥱ ᧐ ⌒ ⌐₆ ⟍ ⟍

constantly
: *enumeration* ᵧᵒ ‿ ⟍ ᧐ ⌒᧐ ⊙ ① ⟍ ⟋ ᧐

‿ ‿ ⟍ᥱ ⎝ᥱ ⎝ᥱ ᠊ ᵧ ᠈ ② ⟍

low-price ⟍ ⌐ ᠈ ᠊ ⌐ ⌐ᥱᥱ ⟍ᥱ ᠈ ③ ⟍

hyphenated
before noun ‿ ‿ = ⎝ᥱ ⌐₆ ⌐ ℬ ᠊

⎝ ⟋ ⌐ ⟍ ⎝ ⟋ ᠊⌐ ⟍ᵧ

ᥱᧄ ᠈ ④ ⟍ ⟋ ᠊⌐ ᒐ ᥱ ⟋ ⎠

available
, *intervening*
phrase ⎝⟋ ⟍ ⟍ ⎝᥉ ᠊ ⎝ᥱ ᥱ ᠊

9 ⊙ ⌐ ‿ ‿ ⌐ ⊙ ⌐ ⟍ ⌐ ⟍ᥱ ᠈ ⎬

⟍ ᥅ᵧ ᠂ ᥱ ᶆᵧ ⌒ ᥱ ⟍ ⌐ ⎝ᥱ

ᵧ ᥅ᵧ ⟍ ⎠ ᥱᵌ ⟍ ᥲ ⟍ ᶆ — ⟍

ᵧᵌ ⟍ ᶆ (153)

154. Penmanship Practice. The drills in this lesson are designed to help you join circles to straight lines correctly. Follow the practice suggestions given on page 36.

In practicing these groups:

1. Keep the straight lines *straight*.
2. Close each circle.
3. Make the A circles *large*; the E circles *tiny*.

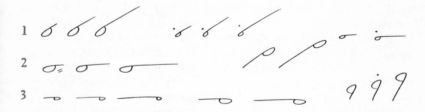

1. Ate, add, added; heat, heed, heeded; when, him.
2. Ann, I am, amend; day, today.
3. Any, me, many; may, memoranda; I shall, hatch, age.

▶ **Progressive Speed Builder (60-100)**

155. Preview

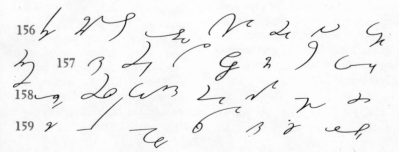

103

156. Just, if you would like to have, let us know, dividends, first, toward, profits, for your convenience.
157. Thank you for, very much, to me, appreciate, issue, advantage, promotion.
158. Requested, variety, products, forms, your orders, in the future, Sincerely yours.
159. Yesterday, indeed, impressed, items, to us, whether, relationship.
160. Interested, to know, amounting, account, next time, in fact, worth while.

(1 Minute at 60)

156. Dear Mr. Gray: Our new supply of catalogues just arrived. If you would like to have/a copy, please let us know.

It will pay you big dividends to place your food business//with us. You can take the first step toward greater profits by sending for one of our catalogues///at once. A stamped envelope is enclosed for your convenience. Sincerely yours, (1)

(1 Minute at 70)

157. Gentlemen: Thank you for writing me about your catalogue. I should like very much to have a/ copy. Please send it to me personally, so that I shall be sure to see it.

I should also//appreciate it if you would place my name on your mailing list to receive all the sales helps that you///issue to food stores. We can use these helps to good advantage in our promotion work. Sincerely yours, (2)

(1 Minute at 80)

158. Dear Mr. Gray: As you requested, we have mailed you today a copy of our new catalogue. I think you will/be pleased with the large variety of food products it lists. In the back of the catalogue you will find a number//of forms that you can use in placing your orders. These forms will save you a great deal of time.

Your name has been placed/// on our mailing list, and in the future you will receive all sales helps that we issue to food stores. Sincerely yours, (3)

(1 Minute at 90)

159. Gentlemen: The catalogue you sent me arrived yesterday, and I have spent several hours examining it. I was, indeed,/impressed with your large variety of food products. I found many items that I am sure we can handle with profit to// you as well as to us.

I wonder whether you would be good enough to send me two more copies of the catalogue. I have/// the feeling that this is the beginning of a profitable business relationship for both of us. Very cordially yours, (4)

160. Mr. Ames. You will be interested to know that some weeks ago we received a request for one of our catalogues from Mr. E. H./ Gray, of the New York Food Stores. We sent him a copy, and today we received an order from him amounting to $355.// If we give him the right kind of service, we can build this into a very profitable account.

May I suggest that the next time you/// are in New York you stop in to see Mr. Gray. In fact, it might even be worth while for you to make a special trip to see him. Charles H. West. (5) (400)

Reading and Writing Practice

161.

. inside quote
, parenthetical

swapped

, intervening
  phrase

health
; because of comma
, parenthetical

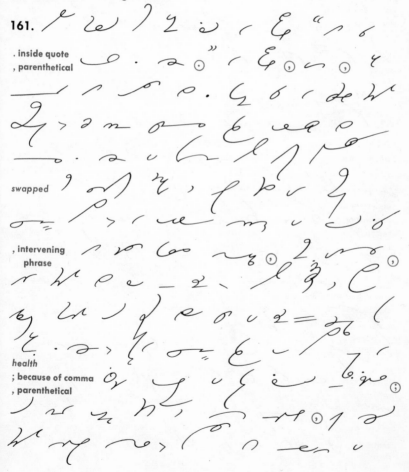

162.

loosely
, when clause

: enumeration
, conjunction
cheerfully

, introductory
urge

, contrast

(108)

Dictation Problems

Every shorthand writer, while he is in the process of developing his shorthand speed, at one time or another encounters three problems that he must learn to handle if he is to make progress:

1. What to do when he falls behind,

2. What to do when the dictator uses an unfamiliar word,

3. What to do when he does not hear (or mishears) some part of the dictation. No doubt you have already encountered these problems in your speed-development practice.

Here are some suggestions that will help you cope with these problems.

1. You fall behind. It should not be a source of distress to you when you *occasionally* fall behind your dictator in your practice. It is only natural for you to fall behind sometimes when you are striving to reach a higher speed than the one at which you are writing. If you were always able to get all the dictation easily, it would be a sign that the dictation rate is not rapid enough and that consequently your speed is not increasing. (Of course, falling behind consistently is a different and more serious matter!) When you find yourself falling behind:

 (a) Hang on as long as you can. Very often the dictator may pause to take a breath or to clear his throat, and the few seconds that it takes him to do this may be sufficient for you to catch up.

(b) When you can hold on no longer, skip the words that you have not written and leave a line or two blank. (When you transcribe, this blank space will indicate the point at which you have a break.)

(*c*) Pick up the dictation at the new point. (Never stop writing during a speed take. If you do, you will never become a really rapid writer.)

(*d*) When you transcribe, try, with the help of context, to supply some of the words that you had to leave out.

2. You meet an unfamiliar word. The most expert writer will occasionally have to write a shorthand outline for a word that is unfamiliar to him. When this happens to you, follow these suggestions:

(*a*) Try to write the word in full, alphabetically.

(*b*) If you cannot write it in full, try to get at least the beginning of the word. This beginning may help you locate the correct word in the dictionary when you transcribe.

(*c*) If the word completely escapes you, leave a space or even skip a line (so that you can readily locate the spot at which the word occurs) and keep on writing. The important consideration is that you do not become flustered and lose precious time worrying about the word as the dictation runs on ahead of you.

When you transcribe, you may be able to substitute a synonym for the word you missed that will not impair the meaning of the dictation.

The larger your English vocabulary, the less frequently will this problem confront you. Consequently, do all you can to build your vocabulary through extensive reading.

3. You do not hear a word (or you mis-hear it). Even a writer with the most acute hearing will occasionally fail to hear (or will mis-hear) a word, either because the dictator did not enunciate clearly or because some noise interfered with hearing. These suggestions will help you to handle this problem.

(a) Leave a space or even skip a line when you do not hear a word. Once again, context may help you supply the word—or at least a satisfactory substitute—when you are transcribing. Do not stop writing with the hope that the context of the next few words may suggest the word you missed. If you stop writing, you may fall hopelessly behind the dictator.

(b) If you *think* you hear a word but the context tells you that it could not possibly be the correct one, write what you think you hear anyway and, if you can, encircle the outline quickly. If you are pressed, leave a space or skip a line. By writing what you think you hear, your outline will often suggest the actual word that was dictated.

 For example, if you thought you heard, "There was a large increase in the building industry's reduction rate," write just that; when you transcribe, your outline for *reduction* will suggest to you that the correct transcription of the sentence is, "There was a large increase in the building industry's *production* rate."

(c) There will be occasions when a word that you mis-heard or did not hear it all, will occur to you words or even sentences later. When this happens, resist the temptation to go back and insert it. The dictation will not wait while you do so, and you may lose more than you gain. Better to hope that you will still remember the word when you transcribe — and the chances are that you will.

Of course, the above suggestions are intended to apply only to your speed-development work. When you fall behind, encounter an unfamiliar word, or do not hear a word while you are taking dictation from your employer in the business office, you will interrupt the dictation, for you must not risk the possibility of turning in an imperfect transcript.

LESSON **21**

▶ **Principles of Outline Construction**

163. Omission of vowel in word endings -ANT, -ENT. *The vowel is omitted in* -ANT, -ENT *in the following families:*

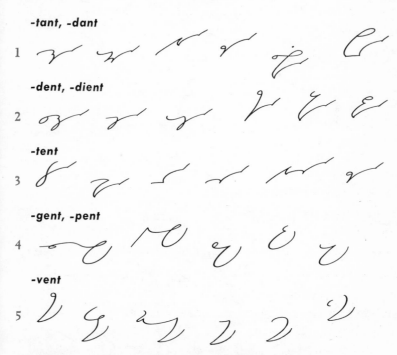

-tant, -dant

1

-dent, -dient

2

-tent

3

-gent, -pent

4

-vent

5

1. Constant, resultant, distant, extant, inhabitant, abundant.
2. Accident, incident, resident, evident, obedient, expedient.
3. Patent, competent, intent, content, discontent, extent.
4. Negligent, diligent, urgent, spent, repent.
5. Event, prevent, solvent, invent, convent, circumvent.

164. Proofreading the Transcript

(shorthand outlines) —E. Lillian Hutchinson   (344)

Letters

165. *(shorthand outlines)* 19, 1915 *(shorthand outlines)*

(shorthand outlines)

, conjunction

[shorthand notation]

, apposition

[shorthand notation] (97)

166. *[shorthand notation]*

, introductory
: enumeration
. inside quote

[shorthand notation]

two-year
  hyphenated
  before noun

[shorthand notation]

. inside quote
, contrast
practical

[shorthand notation] "25 *[shorthand]*"

[shorthand notation]

, if clause *[shorthand notation]* (122)

167. Recall Drill (N). In this drill you will review the several uses of the alphabetic stroke N.

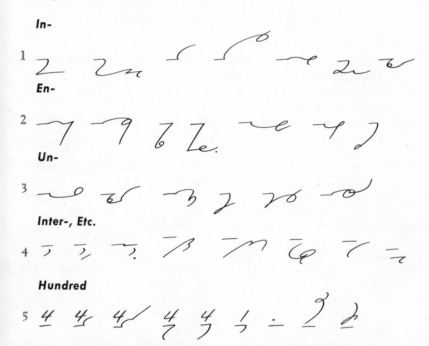

In-

1

En-

2

Un-

3

Inter-, Etc.

4

Hundred

5

1. Inform, influence, intend, intimate, increase, inferior, insert.
2. Encourage, engage, enjoy, engineering, enlist, enrich, envy.
3. Unlike, uncertain, unconscious, unfit, unfortunate, unkind.
4. Interest, interested, uninteresting; introduce, introduction; enterprise, entertain, entrance.
5. 400, 400,000, $400,000, 400 pounds, 400 feet, 100 per cent, a hundred, several hundred, few hundred.

169

170

171

172

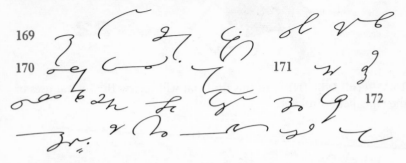

169. Considerable, timer, assembling, prohibitive, adapt, I should like to see.
170. Emergencies, permanent, will be glad.
171. Result, efficiency, accurately, we are sure, machines, procedure, consequently, private.
172. Manufacturing, yesterday, difficulty, months ago, recently, will you please.

169. Dear Mr. Fairview: I have spent considerable time with our Engineering Department at the factory[1] discussing the possibility of making a timer of the type that you have in mind. Our engineers tell[2] me that the expense of assembling the necessary machinery would be prohibitive.

We do manufacture[3] a timer that is not automatic, and we might be able to adapt it to your needs.

If you will[4] be in your office during the coming week, I should like to see you to discuss the matter. Cordially yours,[5]

---

170. Dear Mr. Miles: Is there someone in your organization who thinks he is saving money for you but is[6] actually losing money? Is there someone who meets the emergencies that arise each month by having the[7] staff work overtime instead of seeking a permanent solution to your problems?

Our representative will[8] be glad to call and explain how our office machines will enable you to do your accounting work more rapidly[9] and at reduced cost. If you will return the enclosed card, our salesman will call at your convenience. Sincerely yours,[10]

---

171. Dear Mr. Harrison: As we all know, profits result from business efficiency. A business that is not run[11] efficiently seldom makes a profit.

For the past 100 years our organization has been helping[12] businessmen run their businesses more efficiently. It has done this through its complete line of business machines, which[13] enable businessmen to keep records accurately and rapidly.

We are sure that you are interested[14] in seeing the latest models of our machines and in learning how they will fit into your office procedure.[15] Consequently, we are inviting you to attend our private business show during the week of October[16] 27. I am enclosing four tickets for you.

If you would like to have more, please ask us for them. Sincerely yours,[17]

---

172. Dear Mr. Jackson. Mr. A. J.

Palmer, who is head of the Service Department of the Wells Manufacturing[18] Company, was in my office yesterday. He tells me that they are still having difficulty with the time[19] clock that we installed some months ago, even after the repairs made recently.

Will you please visit Wells as soon[20] as possible to investigate the situation. This organization has been a fine customer, and[21] we would like to see them completely satisfied.

Please write to Mr. Palmer that you will visit him. Sincerely yours,[22] (440)

Reading and Writing Practice

173.

Transcribé:
 June 12
referred

unfortunately
, introductory

, parenthetical
factory

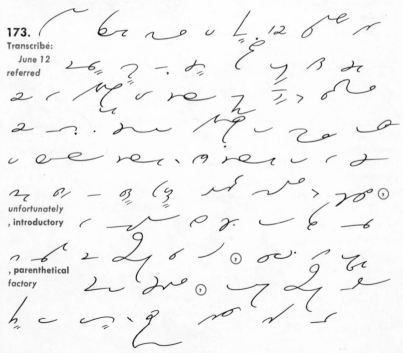

, parenthetical

inquiry
, intervening
   phrase (138)

174.

, introductory
, nonrestrictive

, introductory
automatic

, conjunction
; no conjunction
, word omitted
85/   120/

(114)

LESSON **23**

▶ **Word Families**

175. -claimed

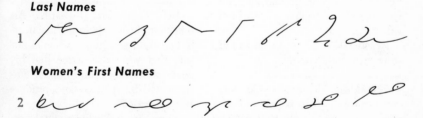

Claimed, acclaimed, reclaimed, disclaimed.

176. -tional

Professional, national, rational, sensational, fictional, fractional.

177. Frequent Names

Last Names

1

Women's First Names

2

1. Driscoll, Duffy, Duncan, Dunne, Edwards, Evans, Farrell.
2. Charlotte, Clara, Constance, Cora, Cynthia, Delia.

178. Previews and Writing Practice

179   180   181

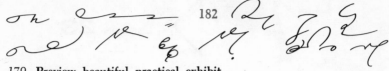

182

179. Preview, beautiful, practical, exhibit.
180. Reflects, employer, throughout the, occupant, fatigue, cushions, experts.
181. Employee, I am sure, Aluminum.
182. Developed, combat, professional, acclaimed, distinct, exercise, disturbing, scientifically, contribute.

179. Dear Mrs. Dunne: On May 27 we are having a special preview of our office furniture products.[1]

We would like you to be among the first to see what we consider the most beautiful and practical office[2] furniture available today. Here, in our new, air-conditioned building, you will find a complete exhibit of[3] our latest models. In addition, you will have an opportunity to discuss your decorating problems with[4] our experts, all of whom will be present.

Reserve May 27 for a visit to our store. Sincerely yours,[5]

---

180. Dear Mr. Evans: Comfort is very important to people in business. Their work reflects this fact. The employer[6] who knows it and acts on his knowledge has the most efficient employees. Smith Posture Chairs provide comfort throughout[7] the day. Every model is adjustable; the occupant himself can adjust his chair to the most comfortable[8] position for him.

The chair is so constructed that it encourages good posture, with the result that[9] it eliminates many of the causes of fatigue. It has rubber cushions that stay cool and clean.

We make posture[10] chairs for all types of office workers. Visit our showroom to see our chairs and obtain posture advice from one[11] of our experts. Our dealer in your neighborhood is located at 416 West 89 Street. Cordially yours,[12]

---

181. Dear Mr. Edwards: An office employee sits in a chair nearly two thousand hours a year. I am sure that you will[13] agree that his chair should be comfortable. Fatigue will be reduced and production increased.

There are five adjustments[14] on a Harris Aluminum Chair. These five adjustments permit each individual to set the chair in[15] the position most comfortable for him.

The Harris Aluminum Chair remains attractive for many years.[16] It has no paint to scratch or wood to chip.

It is good business sense to invest in good office furniture. Yours truly,[17]

182. Dear Mr. Jones: Johnson Comfort Chairs have been developed to combat the poor posture developed by many people[18] who work in offices. Business and professional men have acclaimed these comfortable chairs, which have many[19] distinct features.

In Johnson Comfort Chairs you can exercise while you sit. You can change your position without[20] disturbing your posture.

Johnson Comfort Chair users are enthusiastic about these scientifically designed[21] chairs that contribute to your comfort, health, and greater efficiency.

Write today for our free booklet, "How to[22] Keep Physically Fit." With the booklet, we will send you the name of the nearest Johnson dealer. Cordially yours,[23] (460)

Reading and Writing Practice

183.

300-pound
  hyphenated
  before noun
, if clause

, introductory
released

, when clause
; because of comma
quality

, introductory

, intervening phrase

(156)

184.

yours tastefully

, introducing short quote
. inside quote
, introductory
, contrast

, if clause

. courteous request
, nonrestrictive
equipped

, if clause
handsome

(144)

185. Frequent Phrases

Done

1 [shorthand outlines]

One

2 [shorthand outlines]

1. Be done, to be done, can be done, should be done, could be done, will be done.
2. One of these, one of the, one of those, one of them, one of our, one time, one year.

186. Geographical Expressions

-town

1 [shorthand outlines]

States

2 [shorthand outlines]

Foreign Countries

3 [shorthand outlines]

1. Georgetown, Hagerstown, Jamestown, Norristown, Tarrytown, Youngstown.
2. Texas, Ohio, Nebraska, Maine, Georgia, Alabama, Maryland, Minnesota.
3. Austria, Bulgaria, Finland, Germany, Hungary.

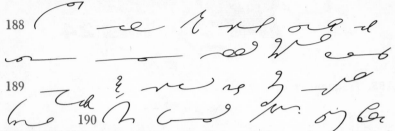

188. Diminish, morale, dispose, installation, analyze, noise, recommend, minimum, guarantee, if you would like, eliminate.

189. Employees, exhausted, controlled, unnecessary, effectively, moderate, booklet.

190. Difficult, permanently, distracting, attractive, appearance.

188. Dear Mr. Mathew: Do not allow noise to diminish your profits. Noise can undermine employee morale. It can[1] slow up work, cause errors, and result in needless hours of overtime.

You can dispose of your noise problem by[2] installing Morse tiles. The cost of installation is very reasonable and the savings in time and money are[3] great.

Here are three things that we will do for you:

1. We will analyze your noise problem and recommend the proper[4] type of tile for your needs.

2. We will install the tiles quickly and with a minimum of inconvenience to you[5] and your staff.

3. We will guarantee our materials and workmanship.

If you would like us to send you a copy[6] of our booklet, "Questions and Answers on How to Eliminate Noise," return the enclosed card. Cordially yours,[7]

189. Dear Mr. Platt: Do you find that many of your employees leave the office exhausted and strained? They are probably[8] suffering from "noise" fatigue. In offices where noise is not controlled, efficiency is often diminished.[9]

Loss of time and efficiency resulting from noise represent unnecessary waste because noise can be[10] effectively controlled. Georgetown Sound Conditioning eliminates noise so that the entire office staff can work more[11] efficiently, with fewer errors and less overtime.

Georgetown Sound Conditioning can be installed at a[12] moderate cost. In a year's time it will more than pay for itself by increasing your employee's production.

Now that[13] you know the facts, shouldn't you act today?

Write for our free booklet, "How to Solve the Noise Problem." Yours sincerely,[14]

190. Dear Mr. Jones: Would you like to increase the efficiency of your office? You can do it by eliminating[15] noise.

This is not difficult to do. Install our special tile, and your noise problem will be permanently solved.[16] Once you have disposed of the distracting sounds that accompany the routine activities of most business[17] offices, you will find that everyone in the office feels better and works more efficiently.

Our tile is[18] sturdily built, but it is not expensive to install. Its surface can be painted without lowering its efficiency.[19] The tile is attractive, moreover, and will improve the general appearance of your office.

If you[20] would like to have our free booklet, "What to Do About Noise," return the enclosed postal card today. Cordially yours,[21] (420)

Reading and Writing Practice

191.

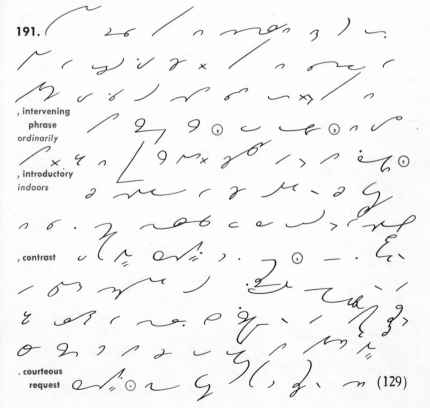

, intervening
  phrase
ordinarily

, introductory
indoors

, contrast

. courteous
  request

(129)

192.

year's
affected

[shorthand outline]

, and **omitted**
drafts

[shorthand outline]

(105)

193.

businessmen
, introductory

[shorthand outline]

discomfort
, and **omitted**

[shorthand outline]

(89)

194. Penmanship Practice. In this drill you will practice the joining of circles to curves. To be sure that you get the most out of your practice, reread the practice suggestions on page 36.

Here are three things to keep in mind as you practice:
1. Make the curves *deep*.
2. Watch the *size* of your circles.
3. *Close* the circles.

1. I can, ago; he can, egg; where, I will, he will.
2. Key, gay; regard, ray; let-letter, like.
3. Handy, empty; either, hint; I want, aimed; how-out, use.

▶ **Progressive Speed Builder (70-110).** Once again, the speed range of the letters in this Progressive Speed Builder has been increased. The letters begin at 70 words a minute and run to 110 words a minute.

If you practice the preview before you take the letters from dictation and pay close attention to the vocabulary of the early letters in this Progressive Speed Builder, the 110-word-a-minute letter will be easy for you.

195. Preview

196 · · · · · ·

· · · · 197 · · · · · · ·

· · 198 · · · · · · · ·

196. Repairman, several days ago, wrong, duplicator, third, further, down, equipment, refund.
197. With reference to the, to him, we have been, unsatisfactory, I hope this, incident, in the future.
198. Difficulty, reports, apparently, touch, few days, regret.
199. Attaching, followed, entirely, reason, instructions, of course, first.
200. Engineering, examined, confirms, unless, users, memorandum, on the subject.

(1 Minute at 70)

196. Gentlemen: Your repairman was here several days ago to see what was wrong with my duplicator./He was the third man to look at it in the last two months. When he left, he said I would have no// further trouble. However, the duplicator broke down again today, and I am ready to///part with it.

Please have your truck pick up this piece of equipment and send me a refund. Very truly yours, (1)

(1 Minute at 80)

197. Mr. Tracy: I am attaching a letter that we received from Mr. Fox with reference to the duplicator/that we sold to him several months ago. We have been asked to take back this equipment because it is//unsatisfactory.

Perhaps the best way to handle this matter is to take back the unit and refund the///purchase price to Mr. Fox.

I hope this incident will not lose

business for us in the future. John H. Baker (2)

(1 Minute at 90)

198. Dear Mr. Fox: We are sorry that you have been having difficulty with the duplicator that you purchased from us several/months ago. Our repairman reports that the unit was in good working condition after his last visit, but apparently//something has again gone wrong.

We are, therefore, asking our Shipping Department to pick up the unit; and they will get in/// touch with you soon. You should receive our check within a few days.

We sincerely regret the trouble you have been caused. Sincerely yours, (3)

(1 Minute at 100)

199. Mr. Baker: I am attaching a copy of the letter I wrote to Mr. Fox. I have followed your suggestion to take back the unit/and issue him a refund.

I have a feeling that the difficulty

is not entirely with our equipment. I think that the real//reason why this unit broke down is that Mr. Fox has not followed the suggestions given in our booklet of instructions. Mr. Fox, of///course, will not admit this.

I have checked on Mr. Fox's orders, and I find that this was the first order we filled for him. John B. Tracy (4)

(1 Minute at 110)

200. Mr. Baker: Our Engineering Department examined the duplicator that Mr. Fox returned. A copy of the report is enclosed. You will/notice that the report confirms my feeling that Mr. Fox did not follow the suggestions given in our instruction book.

I think that in the future our// salesmen should stress the importance of reading the instruction book carefully before starting to operate the duplicator. Unless the users of///our equipment do this, we shall constantly have complaints.

Would you care to have me write a memorandum to our salesmen on the subject? John B. Tracy (5) (450)

Reading and Writing Practice

201.

ruined
, if clause

, introductory
Extinguishing

staining
discoloring

(104)

202.

bravery
fireman's

its
source

, contrast
cripples

(141)

Photo by Ewing Galloway

LESSON **26**

▶ **Principles of Outline Construction**

203. Omission of vowel in syllables CUR, KER. Omitting the slightly sounded vowel in the syllables CUR, KER results in a very fluent joining.

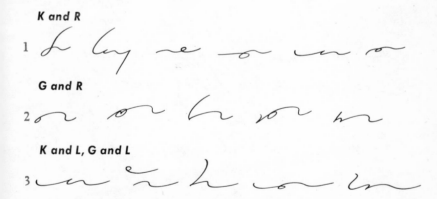

1. Concur, occur, recur, incur, current, curve, courage.
2. Courteous, courtesy, excursion, skirmish, curtail, curtain.

204. The unaccented circle vowel is omitted between:

K and R

G and R

K and L, G and L

1. Baker, brokerage, career, maker, locker, thicker.
2. Eager, tiger, bigger, stagger, sugar.
3. Local, electrical, vocal, legal, frugal.

205. Travel, the Educator

[Shorthand content]

[Shorthand outlines] (270)

Letters

206.
[Shorthand outlines]

local
eager
courteously

[Shorthand outlines] ① *[Shorthand outlines]*

[Shorthand outlines] ② *[Shorthand outlines]*

[Shorthand outlines] ③ *[Shorthand outlines]*

[Shorthand outlines]

fair *[Shorthand outlines]* 25 *[Shorthand outlines]*

[Shorthand outlines]

, parenthetical
advancement *[Shorthand outlines]*

134

ours
, if clause

5. [shorthand outline] (146)

207. [shorthand outline]

Des Moines
, nonrestrictive

, conjunction
outstanding

assistant
experience

, if clause
qualifications

6. [shorthand outline] (134)

208. Recall Drill (Oo). In this lesson you will review the various uses of the oo hook.

Diphthong U

1 *[shorthand outlines]*

Diphthong Ow

2 *[shorthand outlines]*

UI

3 *[shorthand outlines]*

-ulate

4 *[shorthand outlines]*

Under-

5 *[shorthand outlines]*

1. Few, unit, unite, human, view, huge, rescue, pure.
2. Ounce, bow, proud, crowd, loud, blouse, outfit.
3. Ultimate, cultivate, adult, ulterior, insult, result, consult, consultant.
4. Congratulate, circulate, tabulate, speculate, speculation, speculator, speculates.
5. Understand, underground, underestimate, undercurrent, undertaking, understaffed, understatement.

209. Previews and Writing Practice

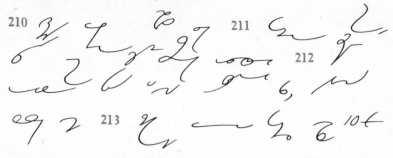

210. Thank you for your order, original, we hope that, enable.

211. Personal, valued, attend, nevertheless, we do not, available, requirements.

212. We have done, loyal, bond, overcoat, entitles, 6 per cent, discount, arrange, comfort.

213. Established, on the market, perfectly, compare, 10 p.m.

210. Dear Sir: Thank you for your order for a dozen shirts and also for your check.

The merchandise has been shipped, and you should[1] receive it soon. The original order is enclosed. Should you find it necessary to write us about this[2] transaction, please return this order with your letter; then we can take action.

We hope that you will like our new method[3] of handling cash orders. It will enable us to give you better and faster service. Sincerely yours,[4]

---

211. Dear Friend: This is a personal invitation to you, one of our valued customers, to attend our fall showing[5] of clothes.

The price of clothing is still climbing and promises to continue climbing. Nevertheless, we can[6] offer you a fine suit for only $60. We should warn you, however, that you must act now as we do[7] not know how long these suits will last.

If you choose your suits now, they will be available to you this winter. We will have[8] them ready for you on May 1.

I shall be here to attend personally to your requirements. Sincerely yours,[9]

---

212. Dear Mr. Wallace: As we have done for many years past, we are showing our appreciation of the business[10] of our loyal friends by presenting them with a Christmas Gift Bond. The attached Bond, which has a value of $5,[11] may be applied toward the purchase of any suit or overcoat. In addition, it entitles you to a[12] 6 per cent discount on all cash purchases you make in any department of our store from now until December[13] 24.

Arrange to do your shopping now while you can still do it in comfort. May we look forward to the[14] pleasure of a visit from you? We are open every weekday evening until eight o'clock. Yours sincerely,[15]

___

213. Dear Mr. West: It is not the policy of our store to conduct sales. When we established the Bell Clothing[16] Company many years ago, we decided that the way to build a successful business was to offer men's clothing[17] at the lowest possible prices every day—not only on sale days. When you buy clothes from us, here are[18] three things of which you may be sure:

1. Each suit will be made from the finest material on the market.

2.[19] Every suit will be made in our own factory and sold direct to you.

3. Every suit that you buy will fit[20] you perfectly.

Of course, we would like to have you come in and let us show you our suits; but before you make your purchase,[21] compare our materials and our prices with those in other clothing stores.

If you are busy during the[22] day, come in to see us any Thursday evening, at which time we are open until 10 p.m. Cordially yours,[23] (460)

Reading and Writing Practice

214.

merchandise
ultimately
appealed

, contrast

, introductory

(89)

215.

absent-minded
, parenthetical

___
: introducing
long quote

search
, conjunction

, parenthetical

. inside quote

, if clause
Philadelphia

(176)

216.

Medical
, introductory

, and omitted
up-to-the-minute
  hyphenated
  before noun

surroundings
, parenthetical

; no conjunction
, word omitted

, introductory

(167)

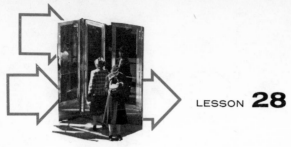

▶ **Word Families**

217. -cation

Location, allocation, complication, indication, education, communication.

218. Out-

Outdone, outcome, outset, outline, outlay, output.

219. Frequent Names

Last Names

1

Men's First Names

2

1. Fisher, Fitzgerald, Foley, Fox, Fraser, Gordon.
2. Duncan, Edgar, Edmond, Edward, Ernest, Eugene.

220. Previews and Writing Practice

221

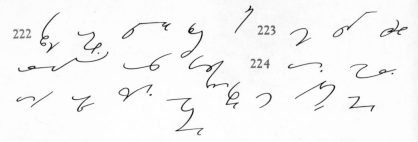

221. Located, Toledo, provide, greater, variety.
222. Busiest, refreshing, atmosphere, survey, suggest.
223. Comfort, outdone, finest, remodeled, laden, pocketbook.
224. Organizing, completing, awkward, report, astonishing, improvements, patience, confident, discovered, information.

221. Dear Madam: This is to notify you that on and after September 10 our office will be located at[1] 16 Main Street, Toledo, Ohio.

So that your payments will be properly charged to your account, please mail all[2] remittances to the new address.

It is our belief that our new location will enable us to provide even[3] finer service. We shall be able to display an even greater variety of goods. Yours sincerely,[4]

---

222. Dear Mr. Fisher: The busiest store in town is the store that is cool in the summer and warm in the winter—and[5] that is the store that gives its customers and employees the convenience and comfort of Taylor Air Conditioning.[6]

Walk into any drug or department store that features air conditioning, and you will find a refreshing[7] atmosphere that is just right

for comfort. The installation of air conditioning results in more customers[8] and in more sales.

There is a Taylor Air Conditioning unit to fit the needs of your business. Let us send[9] one of our engineers to survey your needs and suggest the unit that will be best for your store. Cordially yours,[10]

---

223. Dear Mr. Foley: Several weeks ago things started to happen at our store. Carpenters and painters moved in and[11] gave our store a completely "new look." We hope that you will like the result and that you will be able to shop in[12] greater comfort.

Not to be outdone, our buyers set out for the markets of the world to seek rare and beautiful[13] merchandise. They found some of the finest gifts that it has ever been our pleasure to offer our customers.[14] Our newly remodeled shelves are now laden with merchandise that will suit every shopper and every[15] pocketbook.

If you cannot pay cash for your purchases, you can open a special budget plan. Sincerely yours,[16]

---

224. Dear Mrs. Fox: Organizing and completing our new store has been a little like raising a child. We knew that[17] it would need "dressing up" and "working over" to get it through the "awkward stage."

We are happy to report now that[18] the work is about completed.

The results are really astonishing.

These and many other improvements in[19] the store have taken time and have perhaps tried your patience, but the end result will, we feel confident, be a store[20] that will be a joy to shop in.

Speaking of shopping joys, have you discovered the pleasure of using one of our three[21] credit plans? If not, look through the enclosed pamphlet, which gives complete information about these plans. Cordially yours,[22] (440)

Reading and Writing Practice

225.

, introductory

, parenthetical
; no conjunction
, words omitted

, introductory

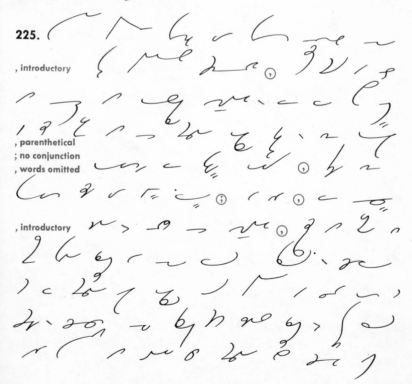

7-5857、 (170)

226.

(118)

227.

(shorthand outline)

efficient
concerns

territory
clothes

nationally advertised
  no hyphen
  after *ly*

(118)

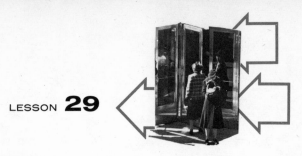

LESSON **29**

228. Frequent Phrases

To

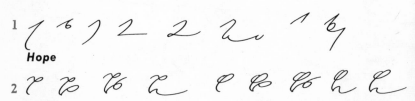

Hope

1. To be, to see, to have, to form, to fill, to follow, to ship, to charge.
2. We hope, we hope that, we hope that the, we hope you will; I hope, I hope that, I hope that the, I hope you are, I hope you will.

229. Geographical Expressions

-ton

States

Foreign Countries

1. Brockton, Charleston, Cranston, Evanston, Galveston.
2. Tennessee, North Dakota, Montana, Louisiana, Florida, Vermont, Delaware.
3. Italy, Japan, Portugal, Romania, Spain, Switzerland, Siam.

230. Previews and Writing Practice

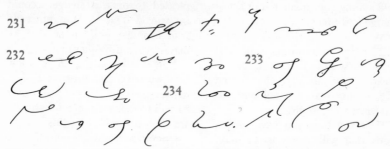

231. Walked, district, merchandise, Chamber of Commerce, of such, community, apart.

232. Realize, comfortable, authorities, consequently.

233. Anniversaries, appreciate, occasions, pleasant, let us know.

234. Frequently, you will be, daily, delivery, request, whenever, payable, following, desire, to make, account.

231. Dear Mr. Thomas: Yesterday I walked through the Evanston business district, visiting all the stores. Never before[1] have I seen them display such a wide variety of merchandise. I am proud to be a member of the[2] Chamber of Commerce of such a business community.

May I suggest that you set apart one or two evenings between[3] now and the end of the year to go downtown for dinner and then visit as many of the stores as possible,[4] to see for yourself how attractively they are decorated and how completely they are stocked.

I know that[5] you, too, will be proud that you live in a city where the stores look after your shopping interests. Cordially yours,[6]

232. Dear Mr. Brockton: Do you

realize how much summer heat actually costs you? It costs you more than you think, because[7] it keeps many customers away.

You can stop this drain on your profits by installing a Vermont Air Conditioner.[8] Not only will this air conditioner stop the drain on your profits, but it will actually make your[9] profits in hot weather greater than those during the comfortable months of the year.

Authorities say that during[10] this coming summer the consumer will be more careful than ever with his money. Consequently, that provides[11] an even more important reason why your business should install a Vermont Air Conditioner. Yours sincerely,[12]

233. Dear Mrs. Warner: Do you like anniversaries? We do. Just a year ago today we had the pleasure of[13] adding your name to our list of charge customers.

We appreciate the fine business you have given us during[14] this past year. We wish to thank you for this business, and we hope that during the coming year you will visit us on[15] many occasions.

If at any time you have suggestions that will enable us to make your shopping at our[16] store more pleasant, please be sure to let us know. We are always happy to hear from our customers. Sincerely yours,[17]

234. Dear Mrs. Ford: We are pleased to open a charge account for you at Tracy's. We appreciate your business and[18] hope that we may serve you frequently.

You will be interested to know that we have established a daily[19] delivery service. All purchases over $1 will be delivered on request. You are invited to[20] use this service whenever you find it a convenience to you.

Our bills are payable on the tenth of the month[21] following the date of purchase. It is our desire to make your account a real convenience to you. Yours truly,[22] (440)

Reading and Writing Practice

235.

; no conjunction

pair

, conjunction

vain

, parenthetical

, apposition

counselor

, parenthetical
recommend

(130)

236.

wear
, nonrestrictive

, introductory
; no conjunction
, words omitted

(109)

237.

, if clause
enclosed

describing
, introductory

(118)

238.

redesigning
condition

, if clause

(59)

239. Penmanship Practice. In this drill you will practice the correct joining of s to other alphabetic strokes. Remember to keep s small and well curved.

1. Ours, else; consider-consideration, goes; its, Dear Sir-desire, dates.
2. Instant-instance, must, men's; puts, business; force, ships, which is.
3. Soon, some; is the, stand; speak, subject.

▶ **Progressive Speed Builder (70-110)**

240. Preview

241. Account, to forget, yours, bother, remind, remittance, however, afford, to do this.
242. Reason, meant, around, at the time, was not, we can understand, collect.

243. You must have, anything, we are sure, don't, relieve, mind, at least, wrong.
244. Manager, lawyers, front, authorize, inclined.
245. Heard, neither, unnecessary, lawsuit, standing.

(1 Minute at 70)

241. Dear Mr. James: We know that your account with us is as good as gold. We know, too, how easy it/is for a person to forget to pay a bill.

If yours were the only account we had, we should never//bother to remind you about a remittance. With many accounts such as yours, however,///we cannot afford to do this.

Won't you please send us a check to balance your account. Sincerely yours, (1)

(1 Minute at 80)

242. Dear Mr. James: Perhaps the reason why we did not receive an answer to our first letter is that you meant to/send us a check but did not get around to it. Perhaps at the time the money was not available. We can// understand that, for it happens in almost any business.

Although we wish to be fair, it is also necessary///that we collect the money that is due us. Won't you please send us your check in the next mail. Sincerely yours, (2)

(1 Minute at 90)

243. Dear Mr. James: You must have a good reason for not having paid anything on your account since October. We are sure of/that. However, don't you think it only fair to tell us that reason?

If we knew the facts, we are con-fident that we could work out// some arrangement that would relieve your mind and satisfy us too.

Could you send us a part payment with your letter? Whether you///enclose a payment or not, however, at least tell us what is wrong. Let us help you if we can.

Don't wait; do it now. Sincerely yours (3)

(1 Minute at 100)

244. Gentlemen: Our credit manager has just suggested that we turn your account over to our lawyers. He placed in front of me copies of/three letters that have been mailed to you since April 5.

I do not wish to authorize such action without personally discussing this matter//with you.

I am inclined to believe that you have some good reason for not writing to us. I will, therefore, hold this correspondence for ten///days to give you an opportunity to send us your check.

You must realize that this matter is most important to you. Very sincerely yours, (4)

(1 Minute at 110)

245. Dear Mr. James: The ten days that I promised to wait before taking legal action on your account have passed, and I have not heard from you. I am, therefore,/authorizing our credit manager to turn the matter over to our lawyers.

I do not like to do this because neither of us will profit by this// action. We shall have to pay a collection fee and your credit standing will suffer.

All this seems so unnecessary. There is still time to prevent a/// lawsuit. You only have to send us your check in the enclosed envelope. When we receive it, your account will once more be in good standing. Sincerely yours, (5) (450)

Reading and Writing Practice

246.
, as clause
instituting
, contrast
preceding
, if clause
unless
; no conjunction

(148)

247.

Transcribe:

No. 3616
$1.50

[shorthand outlines]

3616) 1^50

[shorthand outlines]

receipt
, introductory

[shorthand outlines]

, introductory
canceled

[shorthand outlines]

(142)

248.

, conjunction
, introductory

[shorthand outlines]

(shorthand outlines) (58)

249. _(shorthand outlines)_

(shorthand outlines)

(shorthand outlines)

63 _(shorthand outlines)_

(shorthand outlines)

(shorthand outlines) (113)

▶ **Principles of Outline Construction**

250. Word endings -ION, -EON. *The word endings* -ION, -EON *are expressed by* OO-N *after* N; *by* N *in other cases.*

Expressed by Oo-N

1 [shorthand outlines]

Expressed by N

2 [shorthand outlines]

1. Union, onion, companion, dominion, canyon.
2. Champion, million, billion, criterion, rebellion.

251. Word endings -IOUS, -EOUS. *The word endings* -IOUS, -EOUS *are expressed by* US.

1 [shorthand outlines]
2 [shorthand outlines]

1. Industry, industrious; envy, envious; injury, injurious; study, studious.
2. Serious, various, curious, obvious, previous; erroneous, courteous.

Reading and Writing Practice

252. Six Promises of a Good Citizen

[shorthand outlines]

(Shorthand outlines)

① ② ③ ④ ⑤ ⑥

(177)

Letters

253.

340

(159)

254.

365

, series
knobs

courteous
family

, series
appetizing

(151)

255.

, if clause
: enumeration

Transcribe:
3 cents

control
; no conjunction

, introductory
thorough

(145)

256.

, introductory

low-cost
hyphenated
before noun

(81)

possible
, if clause

160

257. Recall Drill (O). In this drill you will review the different combinations in which o is used.

Oi

1 [shorthand outlines]

Al

2 [shorthand outlines]

Over-

3 [shorthand outlines]

-ort

4 [shorthand outlines]

1. Toy, toil, soil, boy, annoy, destroy, appointment.
2. Almost, alternate, alternative, already, Albany, also, alteration.
3. Over, overcome, overcrowd, overlook, overhead, overrule, overreach, overstay.
4. Sort, assort, port, support, reported, mortal, quart, quarter.

258. Previews and Writing Practice

259 [shorthand outlines]

260 [shorthand outlines]

261 [shorthand outlines]

[shorthand symbols]

259. Williams, early, impossible, solution, faucets, you want, display, local, showroom, I am sure, except.
260. You can be sure, supply, foresighted, to be sure, winter, squeezed, advantage, if you wish, your order.
261. Burner, protected, necessity, assured, prompt, in the world, specializing, operate, described.

259. Dear Mr. Williams: Do you have to shave in cold water in the early morning because it is impossible[1] to heat water fast enough in your present heater?

We think we have the solution to your problem — our new No.[2] 7 water heater, which, at the mere turning of the faucets, supplies you with all the hot water you want[3] when you want it.

This new heater is on display in our local showroom at 415 Main Street. The next time that[4] you are in that neighborhood why not ask our representative to show you this unit. I am sure you will never[5] regret your visit. The showroom is open every day from nine to five except Sunday. Sincerely yours,[6]

---

260. Dear Mrs. Day: Have you given some thought to the heating of your house next winter? Will your family be warm when[7] the snow begins to fly?

You can be sure that you will have a sufficient supply of heat if you get in your[8] supply of coal right now.

Foresighted people are filling their cellars for the winter now for the following reasons:[9]

1. To be sure that next winter they will once again have all the heat they want when they want it.

2. To avoid[10] being squeezed in the rush if cold weather comes early.

3. To take advantage of the present low prices.

If you[11] wish, you can divide the cost of your coal over several months. We have a new budget plan that will make it easy[12] for you to get your coal now. Place your order for coal today by returning the enclosed card. Cordially yours,[13]

---

261. Dear Mr. Harris: As the owner of an oil burner, you realize how important it is for you to be protected[14] by a good service plan. Here are a few of the advantages that you receive when you let us take care of[15] your burner:

1. You save money.

2. You eliminate the necessity for heavy expenses for labor[16] and parts.

3. You increase the life of your unit.

4. You are assured of prompt service during 24 hours of[17] the day.

We have a service plan to meet the desires of every homeowner. In dealing with us, you have the[18] knowledge that you are dealing with one of the oldest and largest organizations in the world specializing[19] in oil heating.

We have two plans under which we operate. Both are described in the enclosed booklet. Cordially yours,[20] (400)

Reading and Writing Practice

262.

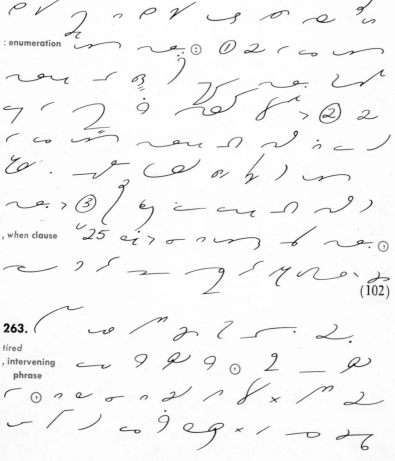

: enumeration

, when clause

(102)

263.

tired

, intervening phrase

completely
, introductory

39^{50}　　59^{50}　(162)

264.
crumbs
oak

lifetime
durability

, introductory
, apposition
, inside quote

(118)

265.
, apposition
, introductory

, introductory
verify

, if clause
immediately

(133)

LESSON 33

▶ **Word Families**

266. -erer

(shorthand outlines)

Wearer, bearer, nearer, dearer, fairer, clearer.

267. -rt

(shorthand outlines)

Shirt, alert, flirt, concert, insert, reinsert.

268. Frequent Names

Last Names

1 *(shorthand outlines)*

Women's First Names

2 *(shorthand outlines)*

1. Graham, Griffin, Hamilton, Hanson, Harris.
2. Dorothy, Edith, Edna, Eleanor, Elizabeth, Esther.

269. Previews and Writing Practice

270 *(shorthand outlines)*

271 *(shorthand outlines)* 272 *(shorthand outlines)*

270. Records, indicate, first-class, temperatures, inspect, determine.
271. Efficiently, uniform, obligation.
272. Costs, as soon as, windows, warm, wonder, long ago.
273. Hard, lowest, stokers, explain, cheaper, sizes, quickly, investment, furthermore, million, dealer.

270. Dear Mr. Graham: Our records indicate that one of our heat-control systems was installed in your home a few years[1] ago. With the high cost of fuel, it is desirable to have your control system in first-class condition. This[2] will result in fuel savings and even temperatures.

We shall be glad to inspect your system at no cost to[3] you to determine whether repairs are needed. Telephone us at Main 9-1702. Sincerely yours,[4]

---

271. Dear Mr. Griffiths: Is your oil burner old and worn? Will it cost you more to heat your house than you can afford?

Let us[5] check the burner for you and tell you whether it is operating efficiently. If it needs replacing, why[6] not consider an Adams Oil Burner, which will help keep your oil bills down. This burner consumes oil efficiently[7] and gives a uniform heat.

Our heating engineers are at your service at no expense or obligation to[8] you. If you act now, you will have no heating problems next winter.

Write or telephone us today. Sincerely yours,[9]

272. Dear Mr. Harris: Fuel costs are going up, but your costs will go down as soon as you have a set of our special windows[10] installed. They keep cold air out and warm air in. The result is that you will be able to keep your house more[11] comfortable at less cost.

One of the features of our windows that has been very popular with our customers[12] is the device that enables them to place their screens in the windows from inside the house, thus saving many hours[13] of labor and annoyance.

We want you to understand fully the many advantages of our windows;[14] consequently, we shall be glad to install a complete set of these windows in your house on approval.

After you[15] have enjoyed the comfort of our windows, you will wonder why you did not install them long ago. Cordially yours,[16]

---

273. Dear Mr. Day: Let your hard-coal dealer show you how hard coal can give you the most heat at the lowest possible[17] cost — more comfort for less money!

Your dealer can give you facts on modern hard-coal stokers, too. He will explain how[18] these stokers burn the cheaper sizes of hard coal and quickly save the entire cost of your investment. Furthermore,[19] they will continue to save up to 20 per cent of your annual fuel bill after they have paid off your[20] investment.

As twenty million users of hard coal have found out, your local dealer is a good man to know. If you[21] are now using hard coal, write him today for a copy of the booklet, "More Heat for Less Money." Sincerely yours,[22] (440)

Reading and Writing Practice

274.

weather
washday
Dryer

, contrast
pieces

, introductory
whether
, if clause

168

, if clause

, conjunction
lost
fair (163)

275.

drawer
laundered

; no conjunction
, word omitted

, when clause

starch
, parenthetical

, when clause
wearer
batch

. courteous request [shorthand] (137)

276.
, conjunction
, parenthetical [shorthand]

, introductory
nowhere [shorthand]

, if clause
discuss [shorthand]

, parenthetical
obligation [shorthand]

(148)

277. Frequent Phrases

To Do

1

Send

2

1. To do, to do it, to do the, to do so, to do this, to do any, to do your.
2. Send us, send you, send the, send this, please send, please send the, please send this.

278. Geographical Expressions

-son

1

States

2

Foreign Cities

3

1. Atchison, Dawson, Ferguson, Harrison, Hutchinson, Madison.
2. Alabama, Georgia, Kentucky, Missouri, North Carolina, South Carolina.
3. Portsmouth, Southampton, Inverness, Birmingham.

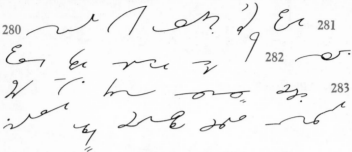

280. Grounds, damage, landscaping, supervision, experts.
281. Experimentation, pests, instructors, newest, agent.
282. Gardening, if you would, entertaining, chuckle, McMann, we are sending you.
283. Hundreds, Research, fertilizer, sanitary, ingredients.

280. Dear Mr. Dawson: The grounds about your home are of great importance to you. I am sure you will want to take the[1] best possible care of them. Perhaps this past winter has done damage to your grounds and you are considering some[2] landscaping work.

Our organization is ready to serve you. It has a staff of well-trained men who will carry[3] out the work under the supervision of one of our experts.

May I have an opportunity of discussing[4] the care of your grounds with you? I know you will find our discussion helpful and interesting. Cordially yours,[5]

281. Dear Mr. Pine: Our organization has always believed that the care of trees is a science.

It has taken[6] years of experimentation to develop the service that we render today. Our research and field experience[7] have aided us in finding ways to kill pests and to help trees grow. Our instructors spend many hours each week[8] teaching our men the newest and most effective ways to take care of trees.

More people than ever are using our[9] service. If you have trees on your grounds, consult your phone book for our nearest agent or write us direct. Sincerely yours,[10]

282. Dear Friend: Would you like to know how you can make your gardening more fun and less work? Would you like to learn how you can[11] do this and be entertained at the same time?

If you would, get a copy of a new book entitled "Gardening[12] for Lazy People." This entertaining book gives you the facts about gardening in a style that will make you chuckle.[13] At the suggestion of your gardener, Harry H. McMann, we are sending you a copy of this new book[14] without charge.

In the back of the book you will find a collection of ideas on how our products contribute to[15] making your gardening more fun.

We hope that you enjoy and profit by this new book. Yours very sincerely,[16]

---

283. Dear Friend: Did you enjoy reading "Gardening for Lazy People"? Hundreds of persons have already told us that[17] the book has not only given them much helpful advice but that it has also provided them with many chuckles.[18]

Our Research Department has recently developed a new type of fertilizer that is clean and sanitary[19] and yet provides every one of the many different ingredients that plants need in order to[20] grow properly.

Your gardener, Harry H. McMann, has this new product in stock and will be glad to supply you[21] with as much as you need.

In the meantime, please tell us how you liked "Gardening for Lazy People." A postal card is all that is necessary. Cordially yours,[22] (440)

Reading and Writing Practice

284.
severe
affected
, introductory

recommend
, parenthetical

; no conjunction
, words omitted
, introductory

, when clause
schedule
past

(112)

173

285.

[shorthand outlines]

[shorthand outlines]

[shorthand outlines]

(142)

286.

[shorthand outlines]

[shorthand outlines]

[shorthand outlines]

, *if clause*
Transcribe:
25 cents

(100)

287.
, *introductory*
: *enumeration*

individuality
, *conjunction*

6-2526,

(121)

LESSON **35**

288. Penmanship Practice. In this lesson you will study the correct joining of circles in the body of a word. There are two things you should remember in practicing the groups in this drill:

1. Try not to put "points" on the beginning or ending of the circle as you join it to the next stroke.

2. If the circle were erased, the stroke that precedes the circle and the stroke that follows it should make a smooth joining.

1. Return, read; rate, raid; late, laid.
2. Take, tag; deck, dig; man, name.
3. Rack, lake; care, gale; pave, beef.

▶ **Progressive Speed Builder (80-120).** The Progressive Speed Builder in this lesson runs from 80 words a minute to 120 words a minute. Does 120 words a minute sound fast to you? You won't find it fast if you practice the preview and pay close attention to the vocabulary of the early letters in this Progressive Speed Builder.

Remember, try to get something down for every word; and under no circumstances stop writing!

289. Preview

290 291

176

290. Delivered, wondering, has been, transit, desperately, elsewhere.
291. Referred, to me, locate, replacement, meantime, continue, efforts, inconvenienced.
292. Second, has not yet, turned, tomorrow, correspondence.
293. One of our; Boston, Massachusetts; I understand, we have not yet, word, handled, reasonable, promised, won't.
294. Original, success, apparently, disappeared, no doubt, subjected, you will understand.

(1 Minute at 80)

290. Gentlemen: On August 20, I ordered one of your No. 16 beds, which is listed on page 18 of/your catalogue. As it is now September 16 and the bed has not yet been delivered, I am wondering//whether my order was lost or whether the bed has been shipped but delayed in transit.

We need the bed desperately;/// and unless you can ship it at once, I shall have to make arrangements to purchase it elsewhere. Sincerely yours, (1)

(1 Minute at 90)

291. Dear Mr. West: Your letter stating that you have not received the No. 16 bed we shipped you on September 3 has been/referred to me.

We have traced this order with the express company, but they can-not seem to locate it. We are, there-fore, sending//you a replacement shipment. This shipment should arrive by September 19. In the meantime, we will continue our efforts///to locate the first ship-ment.

I am sorry that you have been inconvenienced by this delay in delivery. Sincerely yours, (2)

(1 Minute at 100)

292. Mr. Pace: On September 16, Mr. E. H. West wrote us that he had not received the No. 16 bed that he ordered on August/20. As soon as I received his letter, I had a second bed shipped to him and started tracing the first shipment with the express company.//The missing shipment has not yet turned up, and I have had no word from the express company. As I am leav-ing on my vacation tomorrow,///

please follow up this matter to see whether you can locate the missing bed.

All the correspondence on the matter is attached. J. B. White (3)

(1 Minute at 110)

293. Gentlemen: On September 3, we shipped one of our beds to Mr. E.H. West, 416 Beacon Street, Boston, Massachusetts. I understand that Mr./White, of our company, called you about this matter and asked you to trace the shipment. We have not yet had any word from you about the missing shipment.//We are concerned about the way this entire matter has been handled. We have had shipments delayed in transit before, but the shipments have always/// turned up in a reasonable time.

As we promised to let our customer know the cause of the delay, won't you please give this matter your attention. Sincerely yours, (4)

(1 Minute at 120)

294. Dear Mr. West: I have delayed writing to you in the hope that I would soon have news about the original shipment we made to you on September 3. The express/ company has been trying to locate the shipment, but thus far they have met with no success. Apparently, the bed has just disappeared.

By this time, you have no doubt received//the second shipment we made to you on September 16. We are sincerely sorry for the inconvenience to which you have been subjected, but we know that you/// will understand that this was a situation that was beyond our control.

We hope that we may have many opportunities to serve you in the future. Sincerely yours, (5) (500)

Reading and Writing Practice

295.

permanent area

driveway
, if clause

neighborhood
, as clause

(152)

296.
, as clause

, introductory
temporary

, parenthetical
, introductory
interrupt

, apposition
, introductory
interruption

(shorthand outline) (139)

297. *(shorthand outlines)*

up to date
no noun,
no hyphen

(shorthand outlines)

36

, introductory
arrange

4-6345

, nonrestrictive
, series

(shorthand outlines) (121)

LESSON **36**

▶ **Principles of Outline Construction**

298. Word endings -VITY, -CITY. *In the interests of facility, the vowel is omitted in the endings* -VITY, -CITY.

Activity, brevity, captivity, gravity, capacity, electricity.

299. Omission of short ɪ and ᴇ. *In order to obtain outlines that are easy to read, short* ɪ *and* ᴇ *are omitted between:*

P and N, T, D

1

B and N, T, D

2

1. Open, happen, dispense, appetite, perpetual, repetition, competition, rapid.
2. Robin, exhibit, habit, inhabit, prohibit, rabbit, rabid.

Reading and Writing Practice

300. The Biggest Job on Earth

CHAPTER **8** RADIO AND TELEVISION

181

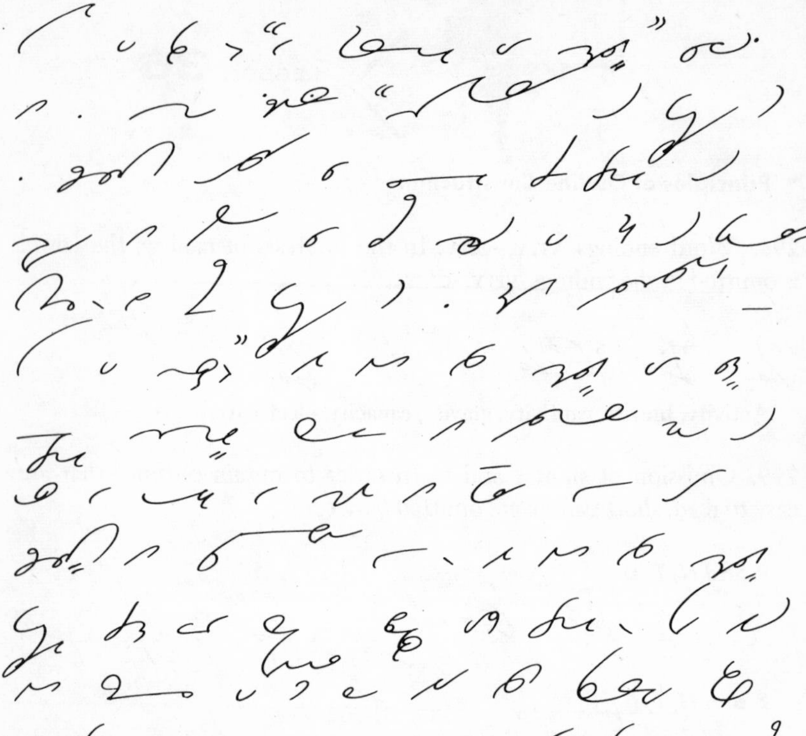

[shorthand] —Ludwell Denny (354)

Letters

301. *[shorthand]*

; because of comma *[shorthand]*

, apposition
, inside quote
, introductory *[shorthand]*

, series
microphones *[shorthand]*

postponing
, if clause
, parenthetical

(147)

302.
becoming
vocalist
popular

, introductory

, series
, if clause
audition

4-1414 (120)

303.
, apposition

, intervening
phrase

13-week
hyphenated
before noun

, as clause
rapidly growing
no hyphen
after *ly*

organizing
, nonrestrictive

(170)

304.

, apposition
advertised

(61)

LESSON 37

305. Recall Drill (E). In this drill you will review the different uses of the alphabetic stroke E.

-ly

1 [shorthand outlines]

-ingly

2 [shorthand outlines]

Incl-

3 [shorthand outlines]

Y-

4 [shorthand outlines]

1. Fairly, greatly, neatly, only, humanly, deadly, simply.
2. Willingly, unwillingly, unfailingly, sparingly, amazingly, knowingly.
3. Incline, inclined, inclination, include, included, including, inclusion, inclusive.
4. Yacht, yawn, young, younger, youngster, youthful, youthfulness.

306. Previews and Writing Practice

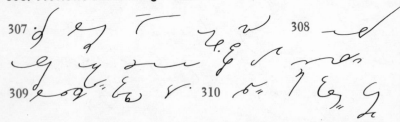

307 [shorthand outlines] 308 [shorthand outlines]

309 [shorthand outlines] 310 [shorthand outlines]

307. **Behalf, television, entertainment, refreshing, won't.**
308. **Enlisted, largely, Robert, similar, especially, audience, congratulate.**
309. **Telecast, sponsored, sustaining.**
310. **Theater, suggestion, Springfield, province, advertiser, network, designates, particular, accordingly, increasing.**

307. Gentlemen: I am writing this letter in behalf of a number of my friends and myself to ask why the[1] show "Betty and Her Friends" is no longer carried over your station. We have followed this show ever since it was[2] first on television. It came in the middle of the day and provided entertainment for us. "Betty and[3] Her Friends" was so refreshing and alive that we looked forward to it each day.

Won't you please tell us what happened to[4] the show and whether we can expect to see it on television again in the near future. Yours sincerely,[5]

308. Gentlemen: Here at Fort Smith, both the enlisted men and the officers depend largely upon television[6] for entertainment.

One of the programs that gives us a great deal of pleasure is the Saturday night telecasts[7] of Robert Nelson. They are interesting and educational; and I am firmly convinced that if similar[8] programs were televised during the daytime hours, especially on weekends, the size of your listening audience[9] would be considerably increased.

Please congratulate Mr. Nelson for us on his entertaining program[10] and assure him that he always has an appreciative audience at Fort Smith. Very cordially yours,[11]

309. Dear Mrs. Lawrence: We are always glad to receive comments from our viewers about the shows that are telecast[12] over our channel.

"Betty and Her Friends" was sponsored by the American Chemical Company. They canceled[13] the show on January 2. Unfortunately, our time for sustaining features is limited, and there[14] was no spot into which we could fit the program.

We hope that some other sponsor will take over "Betty and Her[15] Friends" and that once again you will be able to enjoy the refreshing humor of the show. Cordially yours,[16]

310. Dear Mr. Miller: We appreciate your interest in our show "The Star Theater of the Air" and your suggestion[17] that we make it available over the station that serves Springfield.

Unfortunately, it is not within[18] our province to decide where a given show will be telecast. When an advertiser buys time on a network[19] program, he designates the particular areas where he wishes his message heard, and he is charged accordingly.[20]

Up to the present time, the sponsor of "The Star Theater of the Air" has not included Springfield in the[21] areas in which he is interested.

The number of areas in which this program is being telecast[22] is increasing, and perhaps in the future the Springfield area will also be included. Very cordially yours,[23] (460)

Reading and Writing Practice

311.
, contrast
; because of comma
tonal

, introductory
realize

amazingly
, parenthetical
; because of comma

trade-in
   hyphenated
   before noun

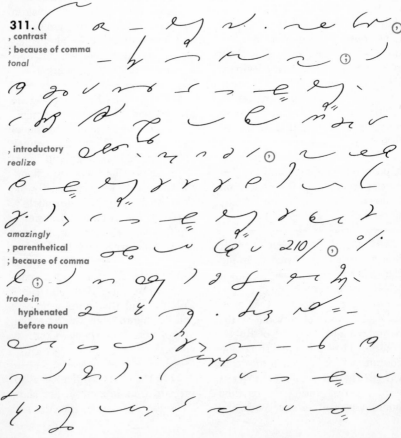

, conjunction [shorthand symbols] (146)

312. [shorthand symbols]

, series
, introductory
rival
[shorthand symbols]

, nonrestrictive [shorthand symbols]

169^{95}, [shorthand symbols] 7-7272 [shorthand symbols]

10-day
easy-payment
  hyphenated
  before noun [shorthand symbols] (142)

313. [shorthand symbols]
[shorthand symbols] KDKK [shorthand symbols]

according
commercial

, if clause
convenience

(141)

314.
8-page
4-column
  hyphenated
  before noun
, and omitted

; no conjunction
, words omitted

▶ **Word Families**

315. -ser

Sponsor, announcer, freezer, razor, bracer, dispenser, tracer.

316. -duct

Conduct, product, induct, deduct, abduct, by-product.

317. Frequent Names

Last Names

1

Men's First Names

2

1. Henderson, Hoffman, Hughes, Hunter, Jackson, Johnson, Johnston.
2. Felix, Francis, Frederick, George, Gilbert, Godfrey.

318. Previews and Writing Practice

319

320

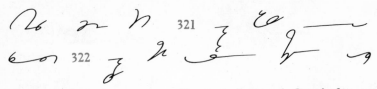

319. Jackson, fiscal, agreement, allotments, indicated, Crawford.
320. Pleased, entitled, schedule, director, definite, we cannot, for this.
321. Newspapers, operate, in the market, selection.
322. In spite, efforts, lemon, adjustment, request.

319. Mr. Jackson: I have completely studied the advertising budget that you prepared for the next fiscal year.[1] I am in agreement with all the allotments you have made except the amount indicated for radio[2] and television advertising.

Before we submit the budget to the Finance Committee, I suggest that[3] we discuss the matter further.

Will Friday at ten o'clock in my office be convenient for you? George H. Hoffman[4]

320. Gentlemen: We shall be pleased to discuss with you the final plans for a new radio series entitled "Great[5] American Heroes." May I schedule a meeting in our office for May 10 at 10 a.m.?

Our program[6] director, Mr. Hughes, and I will be prepared to offer some definite dates for Fall scheduling. Our Publicity[7] Department has agreed to send a representative to our meeting. There should be no reason why we cannot[8] complete the arrangements for this series.

Please let me hear from you if this date is convenient. Cordially yours,[9]

321. Dear Mr. Hunter: We have just learned from the local newspapers that you have purchased a home on West Street. We welcome[10] you to our town and express the hope that you and your family will be happy here.

There will, of course, be times when[11] you will require the services of a radio and television repair shop. When your radio or[12] television does not operate properly, call us; we will have a man at your home within an hour. Our men are[13] well trained, and our prices are reasonable.

If you are in the market for a new radio or television,[14] come in to see the models on our floor. You will be pleased with the wide selection that we offer. Cordially yours,[15]

322. Gentlemen: About a month ago, I purchased one of your television sets and had you install it in my[16] home. I am sorry to report that we have had nothing but trouble with it.

Your records will indicate that your[17] serviceman has been here six times. On each visit he has made some adjustment and on two occasions installed new[18] parts. In spite of his efforts, we still cannot get a clear picture. Every station to which we turn comes in with[19] so much "snow" that it is impossible to sit and watch a program for more than a few minutes.

I feel that our[20] set is a "lemon" and that no amount of adjustment will make it perform satisfactorily. May I request,[21] therefore, that you have your man call for the set and that you replace it with a new one. Sincerely yours,[22] (440)

Reading and Writing Practice

323.

. inside quote

, as clause
; because of comma
participants

. inside quote
, apposition

, nonrestrictive
. inside quote
track

(125)

324.

(90)

325.

, *and omitted*
self-addressed

(124)

326.

, *nonrestrictive*
Transcribe:
1920's

1920's   1930's

some time

, *if clause*

, *if clause*
, *apposition*
  inside quote

30

available
, *conjunction*

-3   (135)

LESSON **39**

327. Frequent Phrases

To

1

Say

2

1. To spend, to sell, to supply, to surrender, to select, to spare, to spell.
2. To say, needless to say, glad to say, I should like to say, I cannot say, would not say.

328. Geographical Expressions

New-

1

States

2

Foreign Cities and Countries

3

1. New York, New Orleans, New London, New Bedford, New Britain, Newark.
2. Arizona, Louisiana, Montana, Minnesota, North Dakota, South Dakota.
3. Glasgow, Wales, Ireland, Belfast, Dublin.

330. Brushing, building, broadcast.
331. Shortcuts, various, popular, stimulated, discontinue, abandon.
332. Possibility, lend, directly, prospects.
333. Family, enjoy, prefers, cowboy, fond, enjoyed, presentation, so much, I had, I hope that the, continue, offer, program.

330. Gentlemen: About two years ago, your station had a program conducted for the benefit of those listeners[1] who were interested in brushing up on their shorthand and building up their speed. The program was conducted[2] by a New York City shorthand teacher, and it was broadcast twice a week between eight and nine o'clock in the evening.[3] If I remember correctly, your station distributed a network booklet free upon request. Are you[4] conducting a similar program now, or do you have any plans for one in the immediate future?

I[5] am interested in such a program because I find it necessary to use shorthand again, after not[6] having used it in several years. I know I would benefit from a radio brush-up course. Cordially yours,[7]

for many years our organization has sponsored a shorthand contest over Station[8] WTKA in which shortcuts were given to students at various levels of shorthand instruction. The[9] program was very popular and stimulated a great deal of interest in shorthand.

We find it necessary,[10] however, to discontinue this contest. In the past the station carried the program on a sustaining[11] basis. It has decided, however, that it can no longer do so. If we wish to continue the contest,[12] we shall have to buy the time at the station's regular rates. Unfortunately, the cost is so great that we[13] have decided to abandon the project.

We thank you for your past interest in these contests. Cordially yours,[14]

---

331. Dear Friend: As you know,

---

332. Dear Mr. Green: As I promised you when you were in my office on June 15, I discussed with our advertising[15] manager the possibility of using television to advertise our products.

It is his feeling[16] that television does not lend itself to advertising products like ours, which are sold directly to schools.[17] He feels that a great portion of the people we would reach would not be prospects for our products and that we will profit[18] more from a direct-mail advertising campaign.

Thank you for taking the time to visit me. Cordially yours,[19]

333. Gentlemen: This is just a note to tell you how much my family and I enjoy your program "History in[20] the Making." It is so interesting that even my 11-year-old son prefers it to the cowboy features[21] of which he is so fond. We enjoyed your Friday night presentation so much that I felt I had to write you[22] about it.

I hope that the sponsor will continue to offer this fine program for many years. Sincerely yours,[23] (460)

Reading and Writing Practice

334.
, introductory
experienced

, contrast

, introductory
management

clearly
Directors

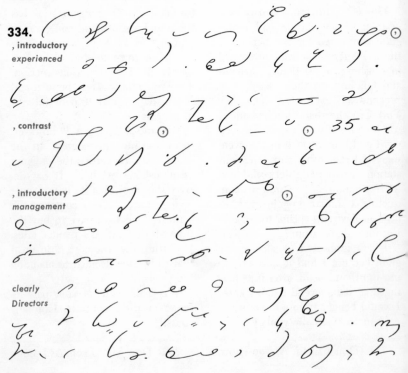

(167)

335.

95,

(168)

336.

families

, as clause

: enumeration

, conjunction

, if clause

medium

5-6III

, introductory

whatsoever

(140)

200

337. Penmanship Practice. In this lesson you will practice the join-ing of circles outside angles. Watch for two things as you practice:

1. Be sure that each ʀ and ʟ begins and ends on the same plane of writing. Don't let the ends of the strokes sag.

2. Be sure that the beginning and end of ᴋ and ɢ are on the same plane of writing before you join the circle. Don't let the ᴋ or ɢ hang in the air.

1. Rash, rich, latch; rain, lean, lame.
2. Cane, came, gain, game; nail, near.

▶ **Progressive Speed Builder (80-120)**

338. Preview

339. Directors, suggested, speaker, convention, Baltimore, 1,500, attend, of course, expenses, count.
340. Accept, invitation, morning, publication, program.

341. Referred, to me, needless to say, topic, things.

342. Mind, qualified, greatest, to speak, six o'clock, as soon as the, has been.

343. Attended, opportunity, officers, very much, worth while, president, offered.

(1 Minute at 80)

339. Dear Mr. Harper: At a meeting of the board of directors of the Book Club, it was suggested that we invite/Mr. Charles Smith of your organization to be the speaker at our convention on May 16 in Baltimore.//We expect more than 1,500 of our members to attend, and I know they would enjoy Mr. Smith's message.///

We shall, of course, be glad to pay Mr. Smith's expenses.

May we count on him to be with us? Cordially yours, (1)

(1 Minute at 90)

340. Mr. Smith: As you will see by the attached letter, you have been invited to speak to the convention of the Book Club in/Baltimore on May 16. If you do not have any other plans for that date, I suggest that you accept this invitation.//You can fly to Baltimore in the morning and return in the evening so that you will lose only one day from the office.///

This will be a fine chance for you to explain the publication program that we have outlined for the coming year. H. R. Harper (2)

(1 Minute at 100)

341. Dear Mr. Casey: Mr. Harper referred to me your letter inviting me to speak at the convention of the Book Club on May 16/in Baltimore. Needless to say, it is a pleasure for me to accept.

If you have not decided on any particular topic that//you would like to have me discuss, I should like to talk about the publication program that we have outlined for the coming year. I think your/// members would enjoy hearing about the things that we have in store for them.

When your final program is ready, please send me a copy. Yours truly, (3)

(1 Minute at 110)

342. Dear Mr. Smith: The board of directors were pleased to learn that you could be with us at the convention of the Book Club on May 16 in Baltimore.

We/have no particular topic in mind for you to discuss. We felt that you would be the one best qualified to decide the topic that would be of greatest//interest to our members. I agree that the members would enjoy hearing about the publication program that your organization has outlined for///the coming year.

Our plans call for you to speak from five to six o'clock. As soon as the program has been printed, I will see that you get a copy. Cordially yours, (4)

343. Mr. Harper: This is just a brief report on my visit to Baltimore to speak to the convention of the Book Club. The meeting was well attended; there were more than /1,500 members present.

As you suggested, I talked about our publication program for the coming year, and the talk was very well received. After the talk,//I had an opportunity to see several of the officers of the Book Club, and all of them felt that the publication program that we have outlined was very///much worth while.

I am submitting my expense report to the president of the Book Club. I am not, however, accepting the fee that he has offered. Charles Smith (5) (500)

Reading and Writing Practice

344.

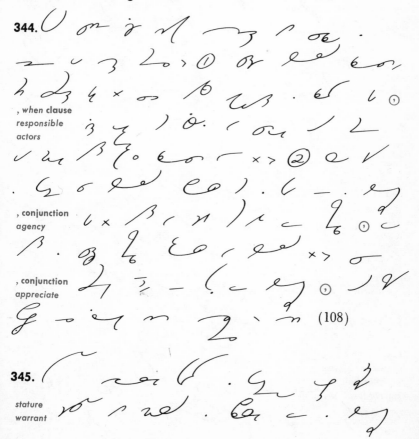

, when clause
responsible
actors

, conjunction
agency

, conjunction
appreciate

(108)

345.

stature
warrant

, introductory
well known
no noun,
no hyphen

, when clause

, introductory
reputation

commercial
, contrast

(124)

346.

sponsors
, parenthetical
: enumeration

essentially
, parenthetical
, introductory

(157)

347.

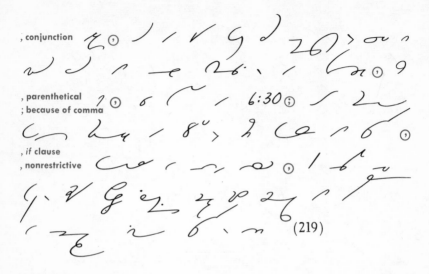

, conjunction

, parenthetical
; because of comma

, if clause
, nonrestrictive

(219)

Turning the Page

Probably the simplest method yet devised for turning the pages of a notebook is to treat the notebook as a solid block until the writer is ready to turn the page and then to consider the *page* as a solid piece of wood.

When using this plan, the writer pushes up the notebook as a block as he writes down the first column. When he is ready to start the second column, the left hand pulls the notebook down toward the right hand, while the right hand comes up until, as a result of the two motions, the right hand is at the top of the second column.

As the writing hand goes down the second column, the other hand pushes up the notebook. When the writing hand is within a few lines of the end of the second column, the other hand prepares for turning the page by turning up the corner of the page. As the writing hand starts on the last line of the second column, the other hand grasps the turned-up corner. When the last outline on the page is written, the one hand turns over the sheet as though it were a solid piece, while the writing hand moves up to begin the new column of the new page.

Left-handed writers will find it most satisfactory to reverse the columns in the notebook, writing in the second column first. Left-handed writers who write from the top of the paper rather than with the hand in the normal writing position will find it more satisfactory to write from the top of the notebook down to the binding.

Devising Shortcuts

Some students have the erroneous impression that all they have to do to increase their shorthand speed is to learn a great many shortcuts. However, shortcuts are not the answer to shorthand speed. Shortcuts can be of value to you only if the words represented by the shortcuts occur regularly in your dictation. If they do not, the shortcuts will be more of a hindrance than a help in the development of your shorthand speed. Why? If the words do not occur very frequently, you will not have an opportunity to use the shortcuts often enough to be able to write them automatically. The moment that a shortcut causes you to hesitate for even a fraction of a second, it is valueless; you will do far better to write the word in full.

 While you are developing your shorthand speed in school, you will be well advised to stay away from shortcuts almost entirely and write everything in accordance with the word-building principles of Gregg Shorthand. Time enough to think of shortcuts when you are on the job.

Even on the job, you should think carefully about any shortcut that you adopt. Before you adopt it, decide whether the shortcut meets the following essential requirements.

1. Is the full outline so long or difficult to execute that you cannot write it in full rapidly? Consider this question carefully, because there are relatively few outlines in Gregg Shorthand that cannot be written rapidly according to the word-beginning principles of the system.

2. Does the word come up in your dictation again and again to justify the additional burden that learning the shortcut imposes on your mind?

3. Is the shortcut distinctive enough to cause you no difficulty when you transcribe?

If the answer to these three questions is "yes," then the adoption of the shortcut may be worth while.

As a rule, it is best to use only shortcuts that you are able to devise at leisure and after some thought.

There is one situation, however, in which you would be justified in forming a new shortcut while the dictation is going on — that is, when a particular word, the outline for which is a lengthy one, is used several times and you have good reason to believe that it will be used many more times in the same letter.

For example, a stenographer was taking dictation in which she was constantly meeting the word *responsibility*. The first time or two, she wrote the outline in full; but when it occurred the third time, she cut the outline to *r-s-p-lity*. It came with such frequency, however, that she finally cut the outline to *r-s-lity*. In this case, the expression occurred so often that the stenographer found it desirable to shorten· the shortcut!

After the dictation, the stenographer took the precaution of making a note of the shortcuts she used for *responsibility* so that if she had to transcribe her notes some days later, when memory was of little help, she would be able to read them.

On page 210 you will find an illustration of shortcuts devised during dictation.

Although shortcuts have their limited place in taking dictation, you will be wise to follow the advice of an experienced shorthand reporter who said, "When in doubt, write it out!"

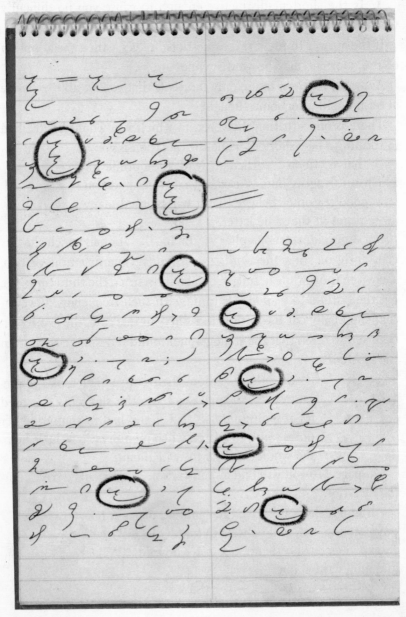

LESSON **41**

▶ **Principles of Outline Construction**

348. Omission of short E between P and K. *In words of more than one syllable, omitting short E between P and K results in a fluent outline.*

Respect, expect, inspect, prospect, suspect, speculate, picture, picnic.

349. Omission of short E in -FECT and -JECT. *Omitting the short E in -FECT and -JECT results in outlines that are easy to write and to read.*

-fect

1

-ject

2

1. Perfect, affect, effect, effective, infect, disinfect, defect, confection.
2. Project, inject, injection, eject, dejected, adjective, conjecture.

Reading and Writing Practice

350. The Fifth Freedom

CHAPTER 9 SCHOOLS AND EDUCATION

(149)

Letters

351.

25'.

25';

, introductory
compliments

(100)

352.

widely known
no hyphen
after ly

— 1912

well-planned
hyphenated
before noun
, and omitted

32

, as clause
; because of comma
beginners

15

already
received
, introductory

, if clause

(175)

353.

well-adjusted
hyphenated
before noun

, contrast
, introductory
ability

, conjunction
perfectly

(138)

354.

, parenthetical
; no conjunction

[shorthand notation]

, conjunction
Transcribe:
   $1,000

[shorthand notation]

(25' .

consequently
, introductory
, if clause

[shorthand notation]

, parenthetical
, series

[shorthand notation]

, if clause
weekday

[shorthand notation]

(162)

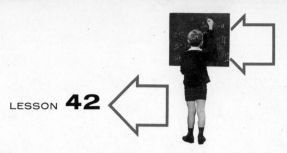

355. Recall Drill (T, D). In this drill you will review the different uses of the alphabetic strokes T and D.

Trans-

1

Past Tense

2

De-

3

-ward

4

1. Transport, transfer, transmit, transform, transatlantic, transcontinental.
2. Interested, neglected, speculated, experimented, advertised, allowed.
3. Depart, delay, depression, depend, deport, debate, deserve, delinquent.
4. Forward, backward, onward, outward, neighborhood, childhood, motherhood.

356. Previews and Writing Practice

357

358   359

360

357. Aviation, unfortunately, we are sending, library, offering, arrange, connection.

358. Questionnaire, graduates, formulating, specific, business world.

359. Alumni, occurred, naturally, to know.

360. Announce, suddenly, it is not, hereafter, first, written, proper, warning, encounter, hesitate.

---

357. Dear Mr. Keys: We are pleased to be of service to you in providing material that will be helpful in[1] your aviation program. Unfortunately, we cannot supply copies of this material for all your[2] students; but we are sending a set for you and another for your reference library. We have made many[3] of our training films available to schools offering instruction in aviation. If you would care to have[4] any of these films, we shall be glad to arrange to get them for you.

If we can be of any further service[5] to you in connection with your courses in aviation, it will be a pleasure to help you. Cordially yours,[6]

---

358. Dear Mr. Rice: The Placement Department of our college is planning to send a questionnaire to several thousand[7] of our graduates who are now teaching. It is our belief that this questionnaire can supply us with information[8] that will be useful to our students and faculty.

We are asking your help in formulating this[9] questionnaire. Are there any specific questions that you would like to have included, questions that will help your present[10] students meet the everyday problems of the business world?

Your questions will be given full attention and[11] consideration. We shall send a copy of the final report to you. Thank you for your help. Cordially yours,[12]

---

359. Dear Mrs. Beck: As you know, the National Teachers Association will hold its annual convention in[13] Detroit, Michigan, from March 28 to 30. This convention will be attended by our alumni[14] from all parts of the United States. It occurred to me that this would be a good time for the alumni to hold a[15] little get-together; and, with that in mind, I am writing you this note.

Mr. Smith, the head of the Business[16] Department, is arranging a luncheon at the College Inn on March 30, to which all alumni are invited.[17] Naturally, before any final plans for this luncheon can be completed, we shall have to know about[18] how many can be present.

Will you please indicate on the attached card whether you will be there. Cordially yours,[19]

---

360. Dear Fellow Worker: Several weeks ago the president of the college decided to make certain changes[20] in the rules of the school. He wished to announce these changes personally at the first meeting of the faculty[21] this fall; but as you know, he was suddenly taken ill and it is not possible for him to be with us this[22] semester. I am therefore listing the changes here:

1. Hereafter no student who does not have an admission[23] card should be permitted to remain in class after the first session.

2. A written mid-term report will be made[24] on each student registered in each of your courses. Failing students should be given proper warning.

If you[25] encounter any problems during the coming year, I hope you will not hesitate to come in to see me. John Green[26] (520)

Reading and Writing Practice

361.
vocational
guidance
, introductory

specializes
, introductory

, introductory

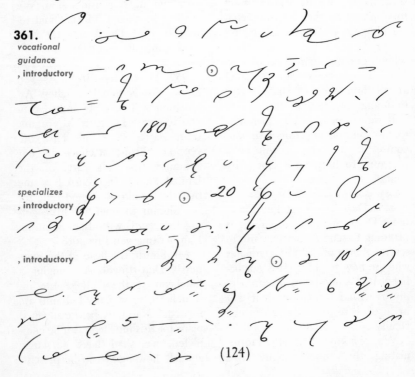

(124)

362.
businessmen
, series
: enumeration

Transcribe:
  $1
, parenthetical

(123)

363.
, as clause
constantly
economics

homemakers
discovered

, introductory
, intervening
phrase

home-economics
hyphenated
before noun

(207)

▶ **Word Families**

364. -sity, -city

[shorthand symbols]

Varsity, scarcity, capacity, publicity, simplicity.

365. -ically

[shorthand symbols]

Physically, technically, medically, radically, chemically.

366. Frequent Names

Last Names

1 *[shorthand symbols]*

Women's First Names

2 *[shorthand symbols]*

1. Kerr, King, Klein, Larsen, Levy, Lynch.
2. Flora, Florence, Georgiana, Gertrude, Harriet, Henrietta.

367. Previews and Writing Practice

368 *[shorthand symbols]* 369 *[shorthand symbols]*

[shorthand symbols] 370 *[shorthand symbols]*

221

368. Daily, good enough, carefully, announcement.
369. Correspondence, demand, ambitious, industry, stimulate.
370. Graduation, let us know, in the past, C.O.D., account.
371. Congratulations, approaching, appropriate, moment, why not, dial, assurance, for your convenience, privilege, parents, entitles.

368. Dear Mr. Lynch: Radio has become an important part of our daily lives. You and your friends are part of[1] a vast radio audience. Because of the size of this audience, most radio programs are planned to appeal[2] to the general public. Every season, however, we offer a series of programs just for students.[3] This program is called "The School of the Air."

As this program is designed for students, we are eager to bring it to[4] the attention of as many boys and girls as possible. With this thought in mind, we ask whether you would be good[5] enough to publish the enclosed carefully worded announcement in your school paper.

If you can do this and will[6] send us a copy of the paper in which the story appears, we shall appreciate it very much. Yours truly,[7]

gained many advantages. I found that I could apply much[9] of what I was learning from your lessons to my work.

The student who knows what he wants and is willing to devote[10] the necessary time to study can get ahead rapidly. Your courses are designed to give the student the[11] most out of each lesson in the least possible time. At least, that is what I found when I took your engineering course.[12]

I found that there is always a demand for ambitious and alert young men in the engineering division[13] of our industry.

If you feel that publication of this letter will encourage or stimulate young men to[14] study in their spare time, I shall be happy to have you use it in any way that you think best. Cordially yours,[15]

369. Gentlemen: You will be interested to know that I took your correspondence course in engineering and found[8] it most helpful.

By studying in my spare time I

370. Dear Mr. Klein: We are writing to ask whether you can tell us how many caps and gowns you will need this June. We should like[16] to have this information now so that we may give you the best possible service.

If it is impossible[17] to give us the date of your graduation, please do not hold up the order. Let us know approximately[18] how many caps and gowns you will want and the sizes.

In the past, school officials have requested that we send the[19] caps and gowns C.O.D. in order that the students may pay the rental cost before receiving these items. On[20] the other hand, if you would prefer to have us send these items on open account, we will do so. Sincerely yours,[21]

---

371. Dear Mr. King: Please accept our congratulations on the approaching graduation of your son. We hope that[22] his future will be a bright one.

No doubt you are planning to give him some appropriate gift to mark this important[23] moment in his life.

Why not make it a Nelson Watch? It is something that your son really wants and will appreciate.[24]

The name Nelson on the dial of the watch is your assurance that it will tell the correct time throughout the[25] years.

For your convenience, I am enclosing a special-privilege card that we give to parents of students who[26] are being graduated from high school. It entitles you to a discount of 15 per cent. Cordially yours,[27] (540)

Reading and Writing Practice

372.

, as clause

architects
accepted
, conjunction

, introductory

(115)

373.
traffic
referred

29

studies
: enumeration
, series

20 25 10

hazard
, if clause

(154)

374.

varsity
, parenthetical
; because of comma
schedule
, parenthetical
represent
physically
, if clause
, if clause
determine
, introductory

(184)

375. Frequent Phrases

In Order

1

As You

2

1. In order, in order to see, in order to say, in order to be, in order to have, in order to be able.
2. As you know, as you may, as you are, as you did, as you say, as you will, as you can.

376. Geographical Expressions

-ville

1

States

2

Foreign Cities

3

1. Asheville, Nashville, Knoxville, Danville, Brownsville, Jacksonville, Evansville.
2. Colorado, Maine, Nebraska, Ohio, Tennessee, Washington, West Virginia.
3. Bordeaux, Marseilles, Cherbourg, Madrid, Lisbon, Brussels.

377. Previews and Writing Practice

378 [shorthand symbols]

379 [shorthand symbols] 380 [shorthand symbols]

[shorthand symbols] 381 [shorthand symbols]

[shorthand symbols]

378. Card, separate, I am sending you, up-to-date, meantime, write me.
379. Advancement, you can be sure, prepared, foresight, executive's.
380. Subscriber, unusual, exclusively, educational, circles, year's.
381. Cummings, parcel post, obtaining, assistance, distributed, if you would like to have, system, requirements.

378. Dear Miss Bond: I have your card of April 10, and I am glad to learn of your interest in Nebraska College. Under[1] separate cover I am sending you today a catalogue and a folder that shows our various buildings[2] and the grounds.

The catalogue will give you up-to-date information concerning our entrance requirements, fees,[3] and the courses that we offer. A little later this fall we expect to have some new folders available[4] that will describe the changes we have made during the past four or five years. I shall be glad to send this material[5] to you on request.

In the meantime, if you have further questions, feel free to write me again. Cordially yours,[6]

---

379. Dear Mr. Green: Perhaps your employer thinks highly of you personally. When an opportunity for[7] advancement comes along, however, will he give it to you or to the other fellow? You can be sure that it will[8] be the other fellow if he is better prepared. Today more than ever, promotions are being given to[9] well-trained people who have had the foresight to prepare themselves to handle bigger jobs.

If you want to hold an[10] executive's position, you must understand accounting and you must know how your product is sold to the public.[11] How can you prepare yourself for advancement to an executive's position with your present firm?

Return the enclosed[12] card, which requires no postage. When we receive it, we will send you our free booklet, "Opportunities in Business.[13]" It will tell you about the training we have been giving to businessmen since 1910.   Yours truly,[14]

---

380. Dear Mr. Bailey: You are invited to become a charter subscriber to Education News, an[15] unusual service prepared exclusively for school executives.

The service is available to you at[16] a time when developments in Washington are becoming increasingly important in educational[17] circles. There are 90 Government agencies in Washington whose activities affect every school and[18] teacher.

The purpose of Education News is to take all the happenings in Washington applying to[19] education and boil them down into one easily read booklet.

I am enclosing a brief outline of the other[20] features that Education News has to offer. When you have examined the outline, I am sure

that you will wish to[21] take advantage of a special offer of a full year's subscription for only $9. Sincerely yours,[22]

---

381. Dear Mr. Cummings: We are sending you by parcel post our new, carefully planned educational unit[23] entitled "The Air Age." The unit contains four parts.

In preparing this material, we were fortunate in[24] obtaining the advice and assistance of Dr. Peter Franklin, who is an expert in this field. We are grateful[25] to him for his many fine suggestions and ideas.

This unit will be distributed without charge through departments[26] of education. If you would like to have this material for use in your school system, let us know how[27] many units you need. We will then try to meet your requirements if it is at all possible. Sincerely,[28] (560)

Reading and Writing Practice

382.

, as clause
adequate

expense
today's

urge
, introductory
, nonrestrictive

(161)

383.
citizens
, introductory
, parenthetical

track
counselor
, parenthetical

10   16

5

, series

12

12

(140)

384.
, as clause
shortage
fortunate

, introductory

substitute
, introductory

, introductory
application

decision
, if clause
convenience

(137)

385. Penmanship Practice. In this lesson you will practice the remaining circle joinings of Gregg Shorthand. Most of the joinings are so simple that they will give you no difficulty.

1. Kit, kid; cat, get, gate; shake, check, jack.
2. Need, matter; nation, match, dash; turn, determine.
3. Pain, bin; fan, vain; pick, fact; map, maybe.

▶ **Progressive Speed Builder (90-125).** The letters in this Progressive Speed Builder begin at 90 words a minute and run to 125 words a minute — or only 5 words a minute more than you wrote in the previous Progressive Speed Builder. Those five words may be brief forms or phrases and therefore should cause you no difficulty. You can do it!

386. Preview

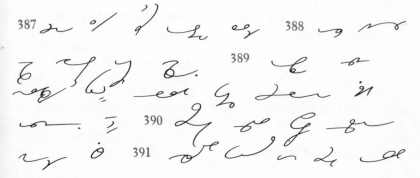

387. Senior, include, supervision, let us know, earliest.
388. Request, together, in the past, colleges, review, compiling.
389. Last year, anyone, criticized, Board, merits, perfectly, familiar, hesitation, recommending, interested.
390. Available, naturally, appreciate, material, you will understand, highly.
391. Kindness, promptly, of course, first, latest.

(1 Minute at 90)

387. Dear Mr. Nelson: Would you please mail me a list of the girls in the senior class who will complete their training in June.

Also,/would you include a list of the teachers under your supervision.We wish to bring our mailing list up to date before sending//out our college catalogues and other materials.

When you list the addresses, please give us the home addresses. If you///do not have the lists ready at this time, please let us know the earliest date on which you think you can send them. Very sincerely yours, (1)

(1 Minute at 100)

388. Mr. Jones: We have just received a request from Baker College for a list of the girls in our senior class who will complete their work in June./They also ask for a list of our teachers, together with their home addresses.

In the past, we have supplied these lists to a number of//colleges. I remember, however, that you raised a question at our last meeting whether we should review our policy on supplying these///lists.

We are now compiling these lists,

and they should be ready soon. When they are ready, shall I send copies to Baker College? Harry Nelson (2)

(1 Minute at 110)

389. Mr. Nelson: I am glad you brought up the matter of supplying mailing lists of our students. Last year, we supplied the list to anyone asking for/it, and this policy was criticized by several members of the Board of Education.

This year, please refer to me all such requests, and I will decide// each case on its merits.

It will be perfectly all right to send the lists to Baker College. I am familiar with the work that they do there, and I///would, have no hesitation in recommending the school highly to any student who is interested in the type of training that they offer. Frank H. Jones (3)

(1 Minute at 120)

390. Dear Mr. Decker: We shall be happy to supply you with the names and home addresses of our students who will complete their work in June. We are now working on this list,/but it will be another week or two before the lists will be available.

As we are naturally interested in the use that is made of these lists, we should//appreciate it if you would send us copies of any material that you mail to our students. I am sure that you will understand our reason for this request.

The///list of our teachers, together with their home addresses, is enclosed.

You will be interested to know that we think highly of the work your school is doing. Cordially yours, (4)

(1 Minute at 125)

391. Dear Mr. Nelson: Many thanks for your kindness in sending us the lists so promptly. Thank you also for your comment that you have no hesitation in recommending our school/to any of your girls who are interested in the type of training that we offer. I may say that we have had the pleasure of enrolling many of your//girls in the past, and almost without exception they have done well.

We shall, of course, be glad to send you copies of all materials that we send to your students. On the first mailing,///we plan to send a copy of our latest catalogue.

If you will let us have your bill for preparing these lists, we will send you a check immediately. Sincerely yours, (5) (545)

Reading and Writing Practice

392.

: introducing
long quote
, parenthetical

. inside quote
, if clause

[shorthand outlines] 15

[shorthand outlines] 50/-

[shorthand outlines] 3 (169)

393. *[shorthand outlines]*

[shorthand outlines]

[shorthand outlines]

[shorthand outlines] 50

[shorthand outlines]

[shorthand outlines]

; no conjunction
, word omitted   (152)

394.

; no conjunction
, introductory

accurately
experience
principal's

(108)

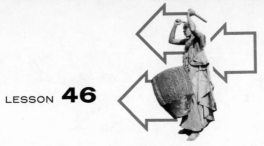

Photo by Ewing Galloway

LESSON **46**

▶ **Principles of Outline Construction**

395. Word endings -TRACT, -TRICT, -TRUCT. The endings -TRACT, -TRICT, -TRUCT are represented by the fluent RK blend.

-tract

-trict, -truct

1. Tract, attract, distract, abstract, detract, extract, contract.
2. Strict, restrict, district, construct, instruct.

396. Omission of o between F, V and K. Omitting the o between F, V and K avoids the rather difficult joinings that would result if the o were written.

Advocate, invoke, provoke, revoke, vocabulary, vocation, vocal.

Reading and Writing Practice

397. Tandem on the Tightrope

CHAPTER 10 COMMUNICATIONS

—F. G. Boyce   (384)

Letters

398.

past
, introductory
; because of comma

effective
, introductory

, contrast

, introductory
district

(147)

399.

, when clause
reducing

, introductory
customers'

(132)

400.

, introductory
impossible

(70)

401. Recall Drill (M). In this drill you will review the different uses of the alphabetic stroke M.

-ment

1

Im-

2

Em-

3

-ingham

4

Million

5

1. Element, supplement, monument, ornamental.
2. Impressed, impair, impart, impending, imperfect, impersonal.
3. Embarrass, embezzle, emblem, embrace, emphasis, emphatic.
4. Framingham, Buckingham, Nottingham, Cunningham, Birmingham.
5. 3 million, $3 million, 3 million bushels, several million dollars.

402. Previews and Writing Practice

403   404

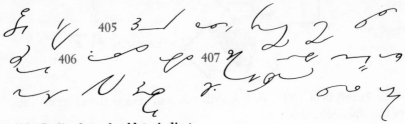

403. Radio, do so, booklets, indicate.
404. Dial, village, expansion, one billion dollars.
405. $3,000,000, erected, Boulevard, convert, adequate, facilities.
406. Holiday, rapidly.
407. Established, increased, Commission, request, you will understand, depend, subscribers, we think, entitled, agree, reasonable.

403. Dear Mr. Wilson: You have been receiving from us booklets in which we have reprinted the talks made by Harry[1] H. Brown over the radio each week. We shall be glad to continue sending these booklets to you if you care[2] to have us do so. Please indicate on the enclosed postal card whether you want us to continue sending them.[3]

It is our plan to drop from the mailing list all those people from whom we do not receive cards. Yours sincerely,[4]

404. Dear Mr. Jones: We are arranging to introduce dial service in your village late this fall.

Dial service for you[5] and our other customers in your area is part of the telephone company's improvement and expansion[6] program, which since 1945 has totaled more than one billion dollars.

We are happy to bring you[7] the convenience of dial service, and

here at the business office we shall be glad to answer any question you might have. Sincerely yours,[8]

405. Dear Mr. Wills: Last January, as you no doubt will recall, fire destroyed the telephone building on Fourth and[9] Main Streets and caused more than $3,000,000 worth of damage.

Soon thereafter we erected a temporary[10] building to serve our customers while we were erecting a new, modern building on Foster Boulevard. That building[11] is now ready.

One of the first things we wish to do is convert the telephones we service to the dial system.[12] In the next ten days our serviceman will install a dial telephone in your home. We ask, however, that you[13] do not operate the dials until we notify you; we do not yet have adequate facilities in our[14] central office for their use. Until further notice, continue to place your calls as you always have. Yours sincerely,[15]

---

406. Dear Customer: If you plan to send holiday greetings to your loved ones by long distance telephone, you will avoid[16] the rush if you call before Christmas eve or after Christmas Day.

In that way, your call will go through rapidly.[17] Even though all our facilities will be available, it will be impossible to avoid delays on[18] Christmas. More calls are made on that day than it is possible to handle promptly.

You will avoid delays and still[19] take advantage of our reduced rates if you call any time on Sunday, December 23, or on any weekday[20] evening after six.

Thousands of telephone people will be on the job Christmas Day, and they will be ready[21] to give you the best possible service. All of them join us in wishing you a Merry Christmas. Cordially yours,[22]

---

407. Dear Mr. Marsh: As you know, there has not been a change in telephone rates since the present rate was established eighteen[23] years ago. From year to year our costs have increased until they are now so high that it is not possible for[24] our company to remain in a healthy financial condition under the present rates. We have placed all the[25] facts before the Public Service Commission with a request for an increase.

You will understand, of course, that the[26] actual increase in your monthly rate will depend on the type of service to which you subscribe.

We feel that, as[27] one of our regular subscribers, you are entitled to know the reason for our request for a rate increase.[28] We think that once you know all the facts you will agree that the increase is a reasonable one. Yours sincerely,[29] (580)

Reading and Writing Practice

408.

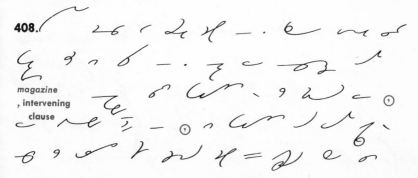

magazine

, intervening

clause

directory
buying

, conjunction
trade-mark

further
, introductory

(137)

409.

prospect
, when clause

, when clause
frequently

(104)

410.

describes
prospect's

unless

, parenthetical

directory

, if clause
local

(153)

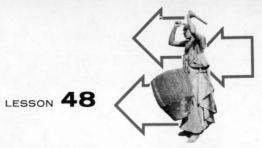

LESSON 48

▶ **Word Families**

411. -way

(shorthand outlines)

Parkway, byway, highway, passageway, driveway, causeway, halfway.

412. -rous

(shorthand outlines)

Prosperous, dangerous, numerous, generous, vigorous, humorous.

413. Frequent Names

Last Names

1 *(shorthand outlines)*

Men's First Names

2 *(shorthand outlines)*

1. Martin, McCarthy, McDonald, McKenzie.
2. Harold, Herbert, Howard, Hugh, Hugo, Isaac, Jacob.

414. Previews and Writing Practice

415 *(shorthand outlines)* 15,

2 416 *(shorthand outlines)*

415. Except, greater, compared, community, without, averages, 15 per cent, we want.

416. In the past, industry, circuit, productive, capacity, defense, communication, in the future, extend, let us know.

417. Auburn, appointment, Ireland, errands, celebrate.

418. Contract, confidence, repeat, why not.

415. Dear Mr. Martin: There may still be a few things that you can buy for only a little more than you paid 10 years ago,[1] but these are mighty few.

The dollar that bought 100 cents' worth back in 1939 won't buy[2] that much today. Higher prices for almost everything you buy have cut that dollar nearly in half—except[3] when it buys telephone service.

The telephone gives you greater value today than 10 years ago. Compared with[4] 1939, customers in the average community today can call twice as many places[5] without a toll charge.

Yet your telephone service fee has increased far less than most things you buy. Its increase[6]averages only 15 per cent since 1939 compared with an 89 per cent rise in[7] prices generally.

We want to assure you that in the days to come we will continue our policy to[8] provide the finest telephone service at the lowest possible price to the consumer. Yours sincerely,[9]

416. Dear Mr. Hughes: In the past 10 years our telephone system has grown rapidly. Millions of people who never[10]had telephones now have them because we have added nearly 20,000,000 new telephones in those 10 years.

Business[11] and industry are better able to serve the country because there are now more than three times as many[12] long-distance circuits.

Most important of all is the value of good telephone service to the productive capacity[13] of the country. Nothing is more important to our defense than quick, rapid communication.

We shall[14] continue to do all in our power to improve and extend our service in the future. If there are any ways[15] in which you think we can improve our service to you, it is our hope that you will let us know. Yours sincerely,[16]

417. Dear Friend: On June 10 in Auburn, New York, one of our men finished a routine telephone installation and went[17] on to his next appointment. That was telephone number 6,000,000, or about as many telephones[18] as there are in England, Scotland, Wales, and Ireland combined.

That telephone is now making the life of a family more[19] comfortable, more pleasant. It is being used for shopping and errands and keeping in touch with friends.

We did not[20] stop to celebrate this milestone. Our men continued installing the cables and other equipment necessary[21] to supply today's telephone needs and to make our service better than ever.

In the days to come, we will[22] continue to improve our service, and we shall appreciate any suggestions you can give us. Yours sincerely,[23]

418. Dear Mr. Isaacs: When the New England Telephone Building is completed, it will be one of the largest buildings[24] of its kind in this part of the country. It will also represent the twenty-fifth building contract that the[25] telephone company has awarded to us in the last ten years. We are pround of the confidence that this "repeat"[26] business indicates on the part of the telephone company.

In the near future you may be planning a[27] new building or an addition to your present factory. When that time comes, why not let us lay out a plan for[28] you and give you an estimate.

We know that we can construct a building of which you will be proud. Yours sincerely,[29] (580)

Reading and Writing Practice

419.

record-breaking
24-inch
hyphenated
before noun

stayed
, introductory

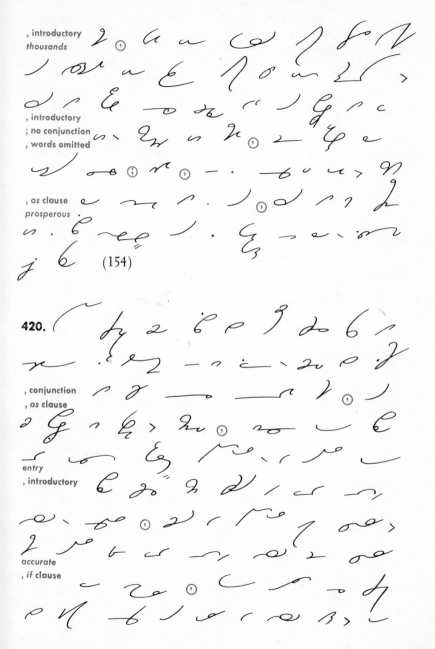

, introductory
thousands

, introductory
; no conjunction
, words omitted

, as clause
prosperous .

(154)

420.

, conjunction
, as clause

entry
, introductory

accurate
, if clause

249

area

(143)

421.

, nonrestrictive
blueprint

passageways
concealed
, introductory

(103)

LESSON 49

422. Frequent Phrases

Words Omitted

1

Several

2

1. Will you please, one of the most, more and more, less and less, one of the best.
2. Several months, several months ago, several days ago, several times, several minutes.

423. Geographical Expressions

-wood

1

States

2

Foreign Cities

3

1. Elwood City, Greenwood, Maplewood, Oakwood, Ridgewood.
2. Connecticut, Idaho, Maryland, Nevada, Oklahoma, Texas, Wisconsin.
3. Berlin, Hamburg, Leipzig, Nuremburg, Munich.

425. We have not been able, telephone, some weeks ago, demand, biggest, expansion, invested, equipment, entirety, patience, in this matter.
426. You will be glad, converted, until, central, greatest, bargain.
427. I am sure, interested, available, answered, no doubt, occasion, if you would like.
428. Considerably, overdue, several times, anxious, it will be, discontinue, however, from you, happen.

425. Dear Mr. Bond: We regret that we have not been able to install the telephone that you requested some weeks[1] ago. It is our hope, however, that we shall be able to take care of this matter soon.

As you know, the growth[2] of your section of the city has been so rapid in the last five years that it has been a great task for us to[3] be able to supply the demand for telephone service.

Our engineers have planned and worked as never before.[4] Meeting this demand for telephones has required the biggest expansion program undertaken by any[5] industry. We have invested almost $800,000,-000 in new equipment, and we have not yet been able[6] to service the area in its entirety.

We appreciate your patience and understanding in this matter. Yours sincerely,[7]

---

426. Dear Customer: You will be glad to know that your telephone will be converted to dial operation at[8] 11 p.m. on August 9. Until that time, please continue to call as usual —by lifting your receiver[9] and giving the number to the operator.

The enclosed folder explains how to dial. It also contains[10] a list of the central offices that you will dial directly. To obtain the greatest benefit from this dialing[11] service, please follow the instructions in the folder.

When the dial goes into operation, party-line numbers[12] will be changed. If you have a party line, please remove the top number plate on your telephone. Underneath, our[13] serviceman has already placed your new dial telephone number.

Your telephone service has always been a bargain.[14] It will be an even bigger bargain when your dialing system goes into operation. Yours sincerely,[15]

---

427. Dear Miss West: I am sure that you will be interested in the new service that we are introducing on a[16] trial basis. This service will be available to all subscribers in your neighborhood.

We call this service the[17] "Message Service"; it makes it possible for you to have your telephone answered by the operator, who will[18] take as well as give short messages.

This new service is described in the enclosed booklet. You will no doubt have[19] occasion to use the service to good advantage.

If you would like further information, call us. Yours sincerely,[20]

---

428. Dear Mr. Scott: As you know, your telephone bill is now considerably overdue. We recently called your[21] attention to this fact by mail, but we have received no word from you as to when you will pay the bill. In addition,[22] we have tried several times to reach you by telephone.

If there is any reason why you cannot pay the[23] bill at this time, please let us know. We are anxious to co-operate with you in arranging for the payment of[24] your account.

We appreciate your business, and we wish you to continue to enjoy the convenience of your[25] telephone service. It will be necessary for us to discontinue your telephone, however, unless[26] we hear from you by January 13; and I am sure that you would not want this to happen. Yours sincerely,[27] (540)

Reading and Writing Practice

429.

10-day
hyphenated
before noun

procedure
described

[Shorthand content]

accurate
gained

(141)

430.

, when clause
reference

, introductory

, and omitted
self-addressed

(105)

254

431.

[shorthand outline passage]

Intercommunication
installation
, introductory

[shorthand outline passage]

two-way
  hyphenated
  before noun

[shorthand outline passage]

unnecessary
, if clause

[shorthand outline passage]

: enumeration
, contrast

[shorthand outline passage]

its
area

[shorthand outline passage]

, introductory

[shorthand outline passage]

(214)

LESSON **50**

432. Penmanship Practice. In this lesson you will practice a number of the fluent, graceful blends of Gregg Shorthand. These blends should be written with one movement of the pen, with no pause between the strokes that constitute the blend.

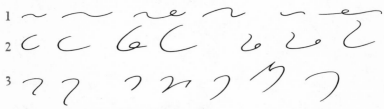

1. Correct, glad; clear, great; work, milk.
2. Present-presence, please; brain, bill; free, flee, value.
3. Keep, can be; confident-confidence, confidential, cover, discover, govern.

▶ **Progressive Speed Builder (90-125)**

433. Preview

434. Tour, telephone, Chicago, we should like to have, double, single, funds, minimum.
435. Thank you for your letter, accommodate, $8, crowded.

436. **Reminder, expecting, eleven o'clock, elevator, second, interest, occur, luncheon, if anything, without.**

437. **Extended, especially, various, wonderful, applications.**

438. **Acted, Springfield, impression, encourage, sources.**

(1 Minute at 90)

434. Gentlemen: On Friday, April 20, I am planning to take my class of twenty girls on a tour of the telephone/building in Chicago. We plan to arrive in Chicago on Thursday, April 19, and to spend the night at your hotel. We should// like to have ten double rooms for the girls and one single room for me. As our funds are rather limited, we should like to have///rooms at your minimum rate.

It would be a special convenience for me if you could place all the girls on one floor. Sincerely yours, (1)

(1 Minute at 100)

435. Dear Miss Lane: Thank you for your letter asking us to reserve ten double rooms and one single room on April 19 for you and the twenty/girls that you are planning to take on a tour of the telephone building in Chicago. It will be a pleasure to accommodate you.

We//can give you the double rooms at $8 a day and the single room at $4.50 a day. All the hotels in Chicago/// will be crowded during the week of April 14; therefore, we cannot promise you that all the rooms will be on the same floor. Sincerely yours, (2)

(1 Minute at 110)

436. Dear Miss Lane: This is just a reminder that we are expecting you and your class of twenty girls at eleven o'clock Friday, April 20. When you/arrive at our building, take the elevator to the second floor and ask for Mr. Green, who will be your guide. He has planned a tour of the various//departments of our organization that I know will be of interest to your students. I hope the girls will feel free to ask him any questions that occur/// to them.

After the tour, you are to be our guests for luncheon.

If anything should happen to change your plans, please let us know without delay. Sincerely yours, (3)

(1 Minute at 120)

437. Dear Mr. Green: I cannot thank you enough for the many courtesies you extended to my girls and to me. We are also very grateful to you for the delicious/luncheon that was served to us in your dining room.

I especially appreciated your fine explanation of the work of the various departments of the//telephone company and the patience with which you answered the many questions that the girls asked. I am sure that the girls will long remember their visit.

Several girls///said that your

257

organization seems to be a wonderful place to work, and I should not be surprised if you receive applications from a number of them. Sincerely yours, (4)

(1 Minute at 125)

438. Mr. Gray: On Friday, April 20, I acted as guide for a class of twenty girls from the East High School in Springfield. The girls and the teacher seemed to enjoy the trip, and I/think they left with a very good impression of our organization. In fact, the teacher, in her letter to me, mentioned that we might expect to receive applications for//positions from several of the girls.

I believe that we should encourage more schools to bring their students to visit our building. Not only will these visits give us an opportunity///to promote public relations, but they may also offer us new sources of supply for office help.

I am attaching the bill for the lunches. William H. Green. (5) (545)

Reading and Writing Practice

439.
Transcribe:
5,000 watts
50,000 watts
, introductory
day-and-night
   hyphenated
   before noun
adjustment
, nonrestrictive

, introductory
segment

, introductory

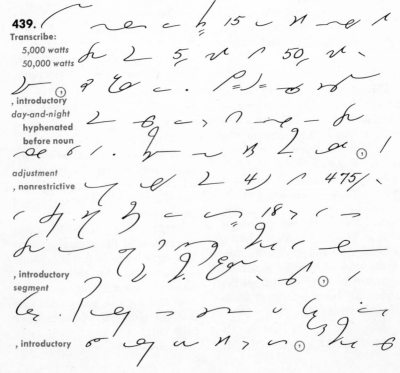

one-year
hyphenated
before noun

(137)

440.

: enumeration
practical
advice

variety
yours

performance
, series

, if clause
personally

(129)

441.

, introductory
radio

Transcribe:
No. 9
, introductory

thousands
, conjunction
, introductory

inasmuch as
, introductory

, when clause
worth while
no noun,
no hyphen

(142)

442.

, introductory

(84)

260

Photo by Ewing Galloway

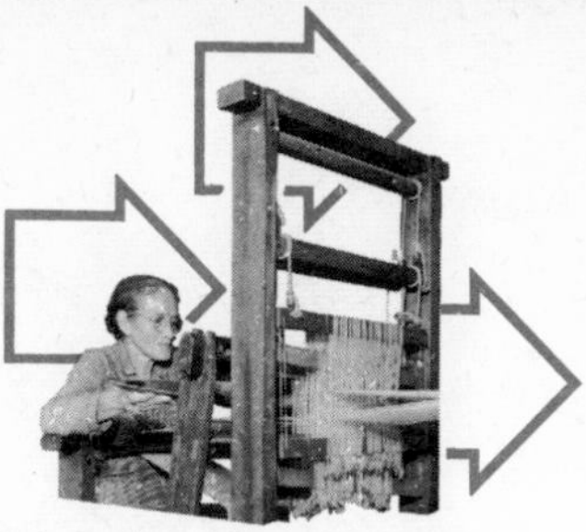

LESSON 51

Principles of Outline Construction

443. Omission of unaccented vowel in word endings -EN, -AN, -ON. *When the endings -EN, -AN, -ON are unaccented, the vowel may be omitted, thus making it possible to obtain fluent, easily readable outlines.*

-en

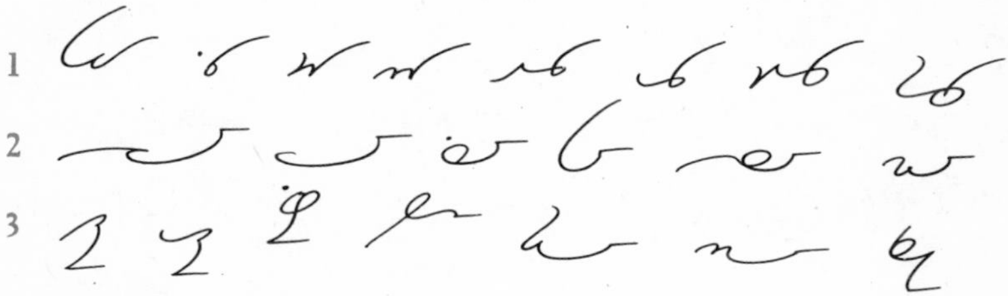

-an, -on

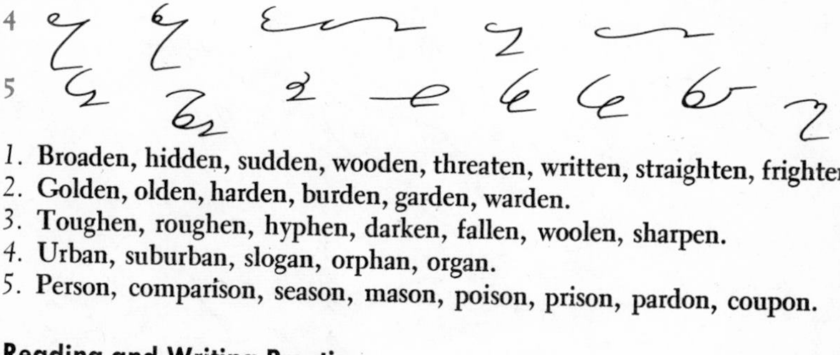

1. Broaden, hidden, sudden, wooden, threaten, written, straighten, frighten.
2. Golden, olden, harden, burden, garden, warden.
3. Toughen, roughen, hyphen, darken, fallen, woolen, sharpen.
4. Urban, suburban, slogan, orphan, organ.
5. Person, comparison, season, mason, poison, prison, pardon, coupon.

Reading and Writing Practice

444. Wanted!

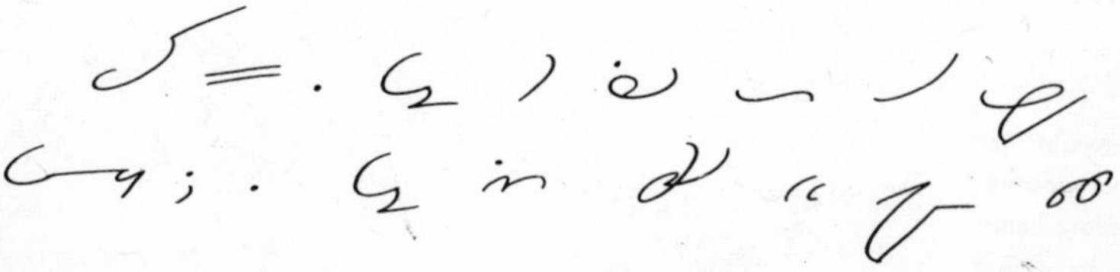

(shorthand outline content)

(192)

Letters

445.

262

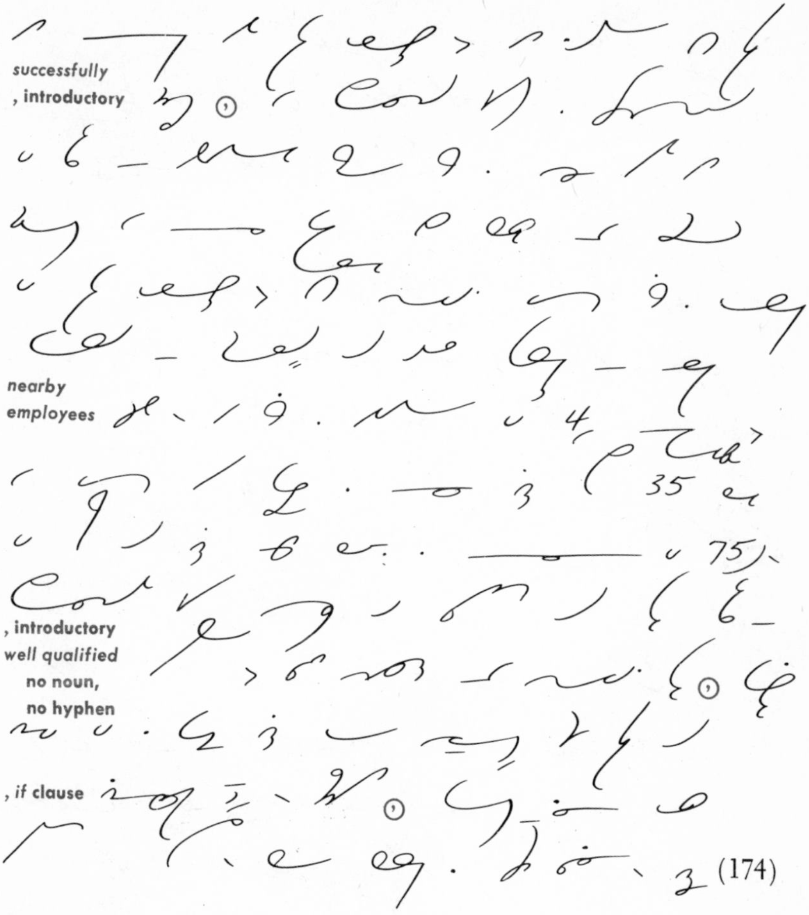

successfully
, introductory
nearby
employees
, introductory
well qualified
no noun,
no hyphen
, if clause

(174)

446.

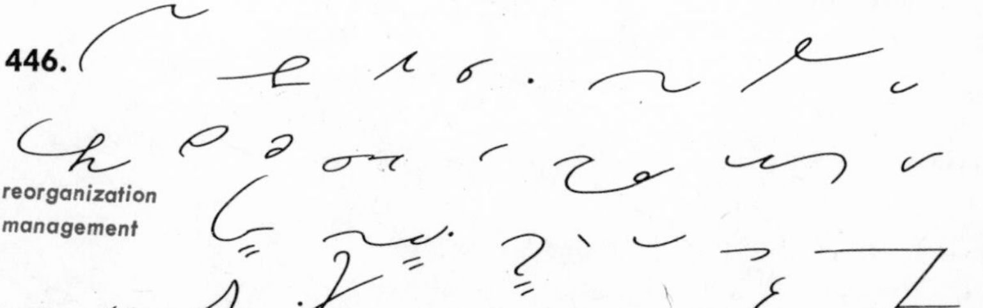

reorganization
management

craftsmen
, nonrestrictive

(118)

447.

reception
, apposition

; no conjunction
, words omitted

, parenthetical
; because of comma

, *if clause*
hesitate

[shorthand symbols]

, *when clause*

[shorthand symbols] (134)

448.

[shorthand symbols]

, *conjunction*
confident

[shorthand symbols]

satisfactory
, *if clause*

[shorthand symbols]

; *no conjunction*

[shorthand symbols] (83)

449.
, *parenthetical*
clothing
clearance

[shorthand symbols] (48)

LESSON **52**

450. Recall Drill (R). In this drill you will review the word beginnings and endings that are represented by the alphabetic stroke R.

Re-

1

-er, -or

2

-rity

3

1. Represent, receipt, repay, receive, reorganize, reorder, react.
2. Advertiser, purchaser, director, governor, greater, writer, speaker.
3. Sincerity, similarity, prosperity, maturity, minority, majority.

451. Previews and Writing Practice

452

453

454

455

456

457

266

452. Thank you for your order, delivery, charge, often.
453. Greatly, exceptionally, stockings, examined, many times, we hope that, equally.
454. Certain, patterns, to us, urgently, astray, expedite.
455. Will you please, determine, proceed, deserved, dispose.
456. Quality, ordinary, shirts, indicate, quantity, bookkeeping, deduct, 2 per cent, of your order.
457. To select, represent, investment, $100.

452. Dear Miss Packard: Thank you for your order for a new coat on which we are to hold delivery until November[1] 2. The coat will be delivered to you on that day.

At the time of delivery you may pay for the[2] coat in cash or charge it, making full payment within 60 days.

We hope we may serve you often. Yours sincerely,[3]

---

453. Dear Miss Carroll: We were greatly pleased to receive your letter of May 19 telling us about the exceptionally[4] fine service you had from a pair of our stockings.

We have been making stockings from the finest materials[5] for more than 30 years. Before a pair of stockings is released, it is examined many times.

We hope that[6] through the years you will continue to use our stockings with equally satisfactory results. Cordially yours,[7]

---

454. Gentlemen: On July 5 we ordered certain dress patterns that we asked you to ship to us by express for use[8] in our Chicago plant. The patterns have not been re-ceived. As the plant urgently needs them, we should appreciate[9] it if you would let us know what has happened to this order. The fact that we have already received the patterns[10] that we ordered on July 20 leads us to believe that our order of July 5 may have gone astray.[11]

Anything that you can do to expedite shipment of these patterns will be appreciated. Cordially yours,[12]

---

455. Gentlemen: Will you please have your driver call at my home for my fur coat, which I wish to put in storage for the[13] summer.

Perhaps one of your men can examine the coat and determine the repairs necessary to renovate[14] it. Before you proceed with the work, however, please let me know what work will have to be done and the cost.

As I[15] am leaving for the summer on May 15 for a well-deserved vacation, I should appreciate it if you[16] would let me hear from you before that date. I should like to dispose of this matter before I leave. Sincerely yours,[17]

456. Dear Customer: Now, for the first time in years, we can offer you high-quality shirts. These are not just ordinary[18] shirts but strong, form-fitting shirts. What is more, we can offer them to you at a price that I know you will agree[19] is reasonable—$3 each.

Enclosed is an order card on which you can indicate the quantity, size,[20] and style that you would like. After you have filled out the card, place it in the envelope that is also enclosed and[21] mail it to us. We don't know how long our supply of these shirts will last, but we do have them now — so don't delay. Make[22] your selection at once and return the card today. Cordially yours,

P.S. If you send us your remittance with[23] your order and thus save us bookkeeping costs, you may deduct 2 per cent from the total cost of your order.[24]

---

457. Dear Mr. Day: It pays to buy a good overcoat. It pays to select a style that will be in good taste for years[25] to come.

Our overcoats represent a long-term investment for the purchaser.

On our floor today you will find[26] excellent buys ranging from $50 to $100. Come in and make your selection. Cordially yours,[27] (540)

Reading and Writing Practice

458.

level
despite

, conjunction
receipt

, introductory
enough

, when clause
Transcribe:
10 per cent

, when clause
Transcribe:
  10 per cent

(145)

459.

men's
, conjunction

; illustrative ,
topcoats

, when clause
; no conjunction
surprised

excessive
, when clause

(99)

460.

269

accessories
, nonrestrictive

equipment
, as clause
boys'

; no conjunction
, introductory
well equipped
　no noun,
　no hyphen
, series

Transcribe:
　June 5
, and omitted

, parenthetical

(125)

461.

opportunity
, conjunction

(84)

LESSON **53**

▶ **Word Families**

462. -coming

[shorthand outlines]

Coming, becoming, welcoming, overcoming, incoming, unbecoming.

463. Coat

[shorthand outlines]

Coat, coatings, topcoat, overcoat, raincoat, turncoat.

464. Frequent Names

Last Names

1 *[shorthand outlines]*

Women's First Names

2 *[shorthand outlines]*

1. Miller, Mitchell, Moore, Morgan.
2. Hortense, Ida, Irene, Jean, Jeannette, Josephine, Judith, Julia.

465. Preview and Writing Practice

466 *[shorthand outlines]*

467 *[shorthand outlines]*

468

469

466. Wearer, Broadway, assembled, comprehensive, outside, invitation, collection, experienced.

467. Century, experts, handsomely, successfully, attractive, England, United States, reasonable.

468. Recently, edition, Career, leisure, in addition, originating, informative, immediately.

469. Celebrate, anniversary, volume, customer, compliments, confident, conducting, largest, account, postponing, purchase, seemed, obtain.

466. Dear Mrs. Moore: As a wearer of Smith shoes, you will be interested in what is happening in our Broadway[1] store.

For this summer season we have assembled the most comprehensive stock of shoe styles to be found in any[2] store outside of New York City.

Like all Smith shoes, these models are styled for beauty and comfort.

Please accept this letter[3] as your personal invitation to come and see our wonderful collection. Mr. Farmer, the manager[4], and his staff are experienced and will be glad to help you make your personal selections. Cordially yours,[5]

---

467. Dear Mr. Miller: Over a quarter of a century ago our raincoat experts decided to do something[6] about the weather. They helped us to establish this policy: Raincoats must be handsomely styled so that the[7] owner will be proud to wear them in any kind of weather. Our experts successfully produced that type of raincoat,[8] and today thousands of men buy their raincoats from us.

At any time during the year you will find attractive[9] raincoats on our racks. Some are made in England; others, in the best tailor shops in the United States.

If you need[10] a raincoat, by all means stop in to see us soon. Our prices are more reasonable than ever. Cordially yours,[11]

---

468. Dear Friend: We recently prepared a new edition of our interesting booklet entitled "A Career in[12] Dress Designing." Copies have just reached us from the printer, and I believe you will be interested in having[13] one to read at your leisure. You will find it profitable reading.

The booklet tells you about dress designing[14] and the opportunities it affords women who want to get ahead. It shows, in addition, how it is[15] possible to enjoy the excitement of originating your own dresses while you are taking the course.

The enclosed[16] postal card requires no postage. If you will mail it at once, your copy of this interesting, informative[17] booklet will be sent to you immediately. This creates no obligation on your part. Cordially yours,[18]

---

469. Dear Mrs. Hill: On January 15 we shall celebrate the twenty-fifth anniversary of the[19] opening of our Main Street store. In honor of the occasion, we have prepared a special volume entitled "Fine[20] Furs," which not only outlines the growth of our organization but also gives an account of the fur industry[21] in general. Because you have been a good customer of ours for many years, we are sending you a copy[22] of this book with our compliments. We are confident that you will find in it much helpful information about[23] furs, as well as many facts about our organization that will interest you.

As part of the celebration[24] of our twenty-fifth anniversary, we are conducting the largest fur sale in our history. This[25] sale will start on January 15 and run for one week. Monday and Tuesday will be reserved for our charge-account[26] customers.

If you have been postponing the purchase of a new fur coat because prices seemed too high for you, come[27] in to see us. You will have the opportunity to obtain a new coat at a saving. Yours sincerely,[28] (560)

Reading and Writing Practice

470.

, introductory
Transcribe:
$20

: enumeration
, when clause
season

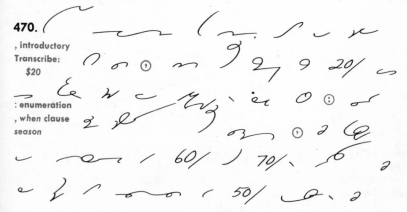

(shorthand outlines)

, parenthetical *(shorthand outlines)*

50/ *(shorthand outlines)*

, parenthetical
regardless *(shorthand outlines)*

, introductory
offering *(shorthand outlines)*

, introductory
, if clause *(shorthand outlines)*
50/ *(shorthand outlines)*

(shorthand outlines) (161)

471. *(shorthand outlines)*
customers'
, introducing
   short quote
. inside quote *(shorthand outlines)*

(shorthand outlines)

, introductory
analyze
; no conjunction *(shorthand outlines)*

past
successes

, introductory
, parenthetical
, introducing
    short quote
. inside quote .   (154)

472.

assembling

, introductory
, apposition

31   5.
    (73)

LESSON 54

473. Frequent Phrases

To

1 [shorthand outlines]

Contractions

2 [shorthand outlines]

1. To make, to him, to our, to us, to me, to be, to form, to see.
2. We couldn't, I couldn't, I don't, you don't, he shouldn't, he didn't, they aren't.

474. Geographical Expressions

-boro, -borough

1 [shorthand outlines]

States

2 [shorthand outlines]

Foreign Cities

3 [shorthand outlines]

1. Attleboro, Goldsboro, Jonesboro, Hillsboro, Marlborough.
2. Arkansas, Illinois, Massachusetts, New Hampshire, Oregon, Utah, Wyoming.
3. Naples, Rome, Sicily, Budapest, Vienna, Prague.

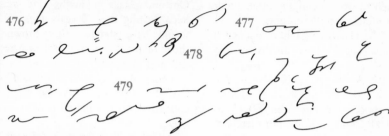

476. Just, Minneapolis, to serve you, identification.

477. Announcement, points, carry, tailoring, altered, wife.

478. Partnership, enviable, reputation, opinion, located, neighborhood.

479. Comment, correctness, self-respecting, relaxes, worn, gradually, conceded, trend, formality, predict.

476. Dear Mr. Taylor: I have just been informed by the manager of our Minneapolis clothing store that you[1] have opened a charge account with us.

Thank you for giving us the opportunity to serve you. I hope the[2] confidence established between you and our store will be a source of pleasure and convenience to[3] you.

Should you wish to shop at any of our other stores, your credit card will serve as an identification.[4]

Feel free to write me if you have any suggestions for improving our service or merchandise. Yours sincerely,[5]

477. Dear Mr. French: In our announcement of the opening of our new store, "Harris and Allan," we failed to make two[6] points clear:

1. Our major line of men's clothes will range in price from $60 to $80. However, we[7] shall also carry fine men's suits that sell for as little as $40.

2. We shall also conduct a complete[8] tailoring service, through which you may have suits pressed, repaired, and altered at reasonable prices.

We invite[9] you to take advantage of this service. Clothes will be called for and delivered at no extra cost.

Make it a point[10] to come in to visit us soon, and bring your wife along. I know that she will like our low prices. Yours sincerely,[11]

478. Dear Mr. Casey: As a man who has always been interested in fine clothes, you will be interested in[12] learning that I am going into partnership with a man who has had an enviable reputation as[13] a tailor in a New York clothing store for more than 20 years.

In my opinion and in the opinion of[14] thousands of men of this city,

Frank Harris knows more about men's clothes than any other tailor in the clothing[15] business.

Mr. Harris and I have opened a shop called "Harris and Allan." It will be located on the corner[16] of Fifth Avenue and 12 Street. We will make the finest men's clothes at prices ranging from $60[17] to $100. Come in to see our merchandise the next time you are in the neighborhood. Cordially yours,[18]

---

479. Dear Mr. Smith: We are often asked to comment on the correctness of brown shoes.

There was a time when only black[19] shoes were correct for wear in the city. No self-respecting man would have been found on the city streets in a pair[20] of brown shoes. Custom relaxes gradually. Had we been writing this 30 years ago, we would have stated[21] that brown shoes might be worn with a brown suit and with nothing else.

Today it is generally conceded that brown[22] shoes may be worn correctly with the lighter shades of gray.

Whether the trend is toward formality or away from[23] it, we predict that 1973 will see one thing unchanged: The Jonesboro Clothing Store will still be the place[24] to come for good clothes – and for good shoes to go with them.

Why not drop in soon to see our latest styles. Cordially yours,[25] (500)

Reading and Writing Practice

480.

Century
, if clause

, if clause

, parenthetical

comfortably

, if clause
remittance

, if clause
cancel

(173)

481.

clothing
, introductory

, introductory
remain

, apposition   250/   250/

(shorthand outline) **(124)**

482. _(shorthand outline)_

, apposition
, nonrestrictive
(shorthand outline)

, nonrestrictive
, introductory
materials
(shorthand outline)

, introductory
(shorthand outline)

(104)

483. _(shorthand outline)_

, introductory
(shorthand outline)

(39)

484. Penmanship Practice. The subject of your practice in this lesson is the letter o. There are two things you should remember in practicing the following groups:

1. Make the o *deep* and *narrow*.

2. The beginning and end of the o should be on the same plane of writing.

1. Of, ocean, was, hope, object; row, low; toe, dough, ditto.
2. No, most, memorandum; what, order, audit; show, jaw.

▶ **Progressive Speed Builder (100-130).** You didn't have difficulty writing 125 words a minute for one minute in the previous Speed Builder, did you? Do you think you can squeeze into one minute just five words more? The last letter in this Progressive Speed Builder is counted at 130 words a minute. If you can get something down for every word in the 130 words a minute letter, you are making progress indeed! You may have some difficulty, however, if you do not first practice the preview.

485. Preview

486

487

488

489

490

486. Inches, we should like to have, position, items, different, judgment. in the matter, schedule, insertion.
487. Thank you for your order, carefully, effective, at this time.
488. Appeared, interested, results, afternoon, 1,200, tribute, power.
489. Report, source, investment, surprise, unusual, amazed, smallest, thoughtfulness.
490. Experience, announced, already, revise, budget, weekly, discontinue.

(1 Minute at 100)

486. Gentlemen: Enclosed is copy for 5 inches of advertising that we should like to have you run in the April 10 issue of your paper./ This is to appear in a top position on your page of personal items. If in your opinion this advertisement could be placed to//advantage in a different position, please feel free to use your judgment in the matter.

I do not at the moment have a schedule///of rates available; therefore, would you please send me a bill for this insertion. I will see that it is paid promptly. Very cordially yours, (1)

(1 Minute at 110)

487. Dear Mr. Trees: Thank you for your order for the advertisement that you asked us to run in the April 10 issue of our newspaper. As you request,/we shall place it in a top position on our page of personal items. After considering the matter carefully, we have decided that that would//be the most effective position for it.

A schedule of our rates is enclosed. The rates decrease as the number of issues in which you run your/// advertising increases.

We are not enclosing a bill for this insertion at this time. You will receive your bill on the first of the month. Sincerely yours, (2)

(1 Minute at 120)

488. Gentlemen: You may remember that, in the April 10 issue of your newspaper, our company placed a small 5-inch advertisement. It appeared in a top position/on your page of personal items.

We believe that you will be interested in the results that we obtained from that small advertisement. During the//afternoon of April 10, we received more than 200 orders by mail. By the end of the week, the advertisement had brought in more than 1,200 orders, ranging from $5///to $10 each. This is a fine tribute to the power of advertising in your newspaper. We are very much pleased with these wonderful results. Sincerely yours, (3)

(1 Minute at 125)

489. Dear Mr. Trees: We were naturally very pleased to receive the report on the results that you obtained from your advertisement in the April 10 issue of our newspaper. /It is a source of pleasure to us to learn that you received so fine a return from such a small investment.

It may surprise you to learn that returns like these are not unusual// for our advertisers. New advertisers are often amazed at the results that they obtain from even the smallest advertisement.

We hope that the results of your first///advertisement in our newspaper will encourage you to place more of your advertising with us.

Thank you for writing us; we appreciate your thoughtfulness. Sincerely yours, (4)

(1 Minute at 130)
490. Mr. Farley: I am sure that

you will be interested in our first experience as advertisers in the Tribune. As an experiment, we placed a small advertisement/in the April 10 issue, in which we announced two of our new products. We have already received more than 1,500 orders as a result of that advertisement, and orders are still// coming in. I believe that this is the greatest return we have ever received from an advertisement of that type.

I believe that it would be wise to revise our advertising///budget and make provision for at least a weekly advertisement in the Tribune. If necessary, we could discontinue some of our present advertising. Henry J. Trees (5) (585)

Reading and Writing Practice

491.

warehouse
substantially

, contrast
100-page
hyphenated
before noun

absorbed
; no conjunction
, introductory

, parenthetical
standards

(150)

492.
, as clause
annual

1930

9 50,

prior
merchandise
, nonrestrictive

(112)

493.

(146)

LESSON 56

▶ **Principles of Outline Construction**

494. Omission of vowel in -VENT, -VENTION. *The vowel is omitted in the endings* -VENT, -VENTION.

1. Inventory, adventure, convent, event, invent, servant, ventilate.
2. Invention, convention, conventional, prevention, intervention.

495. Omission of vowel in word ending -SIVE. *The vowel is omitted in the ending* -SIVE.

Extensive, defensive, expensive, expansive, comprehensive, impulsive, decisive, evasive, excessive.

Reading and Writing Practice

496. An Educated Person

CHAPTER 12 PAPER AND PRINTING

[Shorthand outlines] —Henry Ford (182)

Letters

497. *[Shorthand outlines]*

Transcribe:
No. 16

, parenthetical
previous

(shorthand outlines)

(140)

498.
embarrassed

high-grade
  hyphenated
  before noun

, intervening
  phrase
first-class
  hyphenated
  before noun

, conjunction
promptly

chemicals
, introductory

(137)

499.
, *as clause*
; no conjunction
, words omitted

(133)

500.
cash-with-order
hyphenated
before noun

$9 = 6 =$

guaranteed
, introductory

(96)

501.

, if clause
system

fibers
, series

wear

(123)

502. Recall Drill (L). In this lesson you will review the three word endings represented by the alphabetic stroke *l*.

-less

1 [shorthand outlines]

-lity

2 [shorthand outlines]

-lty

3 [shorthand outlines]

1. Unless, harmless, needless, endless, thoughtless, helpless.
2. Ability, inability, stability, reliability, formality, utility.
3. Penalty, faculty, novelty, loyalty, royalty.

503. Previews and Writing Practice

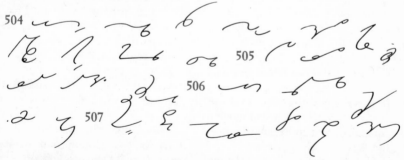

504. Reorganized, glad to say, that time, greater, constantly, to bring, during the past year, doubled, up-to-the-minute, accuracy.

505. **To know**, already, wise, render, entrusting, facilities.
506. **Location**, needless to say, invited, aware, representative.
507. **Civil**, assistance, employment, particularly, capable, constructive.

504. Dear Mr. Brown: As you may know, Jones & Company re-organized two years ago. We are glad to say that things[1] have been going well with us since that time.

Our present volume of business is now ten times greater than it was two[2] years ago. We have five times as many accounts as we had then, and the number is constantly grow-ing. We have[3] made many new friends, and we have been able to bring many old customers back into the fold.

During the past[4] year we have doubled our space and installed many new up-to-the-minute presses that produce more and better work.[5]

Why not let us take care of your printing orders? You will be pleased with our speed and accuracy. Yours sincerely,[6]

---

505. Dear Mr. Hatfield: Even though our business is only four weeks old, you will be interested to know that we[7] already have a large volume of work on hand. The fact that our plant has been kept busy from the day we opened it[8] shows that we were wise to install modern equipment and to decide to render the best possible service.

No[9] doubt you have many print-ing jobs that you want done quickly and attractively. Why not give us a trial by entrusting[10] to us one of your small jobs? When you see what fine work we do and how quickly we do it, we are confident[11] that you will want us to handle your large, important jobs, too.

Will you let me know on the en-closed card when you will[12] have a few minutes to spare. I should like to tell you personally about our facilities. Sincerely yours,[13]

---

506. Dear Mr. Mead: On April 10 the Brown Printing Company is moving to its new location at 162[14] South Street. We have enlarged our facilities and installed equipment that is up to the minute in every[15] respect. Needless to say, you are in-vited to visit us at our new address at any time.

We are aware[16] that in the past year or two some of our deliveries were slow in arriving. You have been very patient[17] with us. From now on we will be able to complete your printing work on schedule.

Our representative, Mr.[18] Brown, will be in to see you soon to tell you about our new presses and other facilities. Yours sincerely,[19]

---

507. Dear Mr. Lawson: The Civil Service Commission wishes to express its appreciation of your help in[20] printing the news releases that we have been issuing from time to time. Your assistance in bringing these releases[21] to the attention of those who may be interested in Government employment is also greatly[22] appreciated.

The co-operation of the press is particularly valuable because the Government[23] urgently needs capable persons for various positions. Never before have there been so many[24] employment opportunities for constructive and interesting positions with the Government. Yours sincerely,[25] (500)

Reading and Writing Practice

508.

, introductory 1910
editor

acquainted
, conjunction
4-53-21

, parenthetical
obligation

century
, conjunction

(157)

509.

, contrast
relieve

well-kept
  hyphenated
  before noun
, series

, introductory
schedule

1902

, parenthetical
, if clause

(143)

510.

, **introductory**
: **enumeration**
flexible

(96)

511.

foreign
regardless

, **if clause**
normally
scrap

, **if clause**
specifications
self-addressed

(89)

personnel

, **conjunction**
difficulty

LESSON **58**

▶ **Word Families**

512. Ind-

[shorthand outlines]

Industry, indistinct, indispensable, indirect, indicate, indisposed, indiscreet.

513. -pression

[shorthand outlines]

Impression, depression, expression, compression, oppression.

514. Frequent Names

Last Names

1 *[shorthand outlines]*

Men's First Names

2 *[shorthand outlines]*

Women's First Names

3 *[shorthand outlines]*

1. Morris, Morrison, Morse, Munroe, Murray.
2. John, Jonathan, Joseph, Julian, Lawrence, Leonard, Louis.
3. Laura, Lillian, Louise, Lucy, Margaret.

515. Previews and Writing Practice

516 [shorthand outlines]

517 [shorthand outlines] 518 [shorthand outlines]

519 [shorthand outlines]

516. Elbow, obligation, representatives, printing, naturally, balanced.
517. Manufactured, billions, era, succeeding.
518. Expansion, in the market, qualifications, executives, potentials.
519. Reception, stationery, concerns, letterheads, advantage, suggestions, if you would like to have, designers, improved, one of the, things, ordinary.

516. Dear Mr. Morris: Would you like to have a printing expert at your elbow when you plan your next advertising[1] campaign? You can have one for the asking. We shall be glad to supply him without obligation to you. Our[2] representatives are experienced men who have spent years helping our customers get the most for the money they[3] spend on printing.

Our representatives average more than 25 years in the printing business. During that[4] time they have naturally acquired a balanced judgment and valuable understanding of the way to obtain[5] the best results from each dollar you spend on printing.

When you start to plan your next campaign, call us. Cordially yours,[6]

---

517. Dear Mr. Morse: In 1910 we sold the first press manufactured in our plant. That press was bought by the[7] Mason Printing Company in Cleveland. Since that time, it has printed billions of sheets. In fact, it is still in use[8] for certain types of work.

Today our model No. 158 is part of a new era in the printing[9] industry. It is manufactured with the same regard for quality printing as our first and all succeeding[10] models, but it is geared to a faster pace. It is designed to make a profit for its owner.

Let one of our[11] representatives explain how our model No. 158 will quickly pay for itself. Yours sincerely,[12]

---

518. Dear Mr. Green: Because of the expansion of our printing business, we are in the market for an experienced[13] salesman to represent us in the states of California, Washington, Oregon, and Nevada. The man[14] we would like to have should possess, among other things, the following qualifications:

1. He should be able[15] to get along well with executives of leading organizations.

2. He should know how to sell services[16] as well as printing.

3. He should possess the potentials to develop into an executive.

If you know[17] of any young man who you think meets our requirements, won't you please have him get in touch with me. Cordially yours,[18]

---

519. Dear Mr. Quinn: Your callers form an impression of your organization from your building, your reception room,[19] or your sales office. Readers of your business letters form their impression from your business stationery alone.[20] The design of your letterhead, the information it contains, and the quality of paper and printing are[21] therefore of vital importance.

That is why so many successful business concerns insist that their letterheads[22] be printed on Mead Paper. That is also why so many executives have sent for our kit of sample[23] letterheads and have used to advantage the suggestions given in it.

If you would like to have one of these kits, all[24] you have to do is ask for it. If you wish, enclose a copy of your present letterhead, and our designers[25] will be glad to show you how it can be improved so that it will make the best impression.

One of the things we think[26] you will like is the fact that Mead Papers cost only a little more than ordinary papers. Cordially yours,[27] (540)

Reading and Writing Practice

520.
, parenthetical
hurry

letterhead
, parenthetical

, parenthetical
toward

, conjunction
well-worded
  hyphenated
  before noun

, conjunction

(154)

521.

, parenthetical

, conjunction
album

(152)

522.

greeting
, conjunction

$\cup$ 50

Transcribe:
15 cents
, if clause

15'

(94)

523. **Frequent Phrases**

Words Omitted

1 [shorthand outlines]

In Addition

2 [shorthand outlines]

1. In the market, on the market, in the future, about the matter, in the world, on the question, on the subject.
2. In addition, in addition to the, in addition to these, in addition to those, in addition to that, in addition to them.

524. **Geographical Expressions**

St.

1 [shorthand outlines]

States

2 [shorthand outlines]

Foreign Cities

3 [shorthand outlines]

1. St. Paul, St. Charles, St. John, St. Augustine, St. Lawrence.
2. Delaware, Indiana, Michigan, New Jersey, Pennsylvania, Vermont.
3. Bucharest, Athens, Moscow, Oslo, Stockholm, Copenhagen.

525. Previews and Writing Practice

526. Textbook, recently, different, schoolbook, competent, illustrated, beautifully, we have made, reputation, standards, in the market.
527. Contribution, competition, appetite, readable, enhance.
528. Different, degrees, quality, craftsmen, fraction, occasion.
529. Confirm, in accordance, cooperation.

526. Dear Mr. Keys: Have you looked at a school textbook recently? We mean, of course, a new textbook. It is quite different[1] from the type of book you and I used in our studies.

Today's modern schoolbook is a treat. It is easy to[2] read, and it is good to look at. It is designed by competent artists and is well illustrated. Finally,[3] it is so beautifully printed that it makes learning a pleasure.

We have specialized in printing fine textbooks[4] of all types. We have made a fine reputation for ourselves because of our high standards.

If you are in the market[5] for quality printing for your textbooks, we are confident that we can meet your requirements. Cordially yours,[6]

527. Dear Mr. Abby: In homes all over the country, books are making a vital contribution to better living.[7] In spite of competition from other fields, this large appetite for books of all kinds has built an industry[8] that does $300,000,000 of business.

For more than 50 years Vermont Papers have played an important[9] part in this expansion. They have helped make books more readable and more attractive.

Vermont Papers enhance the appeal[10] of books and make them attractive to the customer in many ways.

If you are interested in increasing[11] the sale of your books, we can help you do it. Try Vermont Paper in the next book you publish. Cordially yours,[12]

528. Dear Mr. McMann: As I am sure you know, there are many different degrees of quality in printing. Fine[13] quality printing is produced by craftsmen, who take pride in the work they produce.

The cost of a printed piece of[14] material is only a fraction of its value to the buyer. Such material stands or falls on how[15] it looks and what it says. It represents you; it represents your company.

Those who have placed their printing with us[16] have never had occasion to regret their action. We have a record of performance of which we are very[17] proud. Day after day, year after year, our men have been turning out work that is well done and reasonably priced.

May[18] we have an opportunity to show you what we can do the next time you have a printing job. Sincerely yours,[19]

---

529. Dear Mr. Fleming: This will confirm our telephone conversation of April 15.

In accordance with our[20] agreement, we are sending you by truck today 50,000 booklets similar to the one enclosed. It is[21] our understanding that you will mail copies of these booklets to approximately 48,000 druggists[22] on your list. This list, we understand, has been recently revised so that the 48,000 names represent[23] true prospects for our products.

Also, please send 200 of the booklets, in one package, to our San Francisco[24] office. Use the attached label for this purpose.

We are quite anxious to have these booklets distributed; therefore,[25] anything you can do to expedite the mailing will be appreciated. Yours sincerely,

P. S. Our[26] check for $600 to cover the cost of the mailing is enclosed. Thank you for your fine cooperation.[27] (540)

Reading and Writing Practice

530.

, parenthetical
rising
steadily

, introductory
10-month
  hyphenated
  before noun

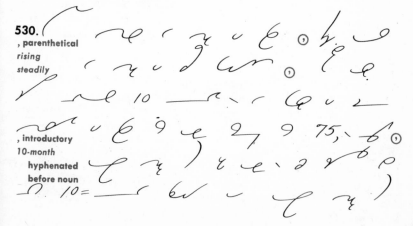

, introductory
absorb
; because of comma
, parenthetical

(132)

531.

minds
, introductory
, introductory
benefit

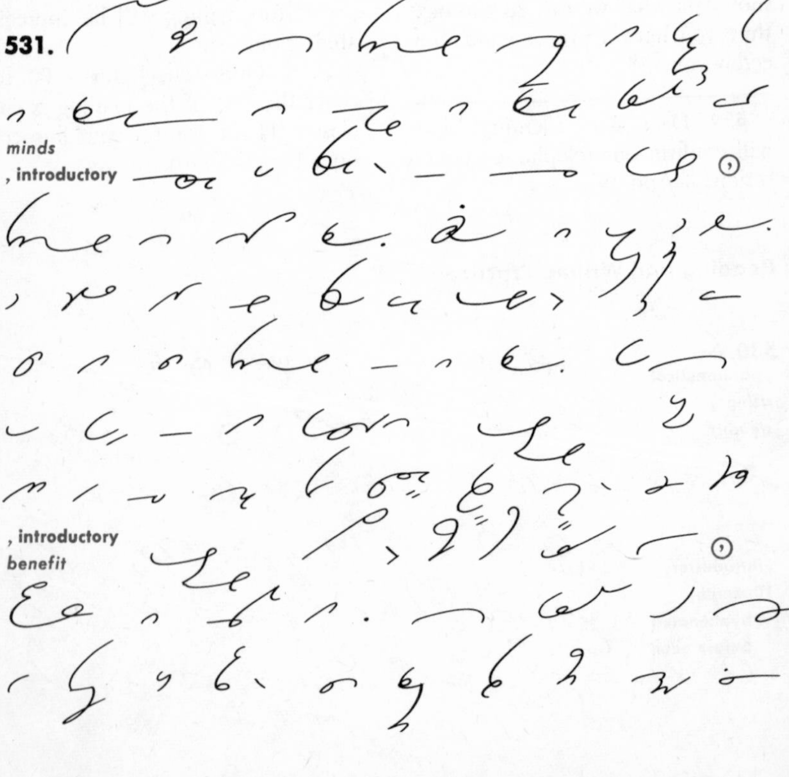

(157)

532.

, when clause
Transcribe:
  No. 6

, apposition
boiled

179

variety

, if clause
, apposition
. inside quote

(133)

LESSON 60

533. Penmanship Practice. In this drill you will work with additional joinings of o. Remember to keep the hook *deep* and *narrow*.

1. Or, whole; oath, want; coal, goal.
2. Paw, pause, body, ball; bottle, bomb; shot, showed.
3. So, sore, fall; of course, organize; of the, ordinary, autumn.

▶ **Progressive Speed Builder (100-130)**

534. Preview

535. You will be glad, to know, I had, several months ago, unable, users, manuscript, opinion.
536. Thank you for your letter, some time ago, anxious, edition, recover, has not yet, judging.
537. Week end, very well, during the past year, I am sure, I hope that.

538. We shall be able, ground, 30,000, reorganization, material, indicated.
539. Town, to him, Chicago, notifying, thought, promotion.

(1 Minute at 100)

535. Dear Mr. Warner: You will be glad to know that I have finally completed the revision of my book, "Money and Banking." I had hoped /to complete the job several months ago, but on May 10 I became ill and was unable to work on it for about a month.

In revising//the book, I have tried to follow all the suggestions that I have received from the present users of the book.

I am sending the manuscript/// to you today by express. After you have read it, I should like very much to have your opinion of it. Very sincerely yours, (1)

(1 Minute at 110)

536. Dear Mr. Clay: Thank you for your letter with the good news that you have completed revision of your book, "Money and Banking." As I wrote you some time/ago, we are very anxious to have this revision because the sales of the present edition are not what they should be. I believe that, with a new edition,//we will soon recover the ground that we have lost.

The manuscript has not yet arrived. I assume that it will reach us either today or tomorrow.///As soon as I receive it, I will read it. Judging by the work you have done in the past, I am sure that this revision will be a fine one. Sincerely yours, (2)

(1 Minute at 120)

537. Mr. Lloyd: Mr. Clay has finally finished the revision of his book, "Money and Banking." The manuscript arrived Friday, and I read it over the week end.

Mr./Clay has done very well, and I am confident that, with this revision, we will be able to recover the ground that we lost during the past year with the first edition.//

Before we place the manuscript into production, I wish that you would read it and let me have your frank opinion. If you feel that any changes should be made, I am/// sure that Mr. Clay will be glad to consider them.

I hope that you can spare the time to read the manuscript as I should like to start production soon. James H. Wilson (3)

(1 Minute at 125)

538. Mr. Wilson: After reading Mr. Clay's revision of his book, "Money and Banking," I, too, am confident that we shall be able to recover the ground that we lost during/the past year with the first edition. If we do not sell at least 30,-000 copies in the first year, I shall be very much surprised.

I particularly like his//reorganization of the material in the book and his treatment of branch banking. I did find a few things that in my opinion could be improved, and I have indicated///them right on the manuscript.

Should I return the manuscript to Mr. Clay, or would it be better to ask him to come in to discuss my suggested changes? John H. Lloyd (4)

(1 Minute at 130)

539. Mr. Wilson: Mr. Clay was in town yesterday and came in to discuss my suggested changes in his book, "Money and Banking." He had hoped to see you while he was here, but I/explained to him that you were in Chicago.

We spent about an hour discussing my suggested changes, and he agreed to them all. In fact, after our meeting, he sat in your office and//made all the changes immediately.

The manuscript is now complete and ready for production. I believe that it will be finished quickly. If all goes well, we may even///have copies by September 1.

I am notifying the Advertising Department that the revision is ready and suggesting that they give some thought to promotion. John H. Lloyd (5) (585)

Reading and Writing Practice

540.

essential
against

record keeping
no noun,
no hyphen

, nonrestrictive

record-keeping
hyphenated
before noun

(127)

541.

bearing
filled

, parenthetical
beginning

, if clause
immediately

(114)

542.

, apposition
. inside quote

local

350

(161)

Shorthand Reporting

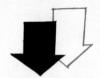

Most people who take up the study of shorthand do so with the sole objective of becoming stenographers and secretaries; from these positions they sometimes work their way up to more responsible jobs in an organization. Some, however, find shorthand so fascinating that they derive great pleasure from writing it at faster and faster speeds and would like to continue their study of the subject.

If you are of the second group, you may want to give some consideration to becoming a shorthand reporter. A shorthand reporter is a person who uses shorthand speed and other abilities to take down word for word speeches at conventions or assemblies, minutes of meetings, and proceedings of a courtroom. His salary is often many times that of the office stenographers.

The two major qualifications of a shorthand reporter are these:

1. He must be able to write shorthand at a high rate of speed — 175 words a minute or more.

2. He must have a good grasp of the English language and a large vocabulary.

Roughly speaking, there are three types of reporting.

 GENERAL REPORTING: the taking down and transcribing of speeches and addresses that become part of the permanent record of a convention, an assembly, or any other type of official gathering. A good example of a general reporter is one who takes down the deliberations of the houses of Congress.

A speed of 175 words a minute on solid matter is usually a minimum shorthand requirement for the person who is to handle satisfactorily this type of reporting.

CONFERENCE REPORTING: the taking down of the deliberations of a group of persons, such as a board of directors, a committee meeting, and the like. This is perhaps the most exacting work of this type because the reporter is required to record and properly identify the comments of a number of people—sometimes as many as twenty or more.

A cool head and a speed of at least 200 words a minute are "musts" for this type of reporting.

COURT REPORTING: the recording of the testimony of a trial. It is the most frequent type of work that a reporter is called upon to do. If you would like to see a court reporter in action, pay a visit to your local courthouse. There you will usually find the reporter seated at a table in front of the witness, taking down all the questions and answers as well as the comments of the lawyers and the judge.

The work of a court reporter is highly interesting; one day he may be reporting the testimony of a doctor; on another day, that of an engineer; and on still another day, that of an architect or an accountant.

Court reporting calls for a speed of at least 200 words a minute, but many reporters write much faster.

If you really like to write shorthand and are willing to put in the necessary time to build your speed to reporting levels, by all means consider shorthand reporting. There are always well-paying positions waiting for competent shorthand writers.

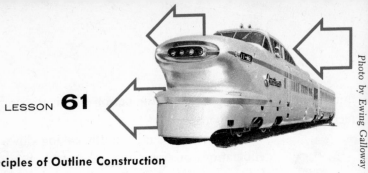

Photo by Ewing Galloway

LESSON **61**

▶ **Principles of Outline Construction**

543. Double consonants. *It is unnecessary to repeat the double consonant in compound words like "bookkeeper."*

Bookkeeping, neckcloth, roommate, headdress, storeroom, nighttime, earring.

544. -NESS after words ending in N or M. *The word ending -NESS is joined to N or M with a jog.*

1. Dimness, slimness, calmness, firmness, meanness.
2. Suddenness, openness, plainness, thinness, sternness.

Reading and Writing Practice

545. Leaners

CHAPTER **13** **TRAVEL AND TRANSPORTATION**

(163)

Letters

546.

stateroom
, nonrestrictive

accept
calmness
, parenthetical

, nonrestrictive
believe

(125)

547.
, introductory
, nonrestrictive

, parenthetical
; because of comma
likelihood

capacity
, conjunction

cancellations
, if clause

(98)

548.
, if clause

journey

traveler
: enumeration

denominations
foreign

① ② ③

(164)

549.

10

, when clause [shorthand outline]

balance
: enumeration [shorthand outline]

receipt [shorthand outline]

, introductory [shorthand outline] (140)

550.
Europe
, if clause [shorthand outline]

, introductory
fare
, nonrestrictive [shorthand outline] (60)

551. Recall Drill (Ten Blend). In this lesson you will review the various combinations represented by the TEN blend.

-ten

1

-den

2

-tain

3

-ington

4

1. Tend, tentative, tenant, attend, tension, attention, retention, intention.
2. Dentist, deny, denote, wooden hidden, sudden, identify, evidence.
3. Contain, maintain, retain, pertain, captain, obtain.
4. Wilmington, Kensington, Huntington, Lexington, Washington.

552. Previews and Writing Practice

553

554

555

556

553. Europe, if you wish, London, pleasant, schedule, obtain, round, if you would like to have, assistance.
554. Scarcely, surprising, designed, quickly, practical, demonstration.
555. Announce, flight, Newark, leisurely, restful, accommodate, altitude, available.
556. Scenic, extreme, central.

---

553. Dear Mr. Case: Have you been thinking of a trip to Europe? If you have, why wait? Reserve a seat on one of our[1] planes. Within hours of the time when you step aboard our four-engine plane, you will be in Ireland, or Paris, or Rome.[2] If you wish, you can fly to London and then on to Paris for the price of a London ticket alone. You fly[3] at five miles a minute, and the trip is smooth and pleasant.

If you will examine the enclosed schedule, you will see[4] that we have sixteen flights a week to Europe. What is more, the rates are lower than ever. You can now obtain a[5] special 30-day round-trip fare that costs only one-third more than a regular one-way ticket.

If you would like[6] to have assistance in planning your trip to Europe, by all means get in touch with us. Planning trips to all parts of[7] Europe is only one of the many services that we offer without charge to our customers. Sincerely yours,[8]

---

554. Dear Mr. Scott: Scarcely a week passes that we do not receive a letter from a business or professional[9] man that reads like this:

"My Johnson Plane is paying for itself. It makes my days more productive and my traveling[10] more comfortable. What is more, it adds many hours to my leisure time."

A surprising number of these men are[11] over forty. That fact pleases us. We designed our latest model as a professional plane that anyone[12] can learn to fly quickly, easily, and safely.

This new model is very practical, too. Four people may fly[13] in it in complete comfort. In addition, it will carry over 100 pounds of luggage.

See your Johnson[14] dealer today for a demonstration fllight in the new model. He will also arrange free flying lessons for you. Sincerely yours,[15]

---

555. Dear Mr. Smith: We are happy to announce the newest addition to our flight schedule, the American Flyer.[16] This flight leaves Newark, New Jersey, daily at 5 p.m. and arrives at Los Angeles, California, at[17] 8 a.m. the next day.

Now you can leave New York leisurely, spend a restful night in your berth, and wake up in time[18] for a hot breakfast before reaching Los Angeles. Our sleepers are large enough to accommodate twenty-one[19] persons, but we limit them to twelve, thus affording you extra comfort.

Remember, when you fly in our planes, you[20] fly at a comfortable altitude. More important, you fly on a line backed by twenty-five years of experience.[21]

We suggest that you retain the enclosed folder, which tells all about our New York-to-Los--Angeles schedules.[22] It also lists the service available to Chicago, Illinois; Kansas City, Missouri; Denver, Colorado;[23] and many other important centers in the United States.

Call us the next time you must make a long[24] trip. The number is Main 4-3201. We shall be happy to make all the necessary arrange-ments for you. Sincerely yours,[25]

---

556. Dear Mr. Burns: Are you planning a trip in the near future to some of the larger cities on the West Coast? If[26] you are, fly by North Airlines. Go by one route and return by another. North Airlines gives you a choice of two senic[27] routes. You can, for example, go out by the extreme northern route, flying over the wonderful scenery[28] of Wisconsin and Montana. You can return by a central route, flying over the states of Idaho,[29] Wyoming, and Nebraska.

Choose the route that suits you best. Then call us, and we will reserve space for you. Sincerely yours,[30] (600)

Reading and Writing Practice

557.

Sydney
, introductory

; no conjunction
, word omitted
commended

(83)

558.

four-engine
    hyphenated .
    before noun

4 =

Transcribe:
    2,100
    , conjunction

survey
    , parenthetical

distant
    , when clause

(143)

559.

itinerary
    , as clause

15

one-day
 hyphenated
  before noun
, series

[shorthand outline]

, parenthetical
; no conjunction
stopovers

round-trip
 hyphenated
  before noun
, if clause

[shorthand outline] (104)

560. *[shorthand outline]*

, parenthetical

, introductory
, conjunction
appreciate

[shorthand outline] (80)

LESSON **63**

▶ **Word Families**

561. -minal

[shorthand outlines]

Terminal, nominal, criminal.

562. -line

[shorthand outlines]

Airline, underline, outline, streamline, headline.

563. Frequent Names

Last Names

1 *[shorthand outlines]*

Women's First Names

2 *[shorthand outlines]*

Men's First Names

3 *[shorthand outlines]*

1. O'Brien, O'Donnell, Olsen, Parker, Phillips, Quinn, Roberts.
2. Marian, Martha, Matilda, Mildred, Norah.
3. Mark, Matthew, Morris, Michael, Nathan, Nathaniel.

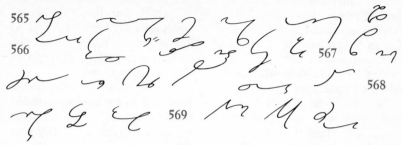

565. Travelers, Columbus, convenient, you will be able, luggage, we hope that.
566. Businessman, readily, unnecessary, benefit, opportunities.
567. I believe, unusual, factual, request, definite, detailed, analysis, indirect.
568. Contribution, prefer, sleeper.
569. Discusses, dependable, facilities.

565. Dear Mr. Olsen: On June 1 we shall place in operation a new plane that you and other travelers have[1] helped to design. The new plane will travel at five miles a minute.

Now you can travel from Chicago to Detroit[2] in an hour; from Cincinnati to Washington in an hour and forty-five minutes; from Cleveland to Columbus[3] in forty minutes.

You will find the new plane convenient in many other ways. For example, you will be able[4] to carry your luggage onto the plane, if the luggage is fairly light, and place it in the convenient racks[5] at the entrance. When you leave, it is immediately available to you; you will lose no time waiting for[6] your luggage.

We hope that you will have occasion to ride on our fine new plane in the near future. Sincerely yours,[7]

---

566. Dear Mr. Morris: As a businessman who flies a good deal, you will be interested in the enclosed folder[8] entitled "More About Air Travel." This folder will give you information that is not readily available[9] to the general public. It will also tell you about our new plan, which makes it unnecessary for[10] you to pick up your reservations in advance. Instead, you can pick them up at the ticket office when you arrive[11] at the airport. This is another move to assure you the greatest possible benefit and convenience[12] from your travel by air.

We hope that you will have many opportunities to use our airlines. Cordially yours,[13]

---

567. Dear Mr. Quinn: If you

travel on business, I believe that you will be interested in an unusual[14] booklet we have just prepared. This booklet is unusual because it presents a factual study of the[15] time, cost, and comfort factors involved in air travel and also in other methods of transportation.

We shall[16] be pleased to send you a copy with our compliments if you will return the enclosed request card. In our opinion,[17] the use of air travel by businessmen will continue to increase only if it offers definite[18] advantages to the traveler. Our booklet shows how in many cases air travel saves the businessman time and[19] money.

The booklet also gives a detailed analysis of direct and indirect travel costs. Cordially yours,[20]

---

568. Dear Mr. Nathan: I am delighted that you are able to be with us for our conference in Greenfield, North[21] Carolina, on July 16. I know that you will enjoy your visit with us and that we will profit by your[22] contribution to the conference.

I am sorry to say that Greenfield is not easily accessible. I[23] suggest that you fly to Raleigh, where I

shall be glad to meet you. I will then drive you to Greenfield. I understand[24] that there are several flights each day from New York to Raleigh. If you prefer to come by train, you can take a sleeper[25] to where I will meet you.

We are reserving for you the guest room in our faculty apartment building, where[26] I am sure that you will be comfortable during your stay.

I shall look forward to hearing from you. Cordially yours,[27]

---

569. Dear Mr. Price: We are enclosing a booklet that discusses in some detail the matter of winter travel[28] by air. We feel that an air traveler like you will be interested in knowing the inside story of how we[29] keep our service so dependable in spite of winter weather.

Perhaps you have already noticed how greatly[30] air-line operation has improved in the last few winters. The booklet gives you some of the reasons for this improvement.[31]

Whether your next trip is for business or for pleasure, we hope that you will use our facilities. Yours truly,[32] (640)

Reading and Writing Practice

570.
, intervening
phrase
questionnaire

, introductory
continuously

, if clause
, parenthetical

, if clause
, parenthetical

envelope
, nonrestrictive

(157)

571.

, introductory
, nonrestrictive

— 1933

[shorthand outlines]

, parenthetical

, introductory
Syracuse

, conjunction
baggage

30

(123)

572.
, apposition
four-engine
   hyphenated
   before noun

Europe
Africa
, series

, if clause
contemplating

(79)

573. Frequent Phrases

Or Omitted

1 [shorthand outlines]

Intersection

2 [shorthand outlines]

1. One or two, two or three, three or four, once or twice, day or two, week or two ago, day or two ago.
2. p.m., a.m., C.O.D., Chamber of Commerce.

574. Geographical Expressions

Fort

1 [shorthand outlines]

States and Territories

2 [shorthand outlines]

Foreign Cities

3 [shorthand outlines]

1. Fort Wayne, Fort Worth, Fort Dodge, Fort Madison, Fort Myers.
2. District of Columbia, Iowa, Minnesota, New Mexico, Virginia, Puerto Rico.
3. Palestine, Singapore, Tokyo, Havana, Santiago, Rio de Janeiro.

575. Previews and Writing Practice

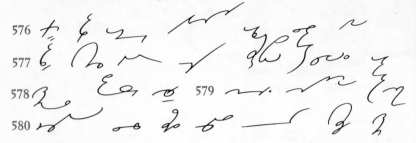

576. Chamber of Commerce, special, resumption, discontinued, reservations, inexpensive, tour.
577. Experienced, difficulty, trunk, instead, aboard, accordingly, responsible.
578. Thank you for your letter, explanation, quite.
579. Commuting, conductor, coupon.
580. Scheduled, immediately, efficiently, naturally, maintain, deficit, thank you for your.

576. Dear Mr. Billings: The Chamber of Commerce invites you and your friends to join us in a special trip to Mexico[1] City from October 3 to October 31. This is a resumption of a practice that was started[2] some years ago but discontinued in 1947. We already have reservations[3] from people from the following cities: Los Angeles, San Francisco, Fort Worth, and Seattle.

This is an[4] inexpensive tour that affords the travelers an opportunity of going to Mexico under the guidance[5] of a staff that is well trained. The party will travel in special coaches that are air-conditioned.

If possible,[6] we should like to know by next Monday whether you or any of your friends are interested in this trip. Yours truly,[7]

577. Dear Mr. Pace: I was sorry to learn that you have experienced some difficulty with your trunk. As soon as[8] I received your letter, I wrote our agent in Boston. He tells me that, through an error on the part of the Miller[9] Express Company, your trunk was delivered to the Eastern Steamship Lines instead of to our railroad station.[10] By the time the error was discovered, it was too late to have the trunk put aboard your train.

Our agent then shipped[11] the trunk to you by freight, at your request, and you were charged accordingly. You will agree, I hope, that we are not[12] responsible. We suggest that you discuss the matter with the Miller Express Company. Very cordially yours,[13]

578. Gentlemen: Thank you for your letter of November 10, explaining the reason for the freight charges on my trunk.[14] From your explanation, it is quite clear that you are not responsible. I shall discuss the matter with the Miller[15] Express Company, as they are obviously responsible for the situation. Very cordially yours,[16]

---

579. Dear Mr. West: During the month of April we are planning a survey to obtain up-to-date information[17] on our commuting service. Therefore, during this particular month we are going to use a special ticket.[18]

This is the plan that we shall follow:

1. If you use our regular monthly service, your April ticket will consist[19] of a book containing 60 coupons. The conductor will detach a coupon for every ride.

The 60[20] coupons should be sufficient for the month. If you need more, however, your ticket agent will supply you with[21] additional tickets.

2. If you now hold a 26-ride ticket, continue to use it until it expires.[22]

As a result of this survey, we are confident that we will be able to improve our service. Cordially yours,[23]

---

580. Dear Mr. Jones: Thank you for your letter suggesting that we add another train to those scheduled between White Plains[24] and New York. It is not possible for us to do this immediately, but we shall do it as soon as we have[25] the necessary equipment.

You may be interested in one of our recent improvements. We have opened[26] six new electric power stations that will enable us to operate our trains faster and light them better.[27]

I am sorry to say, however, that we shall have to apply for an increase in rates. Because of increased costs[28] and payrolls, we have not been able to operate efficiently with our present rates. Naturally, we would[29] like to maintain our rates as low as possible; but you will understand that we cannot continue to operate[30] on a deficit as we have done during the past year.

Again, thank you for your suggestion. Sincerely yours,[31] (620)

Reading and Writing Practice

581.
response
, introductory

year's

; no conjunction
, parenthetical

, as clause
likely

, contrast
, introductory

(110)

582.
, if clause
convenience

, conjunction
disposal

boarding
, introductory
; no conjunction

350

32 =

(146)

583. 26: 16 12

167

4°

5:15 — 9:30

eh (100)

LESSON 65

584. Penmanship Practice. In this lesson you will practice the various joinings of the oo hook. The main point to keep in mind as you practice the oo hook is to keep it *deep* and *narrow*.

1. You-your, world, you can; Yours truly, you would, you did; wood, woman.
2. Shoe, chew; one, whom; you want, you are, you will.
3. New, none, number; nut, mood.
4. Cool, gull; us, you have; rubber, group, up.

▶ **Progressive Speed Builder (110-135).** The letters in this Progressive Speed Builder range in speed from 110 to 135 words a minute. Don't you feel a thrill watching your speed increasing as a result of your practice?

585. Preview

586. Weather, why not, Orient, one of our, few minutes, as long, afford.
587. Daughter, nurse's, graduation, touch, of course, tourist, indicating, ports, grateful.
588. Choice, memorable, I believe, Pacific, San Francisco, special, accommodations.
589. Studied, ideal, $100, deposit, assume, passports, procedure.
590. Promptly, disappoint, except, in the matter, Building.

(1 Minute at 110)

586. Dear Mr. Ogden: Though you might not think so from the weather we have had during the past few weeks, summer is only six weeks away; and you will/soon be making plans for your vacation.

Why not do something really different and relaxing this summer? Why not take a trip to the Orient on//one of our fine liners?

Deviate a few minutes to reading the enclosed booklet, which gives all the details about the trips available and the cost of///each. We have trips that are as short as five weeks, and trips that are as long as three months.

We shall be glad to help you plan a trip that you can afford. Sincerely yours, (1)

(1 Minute at 120)

587. Gentlemen: My daughter will complete her nurse's training on June 15, and I have promised to give her a boat trip to any part of the world as a graduation/present. She has decided that she would like to visit the Orient.

We are interested in a trip that will last about three months and that will touch as many//different ports in the Orient as possible.

Our funds, of course, are limited; therefore, we could not consider anything but tourist class.

Would you outline a suggested /// trip for us, indicating the ports that we would visit. Also, please let us know what the cost would be.

We shall be grateful for any help you can give us. Sincerely yours, (2)

(1 Minute at 125)

588. Dear Mr. Ogden: You have made a fine choice in your gift of a trip to the Orient for your daughter, who will complete her nurse's training in June. It will be a memorable/ experience for her and a relaxing vacation for you and your wife.

I believe we have the perfect trip for you. Our liner, "The Pacific," will leave San Francisco//on June 18 and return on September 18. It will stop at most of the important ports in the Orient.

We have prepared a special folder on this trip, and I am///enclosing a copy. It explains in some detail the types of accommodations that are available on "The Pacific" and the cost of each. Very cordially yours, (3)

(1 Minute at 130)

589. Gentlemen: We have carefully studied the folder that you sent us explaining the types of accommodations that are available on "The Pacific." This trip seems to be/ideal for my daughter; therefore, we have definitely decided to take it. I have checked on the folder the accommodations we should like to have, and I am enclosing my//check for $100 as a deposit.

As this is the first trip of this kind that any of us have taken, we shall, of course, need all the help you can give us in preparing///for the trip. For example, we assume that we shall need passports. Just what is the procedure? Also, when will it be necessary for me to make final payment? Yours very truly, (4)

(1 Minute at 135)

590. Dear Mr. Ogden: I am glad that the trip we suggested pleases your daughter and that you decided so promptly to take it. Space on this trip is going very rapidly; and if you/had delayed reaching a decision, we might have had to disappoint you.

Thank you for your deposit of $100. It will not be necessary to make your final payment until// June 10.

We will make all the necessary arrangements except in the matter of your passports. I suggest that you take immediate steps to obtain these, so that you will have them in///time for the trip.

It is a simple matter to obtain passports. Apply for them on the third floor of the Federal Building in San Francisco.

You will be hearing from us soon. Sincerely yours, (5) (620)

Reading and Writing Practice

591.

, conjunction

, when clause

attending

well-balanced
hyphenated
before noun

(138)

592.

greet
, introductory

, if clause
meals

(121)

593.

director
, apposition

brochure
ideally

, if clause
; no conjunction

; no conjunction
envelope

(143)

338

LESSON **66**

▶ **Principles of Outline Construction**

594. Diphthong ʊ represented by oo hook. *In many words a more facile outline is obtained by writing the oo hook for* ʊ.

Reduce, introduce, produce, induce, subdue, educate, duty, deduce.

595. Word endings -UATE, -UATION, -UITY. *In writing the endings* -UATE, -UATION, -UITY *more legible outlines are obtained by including the* E *in the diphthong.*

-uate

1

-uation, -uity

2

1. Graduate, actuate, punctuate, perpetuate, fluctuate.
2. Graduation, insinuation, punctuation, continuity, ingenuity.

Reading and Writing Practice

596. You Can Do It

CHAPTER **14** PUBLISHING

(shorthand characters) — The Friendly Adventurer (192)

Letters

597. *(shorthand characters)*

, if clause
collection   *(shorthand characters)* 350 *(shorthand characters)*

, and omitted
, apposition
, inside quote

(shorthand outlines)

(153)

598.

choosing
graduation

(shorthand outlines)

(67)

599.

full-page
hyphenated
before noun

[shorthand]

, parenthetical [shorthand]

, intervening
phrase
Transcribe:
a cent , [shorthand] $\frac{1}{3}$

[shorthand]

carrying [shorthand]

[shorthand] 80 [shorthand] 40 [shorthand]

, series [shorthand]
handling
, introductory [shorthand]

, parenthetical [shorthand]
really

[shorthand]

effective
, when clause [shorthand]

[shorthand] (202)

600.

subscription
; no conjunction
, introductory

unless
, parenthetical

, conjunction
receive

(86)

601.

, introductory
enjoys
receive

achieve

(68)

LESSON 67

602. Recall Drill (NT Blend). In this lesson you will review the uses of the NT blend.

-nt

1 *[shorthand outlines]*

-nd

2 *[shorthand outlines]*

Ind-, Int-

3 *[shorthand outlines]*

End-, Ent-, Ant-,

4 *[shorthand outlines]*

Phrases

5 *[shorthand outlines]*

1. Print, rental, client, current, event, different, sent.
2. Brand, ground, thousands, kindness, refined, binder, trend.
3. Independent, index, indicating, indicator, intact, into, intellect.
4. Enduringly, endurance, entitle, entrust, entry, anticipate.
5. It is not, there is not, there was not, was not, I was not, he was not, $400.

603. Previews and Writing Practice

604 *[shorthand outlines]* 605 *[shorthand outlines]*

604. Dear Mr. Brown: Enclosed you will find an up-to-date list of books that we have issued on various phases of[1] music. You will notice that for each book we have provided a brief description as well as a quotation or[2] two from authorities who have read the book.

As a music lover, you will want many of these books in your music[3] library.

You may use the convenient form that is also enclosed to send us your order. Cordially yours,[4]

605. Dear Friend: If all the superlatives in the dictionary were placed end to end, the result would be a dull,[5] monotonous piece of writing to read.

Frankly, a description of the "American Cookbook" calls for the use of[6] a great many superlatives; but if I were to use them, you probably would not believe that this book on cooking[7] could be all that

we claim.

Therefore, I am asking you to be judge and jury and decide for yourself by taking[8] advantage of a free ten-day examination of the "American Cookbook." There are absolutely[9] no strings attached.

You make no commitments by sending for this fine volume. Quite likely, you will find that you have made[10] a delightful discovery.

Will you, therefore, accept my invitation to examine the book for yourself[11] by sending in the enclosed postal card.

The card is ready for mailing; no postage is required. Sincerely yours,[12]

606. Dear Friend: It is a pleasure to send you our new cookbook. I am sure that you will find in it many recipes[13] that will solve your meal-planning problems.

You will find not only that the tested recipes in this booklet are helpful[14] in themselves but also that they suggest many new and different ways in which you can use our milk in your cooking.[15] Thousands of good cooks know that our condensed milk gives a special richness to all recipes that call for milk.[16] Furthermore, our condensed milk is nutritious — twice as rich as good whole milk.

Perhaps you will also be interested[17] in our enlarged, binder-type cookbook described on page 32. It includes more than 300 recipes of[18] all types, and it is illustrated throughout with beautiful full-page pictures of more than 100 dishes.[19] All that this fine cookbook costs is 15 cents, either in stamps or coin, to cover the cost of mailing and handling.

Please[20] feel free to write to me whenever I can be of assistance to you with your cooking problems. Cordially yours,[21]

---

607. Dear Mr. Riley: The publication date of "Smith's Tax Guide" has been moved forward from January 1 to[22] November 1. We have advanced the date so that our friends will have plenty of time to take advantage of the new[23] tax savings described in the guide. These new tax savings are based on up-to-the-minute rulings, decisions, and[24] opinions that will directly affect your business this year.

To help you prepare your tax returns and take advantage[25] of the new savings now available, we have reserved a copy of our tax guide for you. As our special[26] customer, you are entitled to have the new guide on the following plan:

1. On November 1 you will receive[27] the new guide, ready for instant reference on tax problems.

2. For a period of a year you will receive[28] reports that will keep your guide up to date.

3. You are entitled to the special rate of $3 a month.

Please[29] look through the attached pages showing the kind of help that our tax guide will bring to you. Then, to be sure that your copy[30] comes in time, return the enclosed card. We anticipate a heavy demand for this tax guide. Cordially yours,[31] (620)

Reading and Writing Practice

608.

, contrast

[Shorthand outlines]

titles
, introductory

, conjunction

, introductory

(161)

609.
employs
, introductory

, and omitted
up-to-the-minute
hyphenated
before noun

, apposition

347

(shorthand outline) (145)

610.

(shorthand outline)

(shorthand outline) (93)

▶ **Word Families**

611. -mentary

Elementary, supplementary, complimentary, rudimentary.

612. -form

Form, transform, inform, perform, reform, conform.

613. Frequent Names

Last Names

1

Men's First Names

2

Women's First Names

3

1. Robertson, Robinson, Rogers, Russell, Ryan, Schmidt, Schneider, Scott.
2. Norman, Nicholas, Oliver, Oscar, Owen, Patrick, Peter.
3. Ophelia, Pauline, Pearl, Phyllis, Rachel, Rebecca.

614. Previews and Writing Practice

615. Credited, apology, invoice, you will understand, occasionally, patronage, endeavor, in the future.
616. Effect, confidential, revise, consequently, allowances.
617. Fond, detective, happiest, magazine, overwhelmingly.
618. Newcomer, rendered, eligible, renewed, we hope that, whenever.
619. Principles, checker, Elementary, students, handicap, won't, immediately.

615. Dear Mr. Schmidt: Thank you for your remittance of $1 for the book we shipped you on March 18. It has been[1] credited to your account.

Will you please accept our apology for the $2 invoice that was enclosed[2] with your March book. This invoice was sent through an oversight on our part; we received your remittance in payment of[3] the February book some time before the March book was shipped. We regret the error, but we believe that you will[4] understand that mistakes will occasionally happen.

We appreciate your patronage, Mr. Schmidt, and we[5] assure you that we shall endeavor to give you the best possible service in the future. Sincerely yours,[6]

---

616. Mr. Baker: We are planning to increase our prices on a number of books, to take effect on August 1.[7] This information is confidential for the present, however, as no announcement will be made until we[8] revise our price list and have it printed.

After we increased our prices on February 1, we did not wish[9] to increase them any further; but binding and printing costs continue to rise. Consequently, another increase[10] is now necessary.

Also, since February 1 we have been quoting exchange allowances of only[11] 2 per cent of the list price. We have already made this 2 per cent exchange allowance to several important[12] customers in this territory.

I will send you more information on this matter in a few days. John Green[13]

---

617. Dear Mr. Ryan: Are you fond of detective stories? Almost every family has at least one person[14] who is; and the happiest detective-story fans are those who read the Post.

A survey made several months ago[15] by one of the leading research organizations in the world asked: "Which magazine publishes the best[16] mystery stories?" Mystery fans voted so overwhelmingly for the Post that it was almost a crime!

Of course,[17] each issue of the Post contains many other features that are of interest to the entire family.

Why[18] not have the Post delivered to your door each week. For only $5 a year you will receive hundreds of pages[19] of fine entertainment.

The enclosed envelope will bring your order and remittance to me. Sincerely yours,[20]

---

618. Dear Mr. Russell: As a newcomer to Greenfield, you will be interested in the services rendered by[21] our library. Any person whose home or business is in Greenfield is eligible to use the library[22] without charge.

The library is open on Mondays and Wednesdays from 1 p.m. to 9 p.m.; on Tuesdays, Thursdays,[23] Fridays, and Saturdays from 10 a.m. to 6 p.m.

Books are issued for two weeks and may be renewed for[24] another two weeks.

We hope that you will make use of our library and will let us know whenever we can render[25] some special service. Remember that the library is here to serve your reading needs. Very cordially yours,[26]

---

619. Gentlemen: On February 1 we ordered from your New York Office 200 copies of Scott's "Principles[27] of Accounting." When your shipment arrived on February 12, our checker found that you had sent us only[28] 100 copies of "Principles of Accounting"; but the shipment also contained 100 copies of West's[29] "Elementary Accounting," which we did not order and cannot use.

Since classes started on February[30] 10, this means that 100 students are now without textbooks and are working under a handicap.

Won't you please[31] send us the additional 100 copies of "Principles of Accounting" immediately. Cordially yours,[32] (640)

Reading and Writing Practice

620. ⌇ 〰 〰 〰 ⌇ 〰 ∿

(130)

621.

, *if clause*
, conjunction

(117)

622.
lover
, introductory

: enumeration
buy

, series
Transcribe:
  25 per cent

(81)

LESSON **69**

623. Frequent Phrases

Many

1 [shorthand outlines]

Would Like

2 [shorthand outlines]

1. Many things, many days, many times, many of them, too many.
2. You would like, he would like to see, I should like to know, you might like to have, I should like to say.

624. Geographical Expressions

-mont

1 [shorthand outlines]

States and Territories

2 [shorthand outlines]

Foreign Cities

3 [shorthand outlines]

1. Oakmont, Edgemont, Piedmont, Dumont.
2. Alaska, Florida, Kansas, Mississippi, New York, Rhode Island, New Jersey.
3. London, Bristol, Manchester, Plymouth, Edinburgh.

625. Previews and Writing Practice

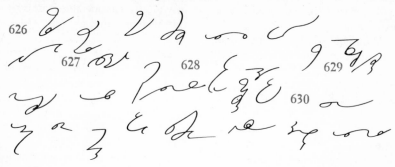

626. Avoid, favorite, event, vacation, regularly, pertinent, impartially, at all times.
627. Thousands, coverage.
628. Publisher, newsstand, advantage.
629. Decisions, you will find, likely, declare, associations, spent.
630. Annual, reasonable, young, inventions, opportunities, advancement, trial, subscription, regret.

626. Dear Mr. Edgemont: You are going to be very busy just before you leave on your well-earned vacation, and[1] you could easily overlook to arrange to have the Times mailed to you while you are away. To avoid finding[2] yourself without your favorite newspaper, why not make immediate use of the form that is enclosed.

So much[3] is happening in the world today that an important event may take place while you are on your vacation. With[4] the Times reaching you regularly, you will have all pertinent facts impartially presented to you at all[5] times.

Fill in the enclosed form, and mail it in the self-addressed envelope that is also enclosed. Cordially yours,[6]

627. Dear Mr. Smith: If you are looking for a Christmas gift for a friend, let us suggest that you give him a subscription[7] to the Daily Sun. Thousands of readers appreciate our complete news coverage and the many features[8] of our newspaper.

Fill out and mail the coupon that is enclosed. The cost of a full year is $12. Sincerely yours,[9]

---

628. Dear Friend: Through a special arrangement that we have made with the publisher, you can now purchase the News Magazine[10] on your charge account with us — and receive a special price.

We offer you two years of the News Magazine for only[11] $4, which represents a saving of $2 on the newsstand cost. In addition, you will receive[12] six extra issues at no extra cost.

We invite you to take immediate advantage of this special offer.[13] The enclosed postal card needs no stamp. Sign it, fill in your account number, and mail it today. Sincerely yours,[14]

---

629. Dear Mr. Cooper: One reason why some men succeed faster than others is that they have more information on[15] which to base their decisions. Among the men who succeed you will find many who read the Financial Daily. For[16] example, there are on our lists several men who make from $10,000 to $20,000 a[17] year. It is quite likely that these men would be successful without the Financial Daily, but many of them declare[18] that it has helped them succeed.

The Financial Daily is more than a newspaper; it is the only business[19] paper served by all four big press associations.

You may have a trial subscription for three months for only[20] $6. Just send us a note with your name and address and enclose your check for $6.

Don't delay. A few dollars[21] spent for the Financial Daily now may mean a considerable increase in your income. Sincerely yours,[22]

---

630. Dear Mr. Brady: A few years ago an annual income of $5,000 was a reasonable[23] goal for a young man. Today, with increased taxes and higher living costs, a person needs $10,000 to[24] buy what $5,000 used to buy.

This increase in values is only one of many changes taking[25] place in America. New inventions, new industries, and new ways of doing business are creating new[26] opportunities for young men who want to increase their incomes.

The Commerce Journal tells you about these opportunities.[27] Because the Commerce Journal is issued every day, our readers are able to seize quickly new[28] opportunities to win advancement or earn more money. The Commerce Journal is a paper for those men who[29] will be the leaders of tomorrow. Will you be one of them?

Fill out the enclosed blank, and enter your order for[30] a trial subscription today. You will be making a move that you will never regret. Very cordially yours,[31] (620)

Reading and Writing Practice

631.

week-after-week
three-month
hyphenated before noun
accepting
, introductory
, introductory
periodic
, parenthetical
receive
, introductory

(170)

632.

received
trial

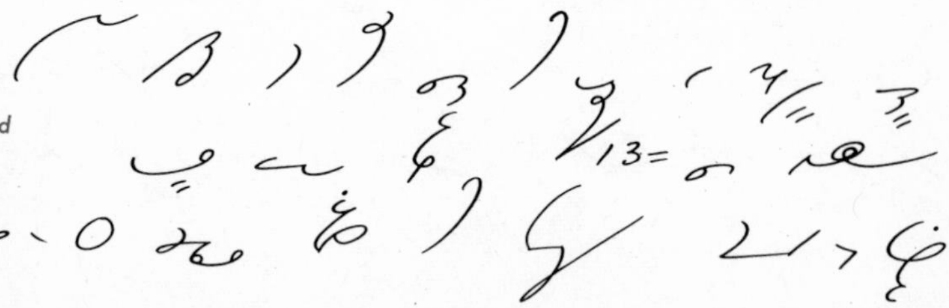

(shorthand outline)

, introductory

, if clause
already

(123)

633.

up-to-the-minute
  hyphenated
  before noun

, introductory
, intervening
  phrase
affect

(110)

634. Penmanship Practice. In this drill you will practice the joining of the two forms of s to other alphabetic strokes of Gregg Shorthand. Remember to give the s a *deep* curve and to keep it *small*.

1 ℰ ℰ ℈ ℈ ⌒ ⌒ ℮ ⌐ ⌐

2 ℓ ℓ ℓ ℓ ℓ ℓ

3 ℓ ℓ ⌐ ⌐ ⌐ ⌐

1. Also, was; whose, who is; uses, how is; eyes; there is, ends.
2. Race, rest; last, lease; mass, next.
3. Sail, sell; keys, guess; case, gas.

▶ **Progressive Speed Builder (110-135)**

635. Preview

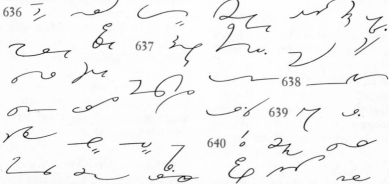

636.
637.
638.
639.
640.

636. Interested, current, Progress, developments, throughout the, for your-self, reporting, compliments, expires.
637. Subscription, ever-growing, informed, forward, eagerly, features, in-formative, welcome.

638. **Months ago, acknowledgment, already, to me, letterhead.**

639. **Trouble, regarding, stencil, Massachusetts, Missouri, enjoying.**

640. **Shortly, we are sure, accurate, up-to-the-minute, single, remind, expiration, to continue, one year.**

(1 Minute at 110)

636. Dear Miss May: As you are a person who is interested in keeping up to date on current events, you will like our weekly magazine, Progress. Progress/will inform you of the latest developments throughout the world.

We should like you to see for yourself the type of reporting that Progress brings you. We are,// therefore, enclosing a copy of the January 12 issue. Please accept it with our compliments. If you are convinced that it is your type of magazine,///take advantage of our offer of 30 issues for only $4. You will have to act soon as this offer expires in ten days. Sincerely yours, (1)

(1 Minute at 120)

637. Dear Miss May: Thank you for accepting our special offer of a trial subscription to Progress at the rate of $4 for 30 issues. Thank you, also, for your check./We are delighted to add your name to our ever-growing list of readers. We are confident that you will depend on Progress to keep informed on the events of the//world; you will look forward eagerly to the arrival of each issue.

We are planning many new features during the coming year that will make Progress even more/// interesting and informative. Watch for these features, and let us know how you like them.

Once again, welcome to our growing family of Progress readers. Sincerely yours, (2)

(1 Minute at 125)

638. Gentlemen: About two months ago, I mailed you my check for a trial subscription of 30 issues to your magazine Progress. I asked that my subscription begin with the/February 2 issue. It is now April 1, and I have not yet received that issue. Nor have I received an acknowledgment of my order, although my check has already// cleared through the bank. Would you be good enough to look into this matter immediately.

Please start my subscription with the April 15 issue, as the back issues will///no longer be of value or interest to me.

Also, please send the magazine to the address given in this letterhead rather than to my home. Very sincerely yours, (3)

(1 Minute at 130)

639. Dear Miss May: We are very sorry that you had to take the time and trouble to write your letter of April 1 regarding the delay in receiving your copy of Progress.

We/investigated the matter immediately and found that an error had been made in the stencil of your name and address. The clerk had typed your address as Springfield, Massachusetts,//instead of Springfield, Missouri. We have made a new stencil and, as you requested, we will mail your copies to your business address rather than to your home address. Your subscription/// will begin with the April 15 issue.

So that you may begin enjoying Progress without further delay, we are enclosing a copy of the April 8 issue. Sincerely yours, (4)

(1 Minute at 135)

640. Dear Miss May: Time passes rapidly. It seems only yesterday that we received your order for a trial subscription to Progress. **Yet,** your subscription will expire shortly — in one more month/, in fact.

We are sure that you have come to depend on Progress to bring you accurate, up-to-the-minute information on the events of the world. We are confident that you would not want//to miss a single issue. That is why we are taking this opportunity to remind you of the expiration date of your subscription and to facilitate your renewal so///that there will be no break in your subscription.

We are enclosing a card on which you need only check whether you would like your subscription to continue for one year or for two years. Sincerely yours, (5) (620)

Reading and Writing Practice

641.

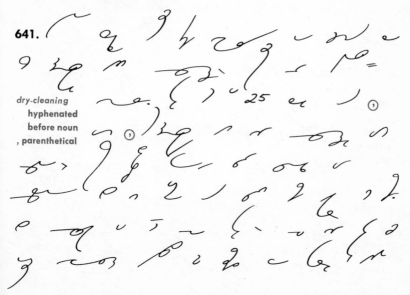

dry-cleaning
hyphenated
before noun

, parenthetical

(124)

642.

, apposition
Construction

compliments
, conjunction

up to date
no noun,
no hyphen
, introductory

(132)

643.
, nonrestrictive
accept
compliments

, if clause
guidance
earners

knowledge

, introductory
amply

(120)

LESSON **71**

▶ **Principles of Outline Construction**

644. Unaccented diphthong ᴜ omitted before ʀ and ʟ. Omitting the diphthong ᴜ before ʀ and ʟ results in fluent outlines for many useful words.

1. Accurate, accuracy, vocabulary, ridiculous, popular.
2. Singular, inaugurate, stimulant, pendulum.

645. Diphthong ᴜ omitted in -ᴜᴛɪᴏɴ, -ᴜsɪᴏɴ. The diphthong is also omitted in the endings -ᴜᴛɪᴏɴ, ᴜsɪᴏɴ.

1. Contribution, distribution, constitution, institution, substitution, retribution.
2. Solution, revolution, resolution, execution, elocution.

Reading and Writing Practice

646. The Land of Inventions

CHAPTER 15 AUTOMOBILES

(377)

Letters

647.

factory-approved
hyphenated
before noun

[shorthand outlines]

, introductory

[shorthand outlines]

, parenthetical
convenience

[shorthand outlines]

(124)

648. *[shorthand outlines]*

, introductory
surprised

[shorthand outlines]

, contrast

[shorthand outlines]

(101)

649.

essential
luxury

, introductory
duplicate

, when clause
resolution
, introductory

(107)

650.
brake
pedal
, if clause

; no conjunction
(66)

368

LESSON **72**

651. Recall Drill (B). In this drill you will review the various uses of the alphabetic stroke в.

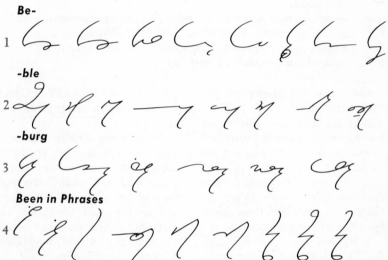

Be-

1

-ble

2

-burg

3

Been in Phrases

4

1. Begin, began, betray, belongings, below, besides, become, benefit.
2. Available, stable, trouble, memorable, honorable, suitable, undesirable, equitable.
3. Pittsburgh, Bloomsburg, Harrisburg, Greensburg, Warrensburg, Plattsburg.
4. Has been, it has been, have been, might have been, should have been, could have been; have not been able, I have not been able, you have not been able.

652. Previews and Writing Practice

653

654

653. Count, next time, highway, maintenance, why not, various, demonstrate, point.
654. Mileage, craftsmen, country, superior, recognized, economy, weekday.
655. Parsons, determine, substantiated, dependability, everyone, wisest.
656. Announcement, terminated, sufficiently, embody, experience.
657. Avoid, advance, capital, list, post card.

653. Dear Mr. Jones: If you count the number of National Trucks the next time you are on the highway, you will learn this[1] simple truth: People who rely on trucks to take care of their shipping use more National Trucks than any other[2] make. Why? Because National gives them lower operating and maintenance costs.

Why not see your National dealer[3] and let him show you the various models we make. Let him demonstrate for you the model that will best meet[4] your own needs.

Make it a point to see him. He will be happy to show you our complete line of trucks. Sincerely yours,[5]

---

654. Dear Mr. King: Are you interested in saving money on the maintenance of your company truck? Would you[6] like to get a full measure of trucking mileage from your equipment?

Of course you would. Then get a powerful new[7] Wilson Truck, built by the world's most painstaking truck craftsmen.

All over the country and on all kinds of work Wilson[8] Trucks are recognized as superior in pulling power and in operating economy. Stop at[9] one of our showrooms now and see the proof. Check into the facts and figures that demonstrate the economy of[10] Wilson Trucks for your type of hauling.

Our showrooms are open every weekday from nine to five. Cordially yours,[11]

---

655. Dear Mr. Trees: About three years ago we purchased our first Parsons Truck. We did it in the nature of an[12] experiment to determine for ourselves whether the claims of your salesman would be substantiated by performance.[13]

We are happy to say that we are completely convinced of the economy and dependability[14] of the Parsons Truck. Every one of our old trucks has now been replaced with a Parsons, and we feel that this is[15] one of the wisest moves we have ever made.

We can recommend your trucks without reservation. Yours sincerely,[16]

---

656. Dear Mr. Grace: As an owner of a Nelson Truck, you have no doubt been interested in our announcement in[17] the local papers: "We have terminated our working agreement with the Nelson Truck Company." This termination[18] is to take place on June 3. The announcement may have brought some questions to your mind regarding the[19] servicing of the truck that you bought from us.

You may rest assured that we will continue to take care of your truck[20] whenever it needs attention. We have a sufficiently large supply of spare parts to last many years.

On July[21] 20 we plan to market our own truck, which will embody improvements resulting from our 20 years'[22] experience. When our new truck is ready, you will receive complete information about it. Cordially yours,[23]

---

657. Dear Mr. Flynn: For many years we have been taking care of the trucking needs of large companies all over the[24] United States. They have hired us to take care of their requirements because by doing so:

1. They avoid service[25] problems or costs.

2. They avoid maintenance costs and know in advance what it will cost to take care of their trucking.[26]

3. They need not invest capital.

There are other reasons why these companies use our service, but we shall not[27] list them at this time. We do, however, want to invite you to send for our booklet that outlines in detail a plan[28] to save your company thousands of dollars each year.

A post card will bring that booklet to you. If you prefer, one[29] of our men will be happy to discuss your trucking problem with the person in charge of transportation. Yours truly,[30] (600)

Reading and Writing Practice

658.

four-door
 hyphenated
 before noun

, introductory
compromise

, if clause
convenient

(127)

659.
past
, introductory

, as clause
whether

, conjunction
guarantee

, if clause
, conjunction
won't

(113)

372

660.

[shorthand outlines]

, when clause
reliability

[shorthand outlines]

, introductory
transportation

30 [shorthand outlines]

; because of comma
, if clause

[shorthand outlines] (128)

661.

[shorthand outlines]

, introductory
checkup

[shorthand outlines]

, conjunction

[shorthand outlines] (64)

LESSON 73

▶ **Word Families**

662. -bility

Durability, ability, inability, reliability, possibility, stability.

663. Rea-

Reassure, reappear, reassert, reappraise, readmit, reapply.

664. Frequent Names

Last Names

1

Women's First Names

2

Men's First Names

3

1. Shaw, Shea, Simpson, Snyder, Stevens, Stewart, Sullivan, Taylor.
2. Rosalie, Ruth, Sarah, Sophia, Susan, Sylvia, Victoria.
3. Philip, Raymond, Robert, Roger, Rudolph, Rufus, Rupert.

665. Previews and Writing Practice

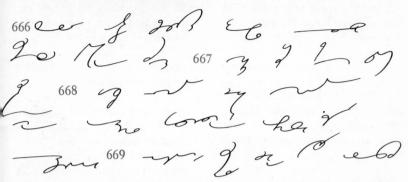

666. Alert, anticipate, executives, slippery, minimize, safeguard, durability, vehicles.
667. Cautious, official, each gallon, attractive, we shall be glad.
668. Occasionally, encounter, snobbish, groundless, quality, luxury, practicality, reassurance, hesitant, manufacturers.
669. Unrestricted, favorite, sincerity, denied, relatively.

666. Gentlemen: Alert businessmen anticipate emergencies. It is not surprising, therefore, that so many[1] business executives carry tire chains in their cars ready for use when roads are slippery.

Furthermore, alert executives[2] insist that the drivers of company cars and trucks use chains to minimize the hazards of winter[3] driving and to safeguard lives and shipments.

Taylor Tire Chains for cars, trucks, and busses offer the best in values[4] in safety and durability. The special metal used in the chains adds extra miles of service. The unique[5] design of the chains gives better traction to keep vehicles moving safely on slippery roads.

In the interest[6] of safety, make sure that you have Taylor Tire Chains for every car and truck used in your business. Cordially yours,[7]

---

667. Dear Mr. Shaw: Every cautious man will ask himself the following questions before he buys a new car:

1.[8] Does it sell for a reasonable price?

2. Will it give good gasoline mileage?

3. Will the upkeep be low?

4.[9] Will the trade-in value always be high?

If you purchase a Steward Car, the answer to all these questions is Yes.[10] Our car is the lowest-priced car in its field. Official tests show that it gives more miles on each gallon of gas than[11] any other car in its price field. The car is so well built that your repair costs throughout the years are very small.[12] A Steward Car keeps its value year after year, thus bringing attractive trade-in allowances.

We shall be glad[13] to have you visit us so that we may give you an opportunity to drive the new Steward. You will then[14] be able to judge for yourself whether the Steward is a car that you would be happy to own. Cordially yours,[15]

---

668. Dear Mr. Stevens: Occasionally we encounter a man who hesitates to buy a Johnson Car lest his[16] friends think him snobbish.

For such people we have reassuring news. The experience of Johnson owners indicates[17] that your fears are groundless. True, the world has long recognized the Johnson Car as a fine possession. Most people[18] understand, however, that quality is not a luxury.

The facts in support of the practicality[19] of our new car are so convincing that the mere recital of a few should be sufficient reassurance for[20] the most hesitant buyer.

Take the matter of cost. There are eight other car manufacturers who have models[21] priced above the lowest priced Johnson. Thousands of motorists on the road actually paid more for their cars than[22] the

man who owns the small Johnson.

If you are ready for a new car, come in and place your order for a Johnson.[23] You will never make a more sensible purchase — and your friends and neighbors will heartily approve. Yours sincerely,[24]

---

669. Dear Mr. Shea: According to a recent survey, almost half the motorcar owners in the United States[25] and Canada would own a Johnson if they had their unrestricted choice. The Johnson was, in fact, voted the[26] favorite car by more than five to one over any other car built.

We are sincerely sorry that all who express[27] their desire to own a Johnson cannot do so. We believe with equal sincerity, however, that a[28] great many have needlessly denied themselves the pleasure of owning a Johnson. The relatively modest price[29] of a Johnson and its unusual operating economy make it a far more practical and[30] sensible possession than many motorists actually realize.

Why not visit your dealer soon and see for[31] yourself. You might be surprised to find that the purchase price of a Johnson is well within your budget. Sincerely yours,[32] (640)

Reading and Writing Practice

670.

flaws
, if clause

, apposition
. inside quote

traffic
, series

, introductory
prejudiced

(131)

671.

capital
, series

: enumeration
nominal

collision

, series

, introductory

(111)

672.

economy
, introductory

25

neighborhood
, conjunction

(99)

673. Frequent Phrases

Let

1 [shorthand outlines]

A Omitted

2 [shorthand outlines]

1. Let us know, let us see, let us make, let us have, please let us, please let us know.
2. For a long time, for a few days, for a day or two, for a few moments, at a time.

674. Geographical Expressions
(United States Cities in Order of Population)

1 [shorthand outlines]

2 [shorthand outlines]

3 [shorthand outlines]

1. New York, Chicago, Philadelphia, Los Angeles, Detroit, Cleveland.
2. St. Louis, Baltimore, Boston, Pittsburgh, San Francisco, Buffalo, Washington, Milwaukee.
3. Newark, Minneapolis, New Orleans, Cincinnati, Kansas City, Seattle.

675. Previews and Writing Practice

676 [shorthand outlines] 677

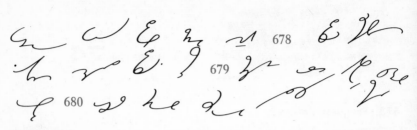

676. **Board, we are sending you, attend, please let us know, arrangements, social.**

677. **Personal, prompt, expiration, issuance, quotation.**

678. **Expired, several days ago, handbook, constantly, expanding, advantages.**

679. **If we do not, renew, disabled, accessories, lapse.**

680. **Recently, fullest, facilities, dedicated, evident.**

676. Dear Mr. Collins: The next regular meeting of the Board of Directors of the Automobile Club will be[1] held at the Hotel Smith in Chicago on June 7. We are sending you this notice well in advance so that[2] you and your staff can make plans to attend. Please let us know how many will attend from your office so that we may[3] make the proper hotel reservations.

There will be a long program of business, but we are making arrangements[4] for a number of social events too. After all, all work and no play would make Jack a dull boy! Sincerely yours,[5]

---

677. Dear Member: Did you know that members of the Auto Club of St. Louis are provided with a fine automobile[6] insurance service?

Personal attention to all insurance problems and a prompt and friendly claim service[7] are available to you 24 hours a day.

If you will note the expiration date of your present[8] insurance on the enclosed card and mail it to us for recording, we will write you about the issuance of[9] a policy at that time.

For an immediate quotation, phone Main 4-8700. Yours sincerely,[10]

---

678. Dear Mr. West: Your membership in the Auto Club expired several days ago. It will take you only a[11] few moments to fill out and return the enclosed card renewing your membership. Why not do it now.

It is with[12] particular pride that we enclose your copy of our new handbook, which contains an outline of our many[13] services. We hope that you will find time to read about the constantly expanding benefits that you will derive[14] from membership in the Auto Club.

One of the main reasons for the growth of our organization is the fact[15] that our members have interested other motorists in the advantages of membership. Yours sincerely,[16]

---

679. Dear Mr. Parker: A few weeks ago we wrote you that on July 31 your membership in the Auto[17] Club would expire. If we do not receive your renewal on or before that date, you will have to pay an additional[18] fee of $5, or a total of $20, to renew your membership. This has been our[19] policy for a long time.

Even more important, after July 31 you will lose the following benefits:[20]

1. Free service when your car is disabled.

2. Access to our dependable Travel Department.

3. Our[21] special insurance policy.

4. The 10 per cent discount on gasoline and automobile accessories.[22]

If you have not already done so, please send your $15 now so that you may continue your membership[23] in good standing.

We are confident that it is not your intention to let your membership lapse. Cordially yours,[24]

---

680. Dear Member: More and better services have became available to you as the number of members of the[25] Auto Club continues to increase.

The purpose of the handbook we recently sent you was to enable you[26] to make the fullest use of all the services at your disposal and to keep you informed of the work being[27] done in your behalf.

The fact that the club membership now numbers over 155,000 is due[28] not only to the many new members who have joined our club in recent years but also to the continued[29] co-operation of old members like yourself. The advantage of having at your command the facilities of[30] an organization dedicated wholly to your interests are more evident today than ever before.[31]

If you have not already renewed your membership for the coming year, you should do so now. Yours sincerely,[32] (640)

Reading and Writing Practice

681.
currently
. inside quote

(141)

682.

, intervening
    phrase

full-sized
    hyphenated
    before noun
, introductory

models
, if clause

(160)

683.

available
    luxury

(75)

LESSON **75**

684. Penmanship Practice. In this lesson you will practice additional joinings of the two forms of s.

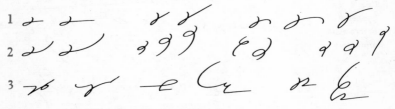

1. Seen, seem; set, said; seek, sag, sadden.
2. Sent, seemed; sees, safe, save; sip; face; session, sash, siege.
3. Institute, resident; mason, blossom; citizen, baptism.

▶ **Progressive Speed Builder (120-140).** The letters in this Progressive Speed Builder range from 120 to 140 words a minute. If you can take these letters from dictation and read them back, you need not fear the dictation of any dictator, even the most rapid.

Remember, don't stop writing!

685. Preview

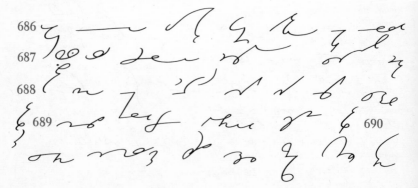

686. Representative, in the market, automobiles, perfect, disposal, in a position, merits.
687. Area, rather, familiar, schedule, week or ten days, as soon as possible.
688. Has been, one of our, engineers, superintendent, condition, your order, in addition, accessories, specifications.
689. Committee, payment, treasurer's, we do not, special.
690. I am sure, congratulations, vitally, consequently, I shall not be able, difficulties, be sure.

(1 Minute at 120)

686. Dear Mr. Pace: Our representative, Mr. Green, has written us that you are in the market for 20 cars as you plan to supply all your salesmen with company/automobiles.

We believe that our business sedan would be perfect for your requirements, and we should like to place one at your disposal so that you may judge the car for//yourself.

We are writing Mr. Green to ask him to make the necessary arrangements if you decide to accept our offer. Mr. Green is in a position to ///quote prices to you and to answer your questions.

We are confident that once you have driven our business sedan, you will be sold on its merits. Sincerely yours, (1)

(1 Minute at 125)

687. Dear Mr. Klein: As Mr. Green has written you, we are in the market for 20 cars for our salesmen in this area. We plan to have all our men drive company cars rather/than their own. I am familiar with your business sedan; in fact, my son, who is also a salesman, has been driving one for more than five years. He is well satisfied with it// and plans to trade it in for a late model soon.

If we should place an order for a fleet of 20 cars, we should like to have delivery by June 15. Would it be possible///for you to meet this delivery schedule?

As we plan to reach a decision within the next week or ten days, please let me know as soon as possible. Sincerely yours, (2)

(1 Minute at 130)

688. Dear Mr. Pace: I am happy to learn that your son has been driving one of our business sedans for the past five years and that he is so well satisfied with it that he plans to trade/it in on our latest model. I know that he will be delighted with the new features that our engineers have built into it.

I talked to the home office about a delivery//schedule for the 20 cars, and the superintendent assures me that we can easily have the cars ready and in driving condition by June 15, if you place your order within///the next two weeks. In addition, we can have any special accessories installed, if you will give us specifications on the date that you place your order. Sincerely yours, (3)

(1 Minute at 135)

689. Dear Mr. Klein: I have good news for you. The order is yours. The committee that was appointed to decide on the make of car we should purchase for our 20 salesmen carefully considered/the merits of five different makes. They tested the cars in every possible way; and, on the basis of their study, they decided on your business sedan.

If you will bring the//necessary papers to my office, I will sign them. Payment for the cars will be made through our treasurer's office on delivery of the cars.

We rely on your promise to have the///cars ready on June 15, the day on which our sales meeting ends. After the sales meeting, I should like the men to drive away in the cars. We do not plan to have special accessories. Yours truly, (4)

(1 Minute at 140)

690. Mr. Green: As I am sure you know by this time, we have received the order for 20 cars from Mr. Pace. All the credit for this order is yours. Congratulations on a fine job of selling./

The superintendent at the home office assures me that the cars will be ready for delivery on June 15. It is vitally important that we keep that promise. I am leaving//on a long business trip in a few days; consequently, I shall not be able to follow up on this matter personally. Would you, therefore, take it upon yourself to see that the cars are ready///on time.

I believe, too, that you should plan to be present when Mr. Pace's salesmen call for the cars.

If any difficulties develop on this order, be sure to call me. Harvey B. Klein (5) (650)

Reading and Writing Practice

691.

thoroughly
, series

unusual
blowout

50   60

40

, introductory
traffic

, nonrestrictive

incident
, conjunction

(177)

692.

(108)

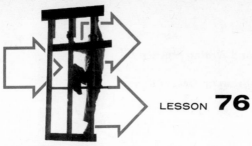

LESSON **76**

▶ **Principles of Outline Construction**

693. Omission of unaccented vowel in word ending -IN. *The unaccented vowel in the word ending -IN is omitted because its omission gives us a better joining.*

1. Origin, margin, imagine, engine, engineer, cousin, raisin.
2. Famine, examine, illumine, determine.

694. Word endings -IUM, -EUM, -DIUM. *The word endings -IUM, -EUM, are expressed by EM; -DIUM, by the DEM blend.*

-ium, -eum

-dium

1. Uranium, chromium, premium, helium.
2. Auditorium, calcium, museum, gymnasium.
3. Radium, stadium, medium.

CHAPTER **16** REAL ESTATE

Reading and Writing Practice

695. Choosing an Occupation

[Shorthand outlines] (381)

Letters

696. *[Shorthand outlines]*

two-year
  hyphenated
  before noun

[Shorthand outlines]

tenant
, if clause

[Shorthand outlines]

416

, parenthetical
museum

, series
baths

; no conjunction
, words omitted

, if clause
anxious

, as clause
appreciate

(164)

697.

, introducing
   short quote
. inside quote

family's
, introductory

[shorthand outline]

[shorthand outline]

approximate
, if clause

[shorthand outline]

appointment
, conjunction

[shorthand outline] (163)

698. [shorthand outline]

, parenthetical
neighbor

[shorthand outline] (78)

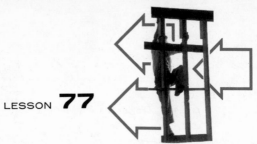

LESSON 77

699. Recall Drill (G). In this drill you will review the different uses of the alphabetic stroke G.

-gate

1

-gram

2

Ago in Phrases

3

Others

4

1. Investigate, navigate, abrogate, delegate, interrogate.
2. Telegram, cablegram, radiogram, monogram, program.
3. Months ago, years ago, days ago, hours ago, minutes ago.
4. A gallon, 3 gallons, Great Britain.

700. Previews and Writing Practice

701

702

703

704

701. I decided, reputation, reasonable, recommended, contract, occupancy, present, did not, considerable, as soon as possible, headway.
702. I am sorry, inconvenienced, has not been able, trouble, obtaining, rectified, sufficiently, garage, confident.
703. Specialists, record, coverage, effecting, assistance, investment, pertaining.
704. Development, Westport, young.

701. Gentlemen: As you know, last June 10 I decided to build a house, and I asked you to recommend a builder.[1] In view of the reputation of your real estate business, I felt that you were in a position to know who[2] would do the best job at the most reasonable price. You recommended the Brown Construction Company, and I[3] gave them the job.

When I signed the contract, I was promised that the house would be ready for occupancy by April[4] 20; and on the basis of that promise, I made arrangements to sell my present house by that time. The[5] Brown Construction Company, however, did not meet the April 20 date; in fact, they now tell me that the[6] house will not be ready until July 1. In the meantime, my family and I have been living at a hotel[7] at considerable inconvenience and expense.

May I appeal to you to see what you can do to get[8] the house completed as soon as possible. I have been able to make no headway with the builder. Cordially yours,[9]

---

702. Dear Mr. Green: I am sorry that you have been inconvenienced by the fact that the Brown Construction Company[10] has not been able to meet its promise to have your house ready by April 20. I have talked to the[11] president, and he tells me that they experienced considerable trouble obtaining building materials;[12] but that situation has now been rectified.

He promises to place all available men on the job and[13] have them work overtime if necessary. He thinks that he will be able to have the house sufficiently finished[14] so that you and your family can move in about June 15. The garage will not be completed and the[15] grounds will still need some work; but these things can be done while you are living in the house.

I have personally visited[16] the house, and I am confident that you will be very happy with it when it is finished. Cordially yours,[17]

---

703. Dear Mr. Evans: Buying and selling farm land is our business. On our staff are 28 farm specialists, who[18] are located in 20 cities and towns of Nebraska and Iowa. These men have a combined sales record[19] of $1,750,000 since January 1. They are specially trained to give[20] down-to-earth advice in the selection and sale of a farm.

Our coverage makes it possible for us to bring[21] buyers from all parts of the country to see your property, often effecting the sale immediately. Therefore,[22] if you have a farm that you would like to sell, let us know; we can be of assistance to you.

We also offer[23] a wide selection of properties, if you are interested in settling in another part of the country.[24] At the present time, we have three farms in the heart of the corn belt that represent a wonderful investment.[25]

For anything pertaining to the purchase or sale of a farm, write us; we are at your service. Yours sincerely,[26]

---

704. Dear Mr. King: As you know, we have built a new apartment development in Westport. We started planning the[27] development two years ago and have put into it the experience of 50 years of building. In planning[28] the development, we have paid special attention to the requirements of young married couples with children.[29]

At our development children can enjoy outdoor life; they have plenty of room to play. The apartments are only[30] a block from the nearest elementary school and a half mile from the nearest high school.

A few blocks away[31] is a new shopping center. Also, the transportation from Westport to the city is excellent.

Come out soon,[32] and let us show you some of the finest apartment dwellings in this part of the country. Yours very sincerely,[33] (660)

Reading and Writing Practice

705.
, conjunction
permanent

suburban
, parenthetical

accommodations
temporary

aware
, conjunction

(158)

706.

neighborhood
, series

, parenthetical
: enumeration

down-to-earth
   hyphenated
   before noun

; no conjunction
, words omitted
typical
: enumeration
, series

70/   4   /   85/   /   5

; no conjunction

(173)

707.

advantages
: enumeration

(90)

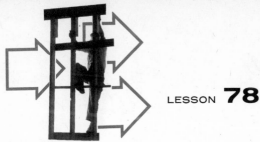

▶ **Word Families**

708. *-spect*

Inspect, inspection, prospect, prospective, respect, respective, disrespect, aspect.

709. *-mination*

Determination, nomination, elimination, domination.

710. Frequent Names

Last Names

1

Men's First Names

2

1. Thomas, Walsh, Ward, Williams, Wood, Wright, Young.
2. Samuel, Stephen, Vincent, Walter, William.

711. Previews and Writing Practice

712   713

712. Transaction, settled, will you please, forwarded, mother-in-law.
713. Inspection, various, event, layouts, representative, we shall be glad.
714. If we can, highly, kind, moderate, consequently, I realize, journey, at this time.
715. Anniversary, opened, it is not, to understand, essential, strongest, prospective, thank you.
716. Outside, to spend, as soon as.

712. Gentlemen: You will be interested to know that Mrs. Watson's house on Market Street has been sold. The final[1] details of this transaction will be settled not later than January 31.

Will you please, therefore, make[2] out a statement of the rent account for this house. A copy need not be forwarded to Mrs. Williams, as she[3] has recently assigned her interest in this house to Mrs. Watson, her mother-in-law. Sincerely yours,[4]

---

713. Dear Mr. Turner: Floor plans for the new 24-story office building at 319 Fifth Avenue are[5] now ready for inspection. Floor space is available for offices of various sizes.

In the event[6] that you are considering changing your office location during the coming year, we urge you to inspect the[7] plans for the new building. Now is the time to make the special layouts required for the smooth operation of your[8] office.

There is someone in my office from 9 a.m. to 9 p.m. every day. If a representative[9] of your organization will call, we shall be glad to go over the building plans with him. Cordially yours,[10]

---

714. Dear Mr. Walsh: We are considering spending the months of February and March in Chicago, if we can[11] find a small furnished house that will meet our needs. The Higgins Real Estate Company has sent me several prospects[12] that they highly recommend.

Would you be kind enough to examine these houses for me. I have received visiting[13] permits, which I am enclosing.

The rental that is asked is moderate — $40 a week. Consequently,[14] we do not expect too much in the way of furniture.

I realize that you are busy, but I am asking[15] you to do this because I find it impossible to make the journey to Chicago at this time. Cordially yours, [16]

---

715. Dear Mr. Ward: Today is our anniversary. Twenty years ago we opened the door of our real estate[17] office at First and Main Streets.

It is not difficult to understand that our profession is an interesting[18] and essential one. It helps to satisfy one of the strongest of man's desires — a plot of ground on which to build[19] a home for his family.

Realizing that a home is a major family investment, we have always made[20] every effort to provide each prospective homeowner with opportunities to secure the home in[21] which he and his family would be happy. This policy has enabled us to make a host of friends during[22] our 20 years of operation.

We wish to thank you and the other homeowners whom we have served and to express[23] the hope that you will not hesitate to call on us whenever we can be of assistance. Yours sincerely,[24]

---

716. Dear Mr. Young: Last Friday, my wife and I drove past a house on West Street, Springfield, in front of which there was a "For[25] Sale" sign. The sign gave your name as the real estate agent.

We are looking for a house in Springfield, and the house on[26] West Street appeals to us. Would you, therefore, be good enough to give us the following information about it:[27]

1. What price is asked?
2. What are the taxes?
3. What is the condition of the house both inside and outside? In[28] other words, how much would we have to spend on the house in addition to the price we pay for it?

As soon as I[29] receive your reply, I will let you know whether we are interested in going through the house. Yours sincerely,[30] (600)

Reading and Writing Practice

717.

assistant
approached
, when clause

, parenthetical

, nonrestrictive

, introductory

, conjunction
recommendations

council
, nonrestrictive

15.

(176)

718.
appropriate
trustees
real estate

(193)

, parenthetical
exception
mortgage

, conjunction
, introductory

heretofore
, conjunction

; no conjunction
treasury

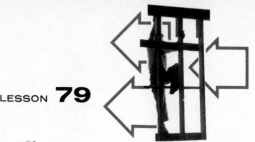

LESSON **79**

719. Frequent Phrases

Understand

1 [shorthand outlines]

Glad

2 [shorthand outlines]

1. Thoroughly understand, fully understand, completely understand, quickly understand, surely understand.
2. We should be glad, I shall be glad, he will be glad, glad to hear, glad to have.

720. Geographical Expressions

(United States Cities in Order of Population — Concluded)

1 [shorthand outlines]
2 [shorthand outlines]
3 [shorthand outlines]

1. Indianapolis, St. Paul, Portland, Louisville, Jersey City, Rochester.
2. Toledo, Columbus, Denver, Providence, Houston, Oakland.
3. Atlanta, Akron, Birmingham, Omaha, Dallas.

721. Previews and Writing Practice

722 [shorthand outlines] 723 [shorthand outlines]
724 [shorthand outlines]

725

722. **Prefer, furnished, you might be able, purposely, thank you for your.**
723. **Appraisal, interior, confirms.**
724. **Certain; Minneapolis, Minnesota; assist, in this matter, similar, possibilities, approximate.**
725. **If you are, handle, reasons, in a position, county, hundreds, genuinely, consists, experience, thoroughly understand, inspect, frankly, on the market.**

---

722. Dear Mr. Mace: My brother and I have decided to spend the months of July and August in Long Beach. During[1] our stay, we should prefer to live in a furnished apartment rather than in a hotel. I thought that you might be[2] able to recommend rooms where we would be comfortable.

We should like to have an apartment overlooking[3] the ocean if possible. We shall be glad to pay any rent within reason. If you know of any such rooms,[4] would you engage them for us. I am purposely writing to you far in advance, as I know the apartments in[5] Long Beach may be difficult to secure later in the year.

Thank you for your assistance. Very sincerely yours,[6]

---

723. Dear Mrs. James: Let me take this opportunity to explain to you our delay in sending you an appraisal[7] of your dwelling. On February 2 one of the insurance company engineers and I went to[8] your house

to make an appraisal. You were not at home, but we were able to make an appraisal by measuring[9] the outside of the house and estimating the value of the interior.

I did not send this appraisal[10] to you immediately because it was much higher than you had estimated. I therefore ordered another[11] appraisal from another company and had hoped to receive it within a few days. That appraisal has[12] just arrived, and it confirms the first one.

In view of these facts, I suggest that you increase your insurance to cover[13] the new value placed on your house. If you will call me, I will prepare a new policy for you. Cordially yours,[14]

---

724. Dear Mr. Clay: Our home office in St. Paul has asked us to obtain for them certain information about the[15] property at 40 Central Avenue, Minneapolis, Minnesota. Mr. Brown, the manager,[16] suggested that you might assist us in this matter. You may recall that some years ago your organization[17] assisted us in a similar matter in Birmingham, Alabama. What we should like to have is a report[18] from a Minneapolis real estate firm on its opinion of the present market value and sales[19] possibilities of the property. We should also like to have its opinion of the physical condition of[20] the building and the approximate cost of any repairs that might be needed.

For similar reports, we[21] have paid a fee of $100. We should be glad to pay the same fee for this report.

When the work is[22] completed, please send the report and bill to me at 312 North Street, Chicago 16, Illinois. Sincerely yours,[23]

---

725. Dear Mr. Wells: Are you interested in selling your home? If you are, why not let us handle the sale for you?[24] Here are a few good reasons why we are in a position to help you sell it at a good price:

1. We have four[25] offices in four of the largest towns in the county. Hundreds of people seeking to buy homes go to these[26] offices each week.

2. Your home will be shown only to those who are genuinely interested in purchasing[27] a house and who are able to pay the price you ask.

3. Our staff consists only of men who have had considerable[28] experience in selling homes in this county and who thoroughly understand the real estate field. These[29] men will be glad to inspect your house and tell you frankly the price that you may expect to receive for it should you[30] place it on the market. There is no charge for this service.

Our office is open from 8 a.m. to 10 p.m.[31] every day. We should be glad to have you visit us. No appointment is necessary. Yours sincerely,[32] (640)

Reading and Writing Practice

726. , introductory

, introductory

sincerely
appreciate [shorthand] (80)

727. [shorthand]

Indianapolis [shorthand]

features
: enumeration [shorthand]

① [shorthand]

② [shorthand]

③ [shorthand]

, conjunction [shorthand]

, parenthetical [shorthand] (161)

728.

telephone
, as clause

(shorthand outline)

, parenthetical
; because of comma
commission

(shorthand outline)

realize
, conjunction
, introductory

(shorthand outline)

(139)

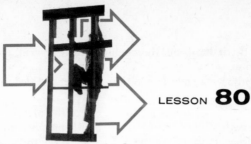

729. Penmanship Practice. In this lesson you will practice the joining of the diphthongs to the various alphabetic strokes of Gregg Shorthand.

1. Use, few, cute, continuation; how, now, loud.
2. Toy, oil, voice, loyal, soil, boil.
3. Tie, might, iron, pine, sign, dine, sight, silence.

▶ **Progressive Speed Builder (120-140)**

730. Preview

731. Possibility, Pleasant, I understand, consists, myself, anxious, appreciate.
732. Occupies, requirements, satisfactorily, if necessary, $600, if you would like, Saturday.
733. Almost, request, apartment, attending, acceptance, rental.

734. Perfectly, it has been, thoroughly, I shall be glad, canoe, conditions, you do so.

735. Promptly, week ends, in addition, prospect, entitled, remaining.

(1 Minute at 120)
731. Dear Mr. Gates: I am considering the possibility of renting a cottage on Lake Pleasant for the coming summer vacation. I understand from some friends/of mine that you have cottages to rent on Lake Pleasant and that you might have something that will meet our needs.

My family consists of my wife, two small children, and myself.// We should like to have a fairly large cottage with at least five rooms.

If you have any cottages available for the months of July, August, and September that would///meet our needs, please let me know.

As I am anxious to make final plans for our vacation, I should appreciate it if you would let me hear from you soon. Sincerely yours, (1)

(1 Minute at 125)
732. Dear Mr. Brown: As your friends have told you, I do have some cottages to rent on Lake Pleasant. I own five cottages, one of which my family occupies every summer./I rent all the others.

All the cottages are directly on the lake.

One of them, I think, will meet your requirements satisfactorily. It has four rooms, but one of them is//very large and can be divided into two rooms by a screen, if necessary.

For the months of July, August, and September, the rental is $600.

I plan///to be at Lake Pleasant on Saturday, March 10, until five o'clock. If you would like to drive up on Saturday, I should be happy to show you the cottage. Sincerely yours, (2)

(1 Minute at 130)
733. Dear Mr. Gates: Thank you for showing my wife and me your cottages on Lake Pleasant.

We have almost decided to take the four-room cottage for the summer. There is one request we/should like to make, however.

As my family will be away for the summer, we shall not be using our apartment in the city. We have, therefore, decided to rent it to a// young man who is attending college in New York during the summer and who would like to have his family with him. His college term starts on June 15, and he would like to have our///apartment on that date.

Would it be possible for us to move into the cottage on June 15? If so, you may consider this letter our acceptance of the rental. Sincerely yours, (3)

(1 Minute at 135)
734. Dear Mr. Brown: It will be perfectly satisfactory to me to have you move into the cottage on June 15. However, it has been my prac-

tice in the past to use the period/ from June 15 to July 1 to have the cottages thoroughly cleaned and to make any necessary repairs. If you wish to move into the cottage and take care of the cleaning//yourself, I shall be glad to let you have it for those two weeks for $50.

There is one other point. A canoe comes with the cottage. I have ordered a new one for the coming summer,///but it will not be delivered until July 1.

If you are willing to move into the cottage on June 15 under these conditions, I should be glad to have you do so. Sincerely yours, (4)

(1 Minute at 140)

735. Dear Mr. Gates: Thank you for writing me so promptly about the possibility of our moving into your cottage on June 15.

Since I wrote you, however, the young man who was going to/rent our apartment in the city has changed his plans and decided to leave his family at home while he attends college. He plans to visit his family on week ends. Therefore, it will no longer//be necessary for us to leave our apartment on June 15. In addition, the prospect of cleaning up the cottage does not appeal to my wife, who feels that she, too, is entitled to///a vacation!

I am enclosing my check for $300. I understand that the remaining $300 is due when we move in.

We are looking forward to the summer. Sincerely yours, (5) (650)

Reading and Writing Practice

736.
readily
, as clause

, parenthetical
certain

, parenthetical

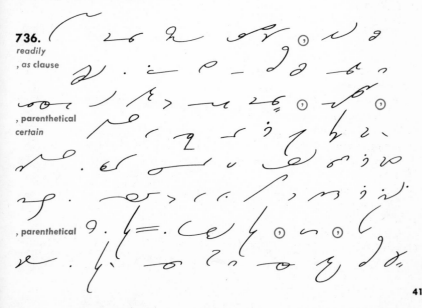

Journal
, apposition

; no conjunction (173)

737.
forgotten
, introductory

; no conjunction
, introductory
answer

, contrast
tenants

, parenthetical

Transcribe:
$10,000
, parenthetical

(shorthand outlines) (122)

738.

, introductory
ample

property
, if clause

, conjunction
arrange

4-3214

convenience
, parenthetical

(shorthand outlines) (95)

APPENDIX

RECALL DRILLS

List of Joined Word Endings

1. -ment

2. -less

3. -tion

4. -tial

5. -ly

6. -ily, -ally

7. -pose, -position

8. -ify

9. -ful

10. -sume, -sumption

11. -ble

12. -ther

13. -ual, -tual

14. -ure, -ture

15. -self, -selves

16. -ort

17. -tain

18. -cient, -ciency

List of Disjoined Word Endings

19. -hood

20. -ward

21. -ship

22. -cle, -cal

23. -ulate

24. -ingly

25. -ings

26. -gram

27. -ification

28. -lity

29. -lty

30. -rity

List of Joined Word Beginnings

31. Per-, Pur-

32. Pro-

33. Em-

34. Im-

35. In-

36. En-

37. Un-

38. Re-

39. Be-

40. De-

41. Dis-

42. Mis-

43. Ex-

44. Com-

45. Con-

46. Sub-

47. After-

48. Al-

49. For-, Fore-

50. Fur-

51. Tern-, etc.

52. Ul

List of Disjoined Word Beginnings

53. Short-

54. Inter-, Intr-, Enter-

55. Electr-, Electric

56. Post-

57. Super-, Supr-

58. Circum-

59. Self-

60. Trans-

61. Incl-

62. Ship-

63. Under-

64. Over-

List of Special Phrases

65. T For To in Phrases

66. Been Represented by B

67. Able Represented by A

68. Want Preceded by Pronoun

69. Ago Represented by G

70. Was Not, Is Not

71. Understand, Understood

72. To Omitted in Phrases

73. The Omitted in Phrases

424

74. Of Omitted in Phrases

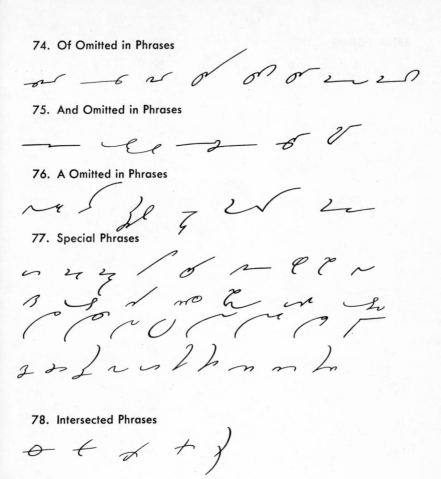

75. And Omitted in Phrases

76. A Omitted in Phrases

77. Special Phrases

78. Intersected Phrases

	A	B	C	D	E	F
1	about	age	AMONG	AUTO	beer	body
2	circle	consider -ation	correspond -ence	glad	enable	ever
3	experience		instant -ance	GREAT	envelope nevertheless	how out
4	must	no.	believer	mr market		most
5	otherwise	a an	every	after	therefore	character
6	be by	mrs	I	BILL	LONG	next
7	correct	general	DESIRE desir-	AM MEN	confer -ence	ELSE
8	GOVERN -MENT	ONE WON	II at	ORGANIZE	convenient -ience	
9	morning	call	company keep business	have advantage	immediate	house
10					opportunity	necessary
11						
12						
13						
14						
15						
16						
17						
18						

	G	H	I	J	K	L
19						
20						
21						
22						
23						
24						
25						
26						
27						
28						
29						
30						
31						

Addresses to be used for mailable transcripts

(These addresses correlate with *Transcription Dictation*.)

Chapter 1

1. Mr. Arnold Day, Electric Appliance Corp., 18 Franklin Square, Pittsburgh 6, Pennsylvania
2. Personnel Department, Carter & Delevan, 200 Spring Street, Euclid, Ohio
3. Mr. Hugh Casey, Casey Stores, Inc., 246 Downer Street, Dayton 2, Ohio
4. Mrs. Harold A. White, 14 Evergreen Circle, Dormont, Pennsylvania
5. Mrs. William Bass, Arcadia Gardens, South Hills, Pennsylvania
6. Mr. Arthur James, Scanlon & James, County Trust Building, Bismarck, North Dakota
7. Mr. Joseph Hayes, Jones Stationery Supplies, Fargo, North Dakota
8. Mr. Kevin Kelly, Credit Department, High-Fashion Styles, Lyric Building, Chicago 3, Illinois
9. Marcus & Lerner, Stationers, 2840 Leonard Avenue, Ann Arbor, Michigan
10. Mr. Herman Green, 222 Greenlawn Drive, Moline, Illinois
11. Sport Togs, Inc., Empire State Building, Room 2397, New York 1, New York
12. Mr. David Simms, Sales Promotion Manager, Kitchen Appliance Company, 2400 State Street, Trenton 10, New Jersey
13. Mr. John O. Macy, Office Equipment & Supply Company, 28 Journal Square, Jersey City 6, New Jersey
14. Mrs. Horace Brown, Smithfield Apartments, Verona, New Jersey
15. Mrs. John Joseph Casey, 47 Mortimer Parkway, Orange, New Jersey
16. Miss Marcia Stevens, 2011 Causeway, Montclair, New Jersey
17. Modern Home Furnishings, 50 Herkimer Street, Albany 2, New York
18. Mr. Truman Bates, Stamford Retail Credit Bureau, 20 Court Street, Stamford, Connecticut
19. Quality Furniture Store, 100 Barnum Square, Bridgeport 5, Connecticut
20. Dr. Clarence Baker, Medical Arts Building, 16 West 56 Street, New York 38, New York
21. Mr. Lawrence Jones, General Publishing Company, 1214 Fourth Avenue, New York 16, New York
22. Mr. Charles Treat, 214 Gateway Road, Ridgewood, New Jersey
23. Creighton's Citrus Cannery, R.F.D. 10, Inverness, Florida

24. Mr. Cabot Palmer, Palmer's Tea Garden, 20 Cypress Road, Macon, Georgia
25. Mrs. Brian Bates, Belmont Apartments, 28 Quaker Avenue, Philadelphia 6, Pennsylvania
26. Mrs. F. L. West, 93-12 168 Street, Jamaica 9, New York
27. Mr. Paul Cooper, R.F.D. 6, Simsbury, Connecticut
28. Miss Sara Jo Lee, 47 Concord Road, Sunnyside, L. I., New York

Chapter 2

29. Mr. Gerald May, Marketing Specialists, 210 Commonwealth Avenue, Boston 4, Massachusetts
30. Conway Construction Company, 380 Penn Avenue, Bethlehem, Pennsylvania
31. Mrs. Joshua Gray, 8 Farrier Street, Charleston 6, West Virginia
32. Mrs. Warren Irving, 364 Terrace Avenue, Richmond, Virginia
33. Mr. Alan Mead, 8 Lowell Street, Providence 11, Rhode Island
34. Mr. Albert Klein, 20 Fennimore Street, New Rochelle, New York
35. Mr. Truman Lee, 92 Cooper Lane, Silver Spring, Maryland
36. Mr. Jasper Pace, 2810 North Park Avenue, Tacoma 10, Washington
37. Mr. Carlton James, 329 Eagan Avenue, Walla Walla, Washington
38. Constant Oil Company, 1400 Beacon Street, Portland 10, Oregon
39. Mr. Everett West, 83 Nugget Lane, Oak Grove, Wisconsin
40. Mr. Warren Field, 219-B Salmon Avenue, Colfax, Washington
41. Mr. George Abbey, Abbey Enterprises, 1400 Price Street, Bremerton, Washington
42. Home Improvement & Remodeling Company, 2300 Glendale Boulevard, Los Angeles 35, California
43. Silver Electric Service, 162 Pacific Avenue, Whittier, California
44. Mr. Stephen Harper, Harper Remodeling Co., 434-436 West Market Street, San Francisco 16, California
45. Mr. Clarence Davis, 18-02 Citrus Lane, Lemon Grove, California
46. Mr. David Abbott, 24-A Capstan Road, Oceanside, California
47. Mrs. Andrew Smith, 23 Glenarm Circle, Palo Alto, California
48. Mr. Wesley James, Evergreen Nursery, Emerson Road, Madison, Connecticut
49. Mr. Gordon Green, Orchard Park Nurseries, Box 74, Heather Lane, Guilford, Connecticut
50. Mr. S. J. Gates, 146 Elm Avenue, Cheshire, Connecticut
51. Mrs. Alison Carr, Box 24, Park Lane, Bristol, Connecticut
52. Mr. Joseph Gray, 326 Barton Street, Jewett City, Connecticut
53. Mr. William F. Mason, Mason Lumber Company, Montpelier, Vermont
54. Mr. Spencer Ames, Ames & Stillwell Mfg. Co., 204 Cooper Street, Boston 20, Massachusetts
55. Mr. Charles E. Baker, 46 River Road, Cambridge 38, Massachusetts

56. Demarest Furniture Company, 30 North Concord Avenue, Lowell, Massachusetts
57. Mr. Conrad Nelson, 439 Mt. Hope Boulevard, Portsmouth, Rhode Island
58. Mr. Townsend Smith, 795 Green End Avenue, Middletown, Rhode Island
59. Mrs. Eric Olson, 322 Rogers Road, Kingston, Rhode Island

Chapter 3

60. Mr. David Ring, Florida Guaranty Trust Company, 1400 Crescent Boulevard, Miami 16, Florida
61. Mr. Thomas Shields, Southern Lumber Company, 288-94 Cypress Avenue, Miami 13, Florida
62. Orange Trust Company, Fifth Avenue at Twelfth Street, Jacksonville 8, Florida
63. Mrs. Milton Green, Everglades Apartments, 1800 Southern Cross Boulevard, Miami 7, Florida
64. Miss Charlene Baker, 23 Cotillion Drive, Columbus, Georgia
65. Mr. Herbert Nelson, Nelson, Wayne & Duff, 58 Davis Avenue, Macon, Georgia
66. Meredith, King & Company, Copper Trust Building, Phoenix 9, Arizona
67. Investment Counselors, 20 Kingman Avenue, Yuma, Arizona
68. Mr. Edward H. Pace, 184 Granite Boulevard, Boulder, Colorado
69. Mr. H. Stanley Brown, 26 Canyon Drive, Estes Park, Colorado
70. Mr. Clayton Baker, 410 Park Avenue, Kingman, Arizona
71. Mr. Elwood White, 11 McArthur Avenue, Chandler, Arizona
72. Mr. Robert N. Green, 46 Wilshire Road, Darien, Connecticut
73. Mr. Thomas E. Hunter, Hunter Packing Company, 640-650 West Bank Street, Moline, Illinois
74. Mr. Roger Lee, 448 Parker Avenue, Racine, Wisconsin
75. Mr. Anderson Smith, 63 Sunset Road, Winter Park, Florida
76. Mr. Francis Jones, Comstock Gardens, 397 Jessup Avenue, St. Petersburg, Florida
77. Mr. Leonard Day, 111 Lindley Avenue, Tenafly, New Jersey
78. Mr. Wilbur Jones, 40 Bradley Circle, Cresskill, New Jersey
79. Mr. Joseph Smith, Personal Loan Department, Fidelity Trust Company, 60 Esplanade, New Orleans, Louisiana
80. Mr. Douglas Jones, 28 Camellia Street, Opelousas, Louisiana
81. Mr. Everett Gray, Manager, Personnel Department, Woodward Trust Company, 1816 Columbus Avenue, Meridian, Mississippi
82. Mr. Joseph Mason, 93 West Main Road, Paris, Mississippi
83. Mr. Maurice A. Brown, 81 Seminole Street, Tampa 8, Florida
84. Mr. Samuel Green, 376 Blackstone Road, Tallahassee, Florida
85. Springfield National Bank, 200 South Third Avenue, Springfield, Ohio

86. Mrs. William E. Baker, 63 Quarrier Road, New Orleans 3, Louisiana
87. Mr. Albert Simms, Simms Furniture Company, 150 Main Street, Albany 7, New York
88. Republic Publishing Company, 104 Simons Avenue, Rochester 3, New York
89. Mr. George W. Chase, 333 Mountain Road, Windham, New York
90. Mr. Theodore Macey, 29 River Street, Hudson, New York

Chapter 4

91. Culver Magazine Agency, 873 Austin Avenue, Detroit 25, Michigan
92. Mr. Robert J. White, President, Ingham County Trust Company, 40 North Michigan Avenue, Lansing 9, Michigan
93. Mr. Thomas C. Walsh, Sheridan Chemical Corporation, 63-67 Columbus Avenue, Muskegon, Michigan
94. Mr. P. T. Samuels, 209 Adams Street, Menasha, Wisconsin
95. Mr. Francis Murphy, Ridge Road, Cliff Lake, Montana
96. Mr. Emerson Gray, Shelby Road, Evaro, Montana
97. Valcourt Publishing Company, 287-289 Sussex Street, Baltimore 40, Maryland
98. Mr. Frank Nelson, Nelson's Book Nook, 500 Calvert Avenue, Cumberland, Maryland
99. Mr. Everett Day, 365 Oak Street, Newbury, New Hampshire
100. Mr. L. E. Cole, Lytton's Bookcase, 40 Oak Street, Manchester 7, New Hampshire
101. Mr. Sidney Kramer, Kramer Personnel Agency, 3040 Chrysler Building, New York 18, New York
102. Mr. Chester Simms, 25 Seaview Road, Stapleton, Staten Island, New York
103. Mr. Albert Snow, The Book Shelf, 54 Nassau Street, New York 25, New York
104. Everett Publishing Company, Inc., 390 Essex Street, Greensboro, North Carolina
105. Mrs. Irene Gates, 144 West Street, Pittsburgh 16, Pennsylvania
106. Mr. Charles Rice, Gilroy Business College, 310 Jefferson Avenue, Spartanburg, South Carolina
107. Mrs. J. C. Strong, 86 Sentinel Street, Maplewood, Oregon
108. Mr. O. M. Jones, Jones Printing & Binding Company, 42-48 Walnut Street, Portland 16, Oregon
109. Duncan School of Business, 60 West Bryant Avenue, Pueblo, Colorado
110. Pyramid Book Company, 436 Fourth Avenue, New York 28, New York
111. Mr. Benjamin Brown, Brown & Bridewell, 100-130 Sunrise Boulevard, Garden City, Long Island, New York
112. Mr. Stanton Green, Green & Noble, Printers, 600 Mercer Street, Jersey City 5, New Jersey

113. Mr. Hobart Baker, Fleetwood Arms, 429 Harvard Street, East Orange, New Jersey
114. Mr. Martin Harvey, Adams High School, Third and Ocean Avenues, Asbury Park, New Jersey
115. Mr. Donald Morris, 119 Blackmer Street, Wilkes-Barre, Pennsylvania
116. Mr. John T. Roy, Roy, Talbott & Adams, 64 Anthracite Building, Harrisburg, Pennsylvania
117. Mr. Sherwood Burns, Essex Printers, Incorporated, Printers Lane, Essex, Connecticut
118. Mr. Andrew Drake, Drake Manufacturing Company, 260 North Street, Portland 6, Maine
119. Mr. Chester Miles, Green Bay Publishing Company, 670 West Superior Street, Green Bay, Wisconsin
120. Mr. Arnold Keith, Keith & Smith, Jewelers, 165 Lee Avenue, Falls Church, Virginia
121. Mr. Marvin Beck, Beck Printing Service, 1800 Salem Street, Providence 10, Rhode Island

Chapter 5

122. Mr. George E. May, 643 Randolph Street, Bridgeport, Indiana
123. Mr. Otto C. Simon, 615 West Main Street, Pittsburgh 16, Pennsylvania
124. Mr. Roger Gray, Gray & Chason, 80-84 Forrest Avenue, Indianapolis 8, Indiana
125. Mr. Charles James, 63 West Madison Street, Des Moines 7, Iowa
126. Mr. Albert Macy, 96 Evans Avenue, Evansville 8, Indiana
127. Mr. Edward H. Smith, Chelsea Arms Apartments, 2860 Lee Avenue, Mason City, Iowa
128. Winecoff & Kashin, Insurance Specialists, 620 Franklin Avenue, Kansas City 10, Kansas
129. Mr. Carlton Barry, 43 Osage Street, Denmark, Kansas
130. Osgood & Parkwell, 604 Tivoli Building, 900 Cherokee Avenue, Wichita 7, Kansas
131. Mr. Eugene M. Adams, 1818 Douglas Boulevard, Irvington, Nebraska
132. Mr. Harry E. Barnes, R.F.D. 3, Raymond, Nebraska
133. Mr. Stephen Crane, 94 South Marion Avenue, Hannibal, Missouri
134. Mr. Roger Jones, Jones Meat Market, 432 Alamo Avenue, Houston 8, Texas
135. Mr. Elwood Smith, Independence Insurance Company, 86 North Jackson Street, Independence, Missouri
136. Pratt & Dickinson, Incorporated, Johnson Building, 900-910 Greeley Avenue, Kansas City 7, Kansas
137. Mr. Theodore A. Jones, 63 Caldwell Street, Hannibal, Missouri
138. Mr. William Abbey, Box 103, Valley Road, Greenwood, Missouri
139. Mr. Sidney M. Travers, 362 Solomon Street, Gaylord, Kansas

140. Mr. Douglas P. Green, Green & Redmond, 47 Mills Street, Houston 11, Texas
141. Mr. Ordwell Macy, 540 North Central Avenue, Fort Worth 8, Texas
142. Mr. Clifford C. Clay, 960 Somerset Avenue, Baltimore 43, Maryland
143. Mr. Vernon A. Kelly, 37 Madison Street, Pine Bluff, Arkansas
144. Mr. Paul L. Donald, 66 Boone Road, Hensley, Arkansas
145. Mrs. J. J. Woods, Beauregard Gardens, 610 De Soto Boulevard, Lafayette, Louisiana
146. Mr. Edward G. Melvin, 418 Fulton Street, Covington, Kentucky
147. Chicago Insurance Company, 450 North Michigan Avenue, Chicago 46, Illinois
148. Mr. Franklin Pace, 23 Oneida Avenue, Lewiston, Idaho
149. Mr. Wilfred Stern, 1428 Canyon Drive, Nampa, Idaho
150. Mr. Charles Macy, 294 Valencia Street, Roswell, New Mexico
151. Mr. Andrew Smith, Silver Smith's Mining Company, 408 Grant, Silver City, New Mexico
152. Mr. Curtis N. Smith, 17 Sierra Glen, Crownpoint, New Mexico
153. Mr. Delbert Jones, El Rio Grande Apartments, 29 Bliss Road, El Paso, Texas

Chapter 6

154. Mr. Everett West, 480 Cascade Boulevard, Sherman, South Dakota
155. Quarry Bank & Trust Company, 150 North Sanborn Avenue, Sioux Falls, South Dakota
156. Mr. John J. May, 79 Perkins Street, Brookings, South Dakota
157. Miss Margaret E. Bailey, Iroquois Gardens, 946 West Park Avenue, Chicago 55, Illinois
158. Mr. Kenneth Nelson, 83 White Horse Pike, Laramie, Wyoming
159. Mr. Ferdinand Clay, Clay Repairs & Accessories, 206 Main Street, Fletcher Park, Wyoming
160. Mr. Keith F. Gates, 409 Palmer Building, Main Street and Edison Avenue, Detroit 33, Michigan
161. Mr. James O. Mills, Caine Motor Company, 600 West Superior Street, Detroit 29, Michigan
162. Mr. Henry Barnes, Barnes Trucking Service, 1428 Bonner Avenue, Missoula, Montana
163. Mr. Joseph E. Lowry, Bluestone Tire Company, 900 Fairlawn Avenue, Akron 5, Ohio
164. Mr. Arthur Simms, 690 Pine Bluff, Hillsdale, Wyoming
165. Mr. Geoffrey Ramsey, Ramsey Motors, Inc., 320 Commerce Street, Sioux Falls, South Dakota
166. Mr. John Andrews, 47 Gold Stone Hill, Havre, Montana
167. Mr. F. Herbert Morris, Kimball Road, De Witt, Nebraska
168. Mrs. George F. Harper, 98 Laurel Lane, Newark, Delaware
169. Mr. Albert Simons, 720 County Road, Milton, Delaware

170. Mr. Robert G. Holt, Holt, Arthur & Heather, 1540 Kent Avenue, Wilmington, Delaware
171. Mr. Duane Wade, 1810 Continental Avenue, S. W., Washington 34, D. C.
172. Mr. Christopher Davis, 273 Cherry Lane, Tacoma Park, South Dakota
173. Mr. Ashley Brown, 312 Talbot Avenue, Cumberland, Maryland
174. Mr. Howard G. Bates, 96 Magnolia Lane, Bethel, Delaware
175. Clinton Motor Service Company, 1470 Fisher Avenue, Dallas 20, Texas
176. Mr. John A. Walsh, Manager, Wilson Brothers, 555 Chestnut Street, Chicago 36, Illinois
177. Mr. John T. Murphy, Jack's Motor Freight, 420 Fulton Street, Cicero, Illinois
178. Mr. Alexander Grace, 368 Marshall Street, Clarksville, Tennessee
179. Mr. Arthur S. Mills, 740 West Clark Street, Chicago 92, Illinois
180. Mr. Chester E. Brown, Brown & Leeds Motor Service, 620 Whitman Avenue, Terre Haute, Indiana
181. Mr. Harry T. Walsh, 216 Carroll Street, Alton Park, Tennessee
182. Comstock De Luxe Car Interiors, 337 Anderson Avenue, Chattanooga 2, Tennessee
183. Drivers Monthly, 46 Clinton Street, Hamtramck, Michigan
184. Mr. Harvey Green, American Baking Company, 1550-1560 Girard Avenue, Philadelphia 25, Pennsylvania
185. Mr. Seymour Karp, Express Trucking Service, 473 Franklin Avenue, Minneapolis 5, Minnesota
186. Mr. Paul M. Lee, Lee Construction Company, 1800 Washington Avenue, Saint Paul 10, Minnesota
187. Mr. Michael Perry, Perry's Motor Service, 720 Pioneer Avenue, Salt Lake City 11, Utah
188. Mr. Samuel D. Jacobs, Motor Express Service, 910 Weber Street, Ogden, Utah

Chapter 7

189. Mr. Conrad L. Simms, Simms Business Institute, 546 Park Avenue, New York 22, New York
190. Sales Efficiency Corporation, 324 Lexington Avenue, New York 19, New York
191. Mr. Ferdinand Day, Harris Trust & Title Company, 300 Lincoln Avenue, Harrisburg, Pennsylvania
192. Mr. Andrew C. Jones, 819 Concord Street, Quincy 68, Massachusetts
193. Mr. John A. Chester, Treadway's Department Store, 98 North Front Street, Sunbury, Pennsylvania
194. Bedford Manufacturing Company, 80 North Clinton Street, Medina, Ohio
195. Mrs. Genevieve Reilly, Manager, Training Specialists, 1800 West Clark Street, Chicago 46, Illinois

196. Mrs. Edward Gates, 23 Freeman Street, Springfield, Illinois
197. Miss Dorothy W. White, Central High School, 900-910 State Street, Chicago 32, Illinois
198. Mr. Thomas Mason, Mason Motors, 620 Jackson Avenue, Waukegan, Illinois
199. Miss Mary C. Allen, 14 Brookdale Road, Brattleboro, Vermont
200. Mrs. Leonard Clay, Bristol Arms Apartments, 64 Bristol Street, Newton 58, Massachusetts
201. Mr. Thomas E. Davis, Davis Toy Company, 17 North Columbia Avenue, Salem, Oregon
202. Mr. T. J. Hoffman, Principal, North High School, 800 Jacinto Street, San Antonio 14, Texas
203. Mrs. Elwell Drake, Manager, Meredith Business Schools, 630 North Plymouth Street, Boston 15, Massachusetts
204. Mr. Charles Abbey, 29 Surrey Road, Morehead City, North Carolina
205. Mr. Harry Blackmore, 87 Florence Street, Lancaster, South Carolina
206. Miss Valerie Jones, Decatur Apartments, 444 Fanning Street, Moultrie, Georgia
207. Mr. Geoffrey Brown, 851 Arlington Boulevard, Alexandria, Virginia
208. Bannister Finance Company, Barnum Building, 40 Trumbull Avenue, Bridgeport 6, Connecticut
209. Mr. Raymond Warner, 680 Roosevelt Street, Freeport, Long Island, New York
210. Mrs. Everett Green, 142 Saxon Lane, Bay Shore, Long Island, New York
211. Miss Madeline Johnson, 30 Garden Circle, Summit, New Jersey
212. Mr. Albert Bailey, 61 Redwood Lane, Elk Grove, California
213. Home Arts Institute, 400-402 Butler Avenue, Cleveland 12, Ohio
214. Miss Bertha Sacks, 792 Warren Street, Belleville, New Jersey
215. Mrs. F. E. Leslie, Principal, Southside High School, Church Street at Blackwood Avenue, Camden 8, New Jersey
216. Miss Alice A. Chase, Riverview Apartments, 1890 Palisade Avenue, Cliffside Park, New Jersey
217. Mr. R. M. Ross, Clark High School, 750 Pershing Avenue, Las Vegas, Nevada
218. Mr. Philip S. Brown, Sheridan High School, Park Avenue at Cass, Freemont, Nebraska
219. Mr. Edmund Klein, Principal, Roosevelt High School, 14 Street at Dawes Avenue, Chadron, Nebraska
220. Mr. Martin Stacy, Principal, Clinton Avenue School, Clinton and Park Avenues, Flushing 31, New York

Chapter 8

221. Business Surveys, Inc., Golden Gate Building, 460 State Street, San Francisco 42, California

222. Air Travel Bureau, Chadwick Building, 320 South Wabash Avenue, Chicago 28, Illinois
223. Mr. Stanton Day, 1448 Parker Avenue, Maywood, New Jersey
224. Mr. Joseph B. Simms, Simms Manufacturing Company, 1200 Warwick Street, Lexington, Virginia
225. Mr. George Palmer, Palmer & Sons, Inc., 100 West Jackson Avenue, Clarksburg, West Virginia
226. Mr. Charles Macy, Jefferson Real Estate Company, 68 North Main Street, New Rochelle, New York
227. Mr. Andrew Smith, Hamilton Court Apartments, 96 Hamilton Avenue, Baltimore 99, Maryland
228. Mr. Anthony Jones, Manager, Smithdeal Department Store, 650 Penobscot Street, Bangor, Maine
229. Mr. Walter Pace, Presbrey & Clarkson Company, 98 Federal Street, Portland 8, Maine
230. Martindales' Hotel Guide, 74 North Erie Street, Albany 6, New York
231. Mr. Clarence Stern, Stern, Stern & Edwards, 402 Humboldt Building, Hawthorne, Nevada
232. Mr. Godfrey Banks, Stadler Publishing Company, 412 Brigham Avenue, Tooele, Utah
233. Mr. J. A. Allen, Allen Ranch, Great Falls, Montana
234. Mr. Everett N. Ray, Elroy Communications, Banks and Marshall Streets, Fond du Lac, Wisconsin
235. Caster Travel Agency, Lucas Building, 900 Railroad Avenue, Toledo 8, Ohio
236. Baker Transportation Company, 46 Comanche Lane, Denver 4, Colorado
237. Dallas Trade Exchange, Pecos and Clay, Dallas 14, Texas
238. Mrs. David C. Glass, Glass Enterprises, 84 Montcalm Street, River Rouge, Michigan
239. Mr. Jonathan Mead, Star Box Company, 46 Oneida Street, Menasha, Wisconsin
240. Mr. Robert M. Simms, Whitehall Apartments, 986 Franklin Avenue, Columbus 14, Ohio
241. Mr. Charles Brooks, Golden Arrow Railway Company, 300 Oakland Street, Topeka, Kansas
242. Mr. Arthur Trees, 42 Ellery Lane, Scarsdale, New York
243. Dr. Thomas L. Green, Medical Arts Building, Hamilton at Arbor Avenues, Hamden, Connecticut
244. Mr. Harold James, James Travel Agency, Iron City Building, Pittsburgh 16, Pennsylvania
245. President Steamship Company, Pier 98, North River, New York 14, New York
246. Mr. John J. Parks, 29 Mountainview Road, Concord, New Hampshire
247. Mr. William Billings, Billings Hardware Store, 40 East 183 Street, Bronx 42, New York

248. Mr. Thomas Kelly, 16 Simons Avenue, Athens, Ohio
249. Mr. Stephen D. Jones, Jones Appliance Company, 75 Morrison Avenue, Mankato, Minnesota
250. Mr. Donald R. Gates, Gates Printing & Publishing Company, 42 Alger Street, Grand Rapids 6, Michigan
251. Mr. Leonard Jones, Sr., 561 Peach Street, Decatur, Georgia
252. Mr. Wilson C. Smith, Smith Chemical Company, Elkhart Street, Valparaiso, Indiana
253. Mr. Edwin C. Jones, 39 Clay Avenue, Paris, Kentucky
254. Mr. Harold G. Brown, 47 Sierra Street, Clovis, New Mexico
255. Mr. Arthur Kramer, 602 Randolph Street, Montgomery, West Virginia

Chapter 9

256. Mr. Philip E. Casey, Retail Merchants of Chicago Association, 46 South Adams Street, Chicago 29, Illinois
257. Mrs. Durand L. Gates, 14-22 Brookdale Circle, Hicksville, Long Island, New York
258. The Connecticut Yankee Shop, 92 Market Street, Hartford 9, Connecticut
259. Mr. Herbert M. Taylor, Euclid Avenue Apartments, 635 Euclid Avenue, Springfield, Ohio
260. Mr. Jason Gates, 411 Campbell Street, Austin, Texas
261. Mrs. Oscar Green, 1818 Seneca Boulevard, Rochester 9, New York
262. Mrs. J. C. Leslie, 23 Lafayette Court, Fall River, Massachusetts
263. Mrs. Victor Kelly, Manager, The Mannequin Shop, 38 Main Street, Chatham, New Jersey
264. Needham's Department Store, 400 Osage Street, Oklahoma City 14, Oklahoma
265. Sara Jo Dress Shop, 87 Palmer Avenue, Fleetwood, New York
266. Mr. Clifford West, 47 Hamilton Avenue, Sherman, South Dakota
267. Mrs. Bradley Park, 863 Morrison Park Avenue, Minneapolis 17, Minnesota
268. Mr. Henry F. Brill, 61 Hennepin Street, Pipestone, Minnesota
269. Mr. Douglas Fox, 290 Knox Avenue, Bennington, Nebraska
270. Mr. Alfred M. Green, Green Clothing Store, 400-410 Decatur Avenue, Memphis 7, Tennessee
271. Mr. Lloyd Johnson, President, Beau Brummel Apparel, 750 Stewart Street, Chattanooga 18, Tennessee
272. Memo to Mr. Johnson from Mr. Jackson
273. Mr. Malcolm Lake, 241 Davis Avenue, South Bend 6, Indiana
274. Mr. Delbert Gray, 96 Cedar Lane, Boone, Iowa
275. Mr. Wilson Smith, 830 Gage Boulevard, Hastings, Nebraska
276. Mrs. C. G. Henry, 629 Hancock Street, Caribou, Maine
277. Mr. Merritt Herman, Hansel & Gretel Shoes, 468-470 Frederick Avenue, Hagerstown, Maryland

278. Little Princess Dress Shoppe, 53 Bedford Street, Falls Church, Virginia
279. The Children's Shop, 81 Simpson Street, Laurel, Mississippi
280. Mrs. Alan E. Craig, 153 Bayou Boulevard, St. Petersburg 4, Florida
281. Mr. George Sanders, 96 Clinton Avenue, Sandusky, Ohio
282. Mr. Albert O. Hodges, Lenoir Avenue Apartments, 117 Lenoir Avenue, Gastonia, North Carolina
283. Mr. Harvey Jones, 55 North Grant Street, Richland, Washington
284. Mr. Richard Baker, 931 Colfax Circle, Los Alamos, New Mexico
285. Freeborn Department Store, 416 West 33 Street, St. Paul 18, Minnesota
286. Mr. Maxwell Tracy, 354 Cliff Street, Trinity Heights, Texas
287. Austin's Department Store, 90 West Market Street, Rapid City, South Dakota
288. Mr. Frederick L. Jones, 67 Lycoming Street, Palmerton, Pennsylvania
289. Mrs. Thomas J. Lee, Garden State Apartments, Plainfield, New Jersey
290. Mr. J. Louis Day, 862 Rockleigh Road, Laconia, New Hampshire

Chapter 10

291. Mr. Chester Williams, County Telephone Service, 98 West Fourth Street, New York 22, New York
292. Mr. Samuel S. Jones, Webster Branch Exchange, 50 West Central Avenue, Allentown, Pennsylvania
293. Mr. Albert Sears, Vernon Telephone Branch, 70 West 14 Street, Los Angeles 65, California
294. Mr. John E. Samuels, 416 Monterey Road, Mount Wilson, California
295. Mr. Daniel James, 504 Wheeler Street, Astoria, Oregon
296. Mr. Roland Dix, 673 Butler Road, Selma, Ohio
297. Mr. Richard Harris, 52 Harding Avenue, Plattsburg, Ohio
298. Mr. A. J. Green, Little River Power & Light Company, 40 Wilcox Street, Little River, Alabama
299. Mr. M. C. Jones, Jones Electrical Service, 71 Graham Street, Bisbee, Arizona
300. Mr. Matthew Ames, Home Appliance Company, 48 North Jackson Street, Trinidad, Colorado
301. Fremont Gas & Electric Company, 370 Cedar Street, Scottsbluff, Nebraska
302. Medway Utilities Company, 64 North Davis Street, Springfield 9, Illinois
303. Mr. E. S. Banker, Mid-State Electric Company, 41 Smith Street, Morristown, New Jersey
304. Mr. Milton Young, 380 Hillside Avenue, Hudson, New York
305. Miss Mary Jane Day, Washington High School, Hopkinsville, Kentucky.
306. Mr. Joseph C. Kelly, Central Gas & Electric Company, 110 Seward Avenue, Chadron, Nebraska

307. Mrs. Stephen Martin, 680 Clark Street, Helena, Montana
308. Miss Marcia Mills, 47-A Lewis Street, Missoula, Montana
309. Galway Construction Company, 20 Broadway, Deming, New Mexico
310. Mr. Louis Nelson, 47 Wills Avenue, Artesia, New Mexico
311. Mr. George Travis, Wheatridge Products Company, 500 Washburn Avenue, Topeka, Kansas
312. Trenton Clarion, 240 South State Street, Trenton 3, New Jersey
313. Mr. William Nelson, Nelson, Graves & Conway, 380 Monroe Street, Jackson 20, Mississippi
314. Dallas Chamber of Commerce, 100 Main Street, Dallas, South Dakota
315. Mrs. Harvey Green, 215 Mercer Street, Halifax, Pennsylvania
316. Mrs. Adam Farley, Modiste Dress Salon, 28 North Bellevue Avenue, Newport, Rhode Island
317. Mr. Edward Paul, 1812 Wilson Avenue, Lexington, North Carolina
318. Mrs. Douglas C. Nelson, 512-A Carteret Street, Linwood, North Carolina
319. Memo to Eric Larson from James Miller
320. Mr. Frank W. Stone, Stone Manufacturing Company, Incorporated, 200 Scott Street, Clinton, Iowa
321. Mr. John G. Bass, Electric Power Company, 310 Lucas Avenue, Davenport, Iowa
322. Mrs. Leroy A. Parks, Louise Court Apartments, 98 Louise Street, Baton Rouge, Louisiana
323. Mr. Clifford White, President, White Tool & Die Works, 1860 New Haven Street, Waterbury 15, Connecticut
324. Mr. Joseph Mann, Mann & Keating, 450 Harris Avenue, Reading, Pennsylvania

Chapter 11

325. Mr. Anthony Ames, Ames Advertising Specialties, 110 Market Street, Newark 3, New Jersey
326. Mr. Frederick A. Thomas, Thomas Furniture Salon, 333 Palm Street, Sarasota, Florida
327. Mr. George Franklin, Franklin Office Furniture, Incorporated, 457 De Kalb Street, Brunswick, Georgia
328. Mr. Conrad Gray, Gray Metal Finishing Company, Jackson & Clark Streets, Wyandotte, Michigan
329. Mr. Herbert Crane, Crane Plumbing Company, 84 Calhoun Street, Fairmont, West Virginia
330. Mr. G. D. Moore, Moore Paper Products, 37 North Marquette Avenue, Green Bay, Wisconsin
331. Mr. Nicholas West, West & Durand, 420 Dodge Street, Madison 5, Wisconsin
332. Mr. Elliott E. Ramsey, Office Specialists, Incorporated, 64 Monroe Street, Green Bay, Wisconsin

333. Mr. Clark Johnson, Tele-Sales Company, 830 LaSalle Street, Chicago 89, Illinois
334. Mr. Otis Brown, Stellar Elevator Company, 1200 Edison Avenue, Lansing 6, Michigan
335. Mr. Garrett Carey, Carey Artists Supplies, 268 Harper Avenue, Detroit 42, Michigan
336. Miss Dorothea Tracy, Tracy Stenographic Service, 340 Custer Avenue, Tulsa 1, Oklahoma
337. Mr. Jeremiah Smith, Household Magazines, Incorporated, 51 Hamilton Street, Macomb, Illinois
338. Mr. Harvey James, James Furniture Company, 211 Newton Street, Fayetteville, Arkansas
339. Memo to Branch Managers from Harry J. Green
340. Mr. George Masters, Conway Book Company, 20 Lee Avenue, Decatur, Georgia
341. National Safe Company, 96 Dodge Street, Fort Madison, Iowa
342. Mr. Robin E. Lee, White Office Building, 28 Fulton Street, Searcy, Arkansas
343. Mr. Hubert Brown, Brown Insurance Underwriters, 600 Pulaski Street, Little Rock, Arkansas
344. Mr. Marvin Brown, Brown Realty Company, Burgess Building, South Norwalk, Connecticut
345. Mr. Walter Jones, President, Ellsworth Department Store, 400 Charles Street, Port Deposit, Maryland
346. Miss Mildred E. Stone, West End High School, West School Street, Wilkes-Barre, Pennsylvania
347. Jayson File Equipment Company, 1800 North Central Avenue, Poughkeepsie, New York
348. Mr. Thomas S. Green, Cane Department Store, 80 North Front Street, Covington, Kentucky
349. Mr. Redmond L. Jones, Jones Motors, Garrett Building, Hancock, Maryland
350. Mr. Robert G. Brown, Brown Confections, 710 Praline Street, Lake Charles, Louisiana
351. Mr. Thomas L. Gray, Kennebec Insurance Company, 400 West Hancock Street, Augusta, Maine
352. Mr. Edward Clay, Moderne Motors, Inc., 607 Ottawa Avenue, Ironwood, Michigan
353. Ridge & Randall, Inc., File Equipment Specialists, Ridge Road, Ridgefield, Connecticut
354. Mr. Carl Lyman, Lyman & Crosswell, 816 Dudley Avenue, Dorchester 72, Massachusetts
355. Mr. William Martin, De Luxe Cleaners & Dyers, 270 North Park Place, Houston 8, Texas
356. Hartwell & Meighan, Chandler Building, Bisbee, Arizona

357. Heirloom Clock Company, 412 South State Street, Hamden, Connecticut
358. Mr. Wilcox Miller, 1612 Brewer Avenue, Bangor, Maine
359. Mr. Harlan Z. Bell, Bell Nationwide Truck Service, 2600 Broad Street, Fairview, New Jersey

Chapter 12

360. Mr. Cecil Andrews, Andrews Advertising Agency, 900 Jewett Street, Muskegon, Michigan
361. Memo to Harry J. Barnes from A. B. Green
362. Mr. Kenneth E. Thomas, Hearthside Publishers, 450 North Hartwell Avenue, Cincinnati 31, Ohio
363. Mr. Alfred M. Foster, Memorial High School, Greenfield, Missouri
364. Mr. Henry Scott, Scott Canneries, Kitsap Avenue, Port Orchard, Washington
365. Mr. Edward Mason, 44 Laketown Drive, Randolph, Utah
366. Mr. David E. Kline, Acme Printing Company, 190 Howard Avenue, Hyattsville, Maryland
367. Mr. Dennis L. Wall, Wall Accounting Service, 67 Washington Avenue, Lewiston, Maine
368. Miss Evelyn C. Miller, Traverse County Consolidated High School, Dumont, Minnesota
369. Mr. Michael Crane, Crane Scientific Research Company, 60 Morris Avenue, New Brunswick, New Jersey
370. Mr. Donald Taylor, Cosmopolitan Drug Company, 200 Montgomery Avenue, Norristown, Pennsylvania
371. Mr. Raymond Davis, Davis & Wentworth, Attorneys, 98 Elizabeth Street, Hampton, Virginia
372. Mr. Everett Rice, Rice Insurance Company, 48 North Adams Street, Portsmouth, New Hampshire
373. Mr. Charles E. Lamb, Lamb Nuts & Bolts Company, 37 Kingman Street, Adams, Kansas
374. Mrs. J. C. Barrett, Duke Plastics, 160 Essex Street, Gloucester, Massachusetts
375. Mrs. James A. Smith, 75 Grove Street, Ann Arbor, Michigan
376. Mr. Charles Kelly, Manager, Miller's Shopper Service, 375 Boulder Avenue, Colorado Springs, Colorado
377. Mr. Matthew E. Jones, Jones Linen Service, 640 Fremont Street, Fort Madison, Iowa
378. Mr. Conrad Lewis, Community Bus Transit Company, 36 West Carroll Avenue, Westminster, Maryland
379. Moore Envelope Company, 1200 Plymouth Street, Dorchester 69, Massachusetts
380. Mr. Edward G. Brooks, Brooks Flower Mart, 391 Fulton Street, East Point, Georgia

381. Miss Clara Harris, Harris Antique Shop, 28 Bristol Street, Attleboro, Massachusetts
382. Mr. George Davis, President, Davis Business Institute, 56 Niagara Square, Buffalo 12, New York
383. Mr. Robert Douglas, Manager, National Equipment Company, 111-86 Parsons Boulevard, Flushing 69, Long Island, New York
384. Mr. George C. Lang, Quality Paper Products Company, 80 Lincoln Street, Livermore, Maine
385. Mr. Walter Ramsey, Ramsey Manufacturing Company, 41 Central Avenue, Sherman, Texas
386. Mr. Henry Walsh, Walsh Stationery & Office Supplies, 320 Harris Avenue, Gainesville, Texas
387. Green Bay Publishers, 404 Taylor Street, Green Bay, Wisconsin
388. Puritan Pencil Company, 512 Worcester Street, Shrewsbury, Massachusetts
389. Mr. Godfrey Fields, 87 Tuxedo Square, Averill Park, New York
390. Mr. Stephen A. Gates, Office Equipment and Supplies, 316 South Main Street, Spartanburg, South Carolina
391. Miss Virginia L. Harris, 63 Jefferson Street, Cullman, Alabama
392. Mr. Rovell A. Meyers, Meyers Jewelry Store, 74 Worth Street, Grand River, Iowa
393. Mr. Louis Johnson, Johnson Envelope & Stationery Company, 622 Erlanger Avenue, Covington, Kentucky
394. Mrs. Arthur Stockton, Stockton's Hosiery, 461 Bristol Street, Framingham, Massachusetts

Chapter 13

395. Mr. E. J. Blair, General Manager, Conway Chain Stores, Conway Building, Lexington, Kentucky
396. Mr. Stanley Hughes, Trade Wind Condiments Company, 1680 South Market Street, San Francisco 4, California
397. Mr. Charles J. Wagner, Wagner & Ewald Market, 490 Blackrock Turnpike, Fairfield, Connecticut
398. Mrs. Harvey Foster, 98 Colonial Drive, Mount Vernon, Iowa
399. Mr. Alex Conroy, West End Supermarket, 400-410 West Monroe Avenue, Johnstown, Pennsylvania
400. Mrs. Catharine Barnes, Cathy's Candy Kitchen, 153 Sumter Avenue, Hartsville, South Carolina
401. Ed & Bill's Sweet Shop, 419 Plymouth Court, Beverly, Massachusetts
402. The Corner Grocery, Main Street at Central Avenue, Dover, New Jersey
403. Mr. Harry Smith, 788 Palm Boulevard, Lake Worth, Florida
404. Mr. Raymond Jones, Steak House, 21 Main Street, Stratford, Connecticut
405. Mrs. Arthur L. Cook, 977 Spring Street, Ossining, New York

406. Mr. Perry Long, Ambrosia Extract Company, Incorporated, 640 Collier Street, Malabar, Florida
407. Mr. Roland Sharp, Sharp Department Store, 3033 Tyler Avenue, Lubbock, Texas
408. Mr. Gary Sands, 940 Lake Drive, Marquette, Wisconsin
409. Mr. Kermit A. Smith, Smith's Market, 1270 Amherst Street, Staunton, Virginia
410. Chicken Heaven, Route 37, Junction 10-A, Springfield, Ohio
411. Mr. Oscar Black, Golden Fruit Orchards, 1980 Valencia Road, Westminster, California
412. Mr. Malcolm Kelly, Manager, Gourmet Delicatessens, Incorporated, 560 Marion Avenue, Oregon City, Oregon
413. Memo to Charles Murray from Edward Smith
414. Miss Josephine E. Allen, Hunter High School, 600 Friendship Street, Huntington, Indiana
415. Mrs. Marion A. Green, 980 Decatur Street, Grand River, Iowa
416. Mrs. Harold Farley, 63 Serpentine Road, Chester Heights, Pennsylvania
417. Mr. Ralph Cooper, Garden Food Products Company, 510 Shawnee Avenue, Pittsburg, Kansas
418. Mrs. Emil T. Lincoln, 46 Windham Road, Colchester, Vermont
419. Mrs. Clarence E. May, 98 Bluestone Lane, Grimms, Wisconsin
420. Mrs. George W. West, Cherokee Gardens, 910 Wilson Avenue, Fort Worth 16, Texas
421. Mrs. Carroll Graham, 20 Spanish Moss Drive, Center Point, Louisiana
422. Mrs. Stephen D. Weeks, 68 Talbot Circle, Royal Oak, Maryland
423. Johnson's Citrus Products Company, Box 545, Crystal River, Florida
424. Mr. Russell Harper, Gold Label Supermarket, 424 Oxford Street, Eastport, Maine
425. Mrs. A. B. Long, 60 Sutter Street, Sacramento 11, California
426. Mrs. Martin G. O'Brien, 47 Scotts Bluff, Lincoln 4, Nebraska
427. Mrs. Francis X. Harris, 248 Polk Street, West Allis, Wisconsin
428. Mrs. Chester R. Jones, Grant Apartments, 430 Grant Avenue, Milwaukee 14, Wisconsin
429. Mr. Irving L. Gray, 38 South Ward Street, Wichita Falls, Texas

Chapter 14

430. Mr. Daniel F. Sullivan, 218 Clayton Avenue, Lancaster, Pennsylvania
431. Mr. A. J. Parks, Sorrento Pastry Shop, 329 Broadway, Seattle 7, Washington
432. Mr. Thomas R. Jones, Morgan & Johnson Real Estate Company, Putnam Avenue at Vine Street, Chattanooga 18, Tennessee
433. Mr. John E. Edwards, 446 Adams Street, New Bern, North Carolina
434. Mr. Randolph Davis, 14 Windsor Towers, 360 Parkside Avenue, Manchester, New Hampshire

435. Chalmers Realty Company, 580 Main Street, Dover, New Jersey
436. Mr. Emory L. Ames, 62 Culpeper Avenue, Greenfield, Virginia
437. Mr. James Thomas, 714 Pine Street, Granby, Connecticut
438. Mr. Andrew Wolf, The Highwood Agency, 20 Grant Street, Ann Arbor, Michigan
439. Mr. Henry Masters, R.F.D. 6, Mooresburg, Tennessee
440. Mr. Gordon L. Ward, 32 Clay Street, Robbins, Illinois
441. Mr. Charles Riggs, 512 Main Street, Florence, Alabama
442. Mr. E. John Hunter, 720 Meadow Lane, Craftsbury, Vermont
443. Mr. Murray Young, 396 Montgomery Street, Fort Worth 17, Texas
444. Mr. Raymond Childress, 42 Baker Street, Westport, Connecticut
445. Industrial Real Estate Company, 410 Buchanan Street, Buffalo 4, New York
446. Mr. David Kelly, Fillmore Apartments, 60 West Douglas Avenue, Omaha 14, Nebraska
447. Mr. C. D. Blair, Blair Real Estate Agency, 320 Archer Street, Dallas 14, Texas
448. Mr. Clayton Payne, 28 Pelham Drive, Westerly, Rhode Island
449. Mr. Edward H. Dale, 123 Burnham Road, Worcester 24, Massachusetts
450. Mr. Louis M. Myers, 26 Carroll Street, Laurel, Maryland
451. Mr. Peter G. Cox, 42 Cumberland Road, Martin City, Missouri
452. Mr. Charles E. James, Woodworth Realty Company, 420 Ocean Boulevard, Deal, New Jersey
453. Mr. Porter Harris, Harris & Mortimer, 648 White Plains Avenue, Pelham, New York
454. Mrs. D. G. Fine, Fine Property Management Company, Inc., 76 Howard Avenue, Clarksville, Maryland
455. Mr. Anderson White, 390 Gila Road, Palo Verde, Arizona
456. Memo to Arthur S. Henry from Edward Johnstone
457. Mr. Elmer P. Strong, 636 Shelby Street, Somerset, Indiana
458. Mr. John H. Allen, 14 Pendleton Street, Crockett, Texas
459. New Deal Realty Company, 161-18 Sunnyside Avenue, Long Island City 4, New York
460. Davidson Publishing Company, Davidson Building, 1700 North Central Avenue, Easton, Pennsylvania
461. Mr. Conrad L. Smith, 75 Lucas Street, Maple Plain, Minnesota
462. Mr. Louis N. Baker, R.F.D. 8, Macon, Illinois
463. Mr. Harold R. Jones, 51 Ridgway Street, Elkins Park, Pennsylvania
464. Mr. David O'Brien, 47 Merriwell Lane, Brentwood, Long Island, New York

Chapter 15

465. Mr. William Smith, Moore, Brown & Smith, 98 North Sussex Street, Jamestown, Virginia

466. Mr. Clayton A. Brown, Professional Building, 430 West End Avenue, Portland 3, Maine
467. Miss Sonya Phillips, 69 Marion Avenue, Dallas, Iowa
468. Mr. S. M. Morris, Morris, Clinton & George, 400 North Huron Boulevard, Pontiac, Michigan
469. Mr. Andrew Gale, 93 Caldwell Road, Carthage, Missouri
470. Mr. John F. Small, 78 Belmont Road, West Warren, Oklahoma
471. Mr. Arthur E. Peters, 35 Oneida Avenue, Elmira Heights, New York
472. Mr. Francis Bates, Curran & Bates, 81 First Street, New Canaan, Connecticut
473. Mrs. Anthony E. Lewis, 750 Mojave Boulevard, Kingman, Arizona
474. Mr. Peter Manning, Manning & Chadwick, 8900 Rhode Island Avenue, S.W., Washington 34, D. C.
475. Mr. Elwood E. Jones, 490 Davis Avenue, Highland Park, Iowa
476. Mr. Matthew Simms, 69 University Gardens, 624 Fountain Drive, Knoxville 7, Tennessee.
477. Mr. Charles E. Palmer, 39 Park Square, Suffolk, Virginia
478. Mr. Fred G. Adams, 697 – 45 Street, Union City, New Jersey
479. Mr. David L. Black, South High School, 900 South Ogden Avenue, Vancouver, Washington
480. Mr. Stephen C. Bates, Bates & Johnson, 40 West Union Avenue, Clovis, New Mexico
481. Nelson Company, 250 Market Street, Sedalia, Ohio
482. Miss Marcia Grace, 76 Magnolia Lane, Bogalusa, Louisiana
483. Mr. Peter Banks, Lapham & Banks, 64 Front Street, Richmond, California
484. Mr. Alvin Hodges, 391 Kent Street, Milton, Delaware
485. Peckham & Muller, 155 Central Avenue, Lenox, Massachusetts
486. Miss Mary Allen, 719 Webster Avenue, Decatur, Mississippi
487. Mr. George Stone, Stone & Brown, 79 North Seventh Avenue, Madison 19, Wisconsin
488. Mr. George Thompson, Thompson & Thompson, 640 West Harris Avenue, Harrisburg, Pennsylvania
489. Mr. Clyde R. Ralph, Ralph Reporting Service, 40 South Mallory Street, Memphis 6, Tennessee
490. Mr. Douglas C. Gates, Cardiff, Gates & Elwell, 690 Fairfield Avenue, Bridgeport 10, Connecticut
491. Mr. Philip M. Webb, Webb, Kendall & Redmond, 510 Battle Street, Concord, New Hampshire
492. Mr. Stanley C. Davis, 37 Belmont Avenue, Williston, North Dakota
493. Dr. Patterson Brown, Oklahoma State College, University Heights, Oklahoma City 18, Oklahoma
494. Mr. Edwin A. Rose, Rose & Martin, 750 Signal Hill, Long Beach 4, California
495. Mr. Clifford Gold, Gold, Tallman & Carroll, 98 Aurora Avenue, Roscoe, South Dakota

496. Mr. Edgar Miller, 436 Clay Street, Elkins, West Virginia
497. Mr. Carter Jones, Jones, Matthews & Jones, 600 North 14 Street, Kalamazoo 10, Michigan
498. Mr. Daniel M. Baker, Baker Motor Express, 49 North Market Street, San Francisco 29, California
499. Mrs. Clifford Evans, 1614 Elmwood Avenue, Syracuse 14, New York

Chapter 16

500. Dr. Amos L. Taylor, 503 Madison Avenue, Billings, Montana
501. Mr. Louis C. Temple, 24 Valley Road, Laurel, Montana
502. Miss Caroline Young, 110 Polk Street, Marianna, Arkansas
503. Mr. Robert L. Davis, 820 Saxon Avenue, Bay Shore, Long Island, New York
504. Mr. Fred Wells, 94 Crescent Way, White Plains, New York
505. Mr. Martin E. Davis, 46 Franklin Street, New Castle, Pennsylvania
506. Mrs. Adam O. Sloan, 71 Becker Street, Osage, Minnesota
507. Dr. O. D. Collins, 146 Ridgewood Circle, Glen Rock, New Jersey
508. Miss Janet D. Miller, 53 Maple Avenue, Westwood, New Jersey
509. Mr. R. S. Brown, 276 Exeter Street, Pittston, Pennsylvania
510. Memo to the Staff from John Barnes, Office Manager
511. Miss Julia Bennett, 320 Clinton Avenue, Richmond Hill, Georgia
512. Mrs. David Mason, Pulaski Gardens, 15 Henry Street, Somerset, Kentucky
513. Dr. Clifford A. Green, 224 Martin Avenue, Madisonville, Kentucky
514. Mr. Archibald Smith, 91 Potter Place, Temple, Pennsylvania
515. Mrs. Joseph D. Mills, 43 Mill Run, Albany, Pennsylvania
516. Mrs. Elmer E. Harvey, Merrick Gardens, 94-26 Merrick Road, Babylon, Long Island, New York
517. Quality Drug Store, 406 Main Street, Rochelle, Illinois
518. Dr. LeRoy A. Lewis, Medical Arts Center, 60 North Central Avenue, Peoria 4, Illinois
519. Dr. Samuel E. Reed, 159 Shawnee Avenue, La Crosse, Wisconsin
520. Mr. Edward C. Peters, 611 Wheeler Street, San Angelo, Texas
521. Mr. Edward C. Perry, 473 Raleigh Street, Burlington, West Virginia
522. Mrs. Sherman P. Brown, 26 Smith Street, Torrington, Connecticut
523. Mr. Charles G. Woods, Principal, Central High School, Lake City, Florida
524. Miss Genevieve Turner, 31 Grove Street, Homestead, Florida
525. Mr. James L. French, French's Machine Shop, 600 Cedar Street, Davenport, Iowa
526. Dr. Kendall Smith, Physicians & Surgeons Building, 406 South State Street, Boston 4, Massachusetts
527. Mr. David O. Harper, 75 Cecil Street, Hancock, Maryland
528. Dr. Milton Farmer, 1650 Lakewood Drive, Dallas 14, Texas
529. Dr. Dennis Collins, Medical Arts Center, 800-810 Tarrant Avenue, Birmingham 10, Alabama

530. Dr. Leo P. Day, 40 Perry Square, Erie, Pennsylvania
531. Dr. Morton Jones, 696 West 14 Street, Chicago 1, Illinois
532. Mr. Henry Smith, Forrest Building, 30 South Fourth Avenue, Pittsburgh 3, Pennsylvania
533. Medical Journal, 604 Norman Street, Rochester 3, Minnesota
534. Mr. Donald R. Smith, 731 Scott Street, Manhattan, Kansas